Civilization® 11

Strategies & Secrets™

THIRD EDITION

JASON R. RICH

SYBEX

SAN FRANCISCO   PARIS   DÜSSELDORF   SOEST

Associate Publisher	GARY MASTERS
Acquisitions Manager	KRISTINE PLACHY
Project Editor	BONNIE BILLS
Production Coordinator	LABRECQUE PUBLISHING SERVICES
Developmental Editor	TERRENCE O'DONNELL
Copy Editor	MARK WOODWORTH
Book Design and Production	WILLIAM SALIT
Proofreader	TORY McLEARN
Cover Designer	ARCHER DESIGN

SYBEX is a registered trademark of SYBEX Inc.

TRADEMARKS: SYBEX has attempted throughout this book to distinguish proprietary trademarks from descriptive terms by following the capitalization style used by the manufacturer.

Library of Congress Card Number: 96-68698

ISBN: 0-7821-1922-0

Manufactured in the United States of America

10 9 8 7 6 5 4 3 2

ACKNOWLEDGMENTS

I would like to thank everyone at MicroProse who was involved in the creation of the *Civilization* game series, especially Sid Meier, the original creator of the game. As the game designers and producers of *Civilization II*, Brian Reynolds, Douglas Caspian-Kaufman, and Jeffery L. Briggs should also be acknowledged for their work. Thanks too to Paula Scarfone, the all-star public relations manager at MicroProse, who keeps me up-to-date on all of MicroProse's latest products.

Without the efforts of Gary Masters and Bonnie Bills at Sybex, along with Terrence O'Donnell and Tory McLearn at Labrecque Publishing, this book could never have been published. I greatly appreciate their hard work and interest in this project.

Finally, I wish to offer my sincere thanks and gratitude to my parents, Lois Rich and Victor Rich, my sister, Melissa Rich, and my two best friends, Mark Giordani and Ellen Bromfield, for their love and support. While computer games are fun, it continues to be my family and friends who make life worth living. No matter how detailed the simulation, no computer could re-create the significance of these people in my life.

Oh, and one word of advice . . . *Civ II* is fun, challenging, and addicting. When you're experiencing a simulation, it's easy to lose track of time and spend many hours playing this game. DON'T LET PLAYING *Civ II*, OR ANY COMPUTER GAME, INTERFERE WITH YOUR PROFESSIONAL OR PERSONAL LIFE!

Jason R. Rich
E mail Address: JR7777@aol.com

TABLE OF CONTENTS

INTRODUCTION

OK, so you own a personal computer and you were looking for a new way to entertain yourself with it, so you purchased some entertainment software. Out of all the games and simulations currently on the market, you selected Sid Meier's *Civilization II*. Perhaps you made this purchasing decision based on the countless hours of fun and challenge that a previous version of the *Civilization* game has already provided. Maybe you heard from a friend that this *Civilization II* game was worth checking out first-hand, or you read one of the extremely positive magazine reviews the game has already received. Whatever the reason, you'll soon discover that you have made an excellent decision.

Unlike many computer games and entertainment packages, *Civilization II* is an intense, strategy-based game. To be a successful player, you're going to have to think, develop strategies, and spend many hours building up an empire that you create from scratch. *Civilization II* contains no fast-paced action, so it does not require lightning fast reflexes, like other popular PC-based games, such as id Software's *Doom II* or *Quake*. Instead, this game demands that you think and plan as you take part in simulations that are affected by each and every decision you make. Best of all, each time you play *Civilization II*, your experience will be totally different. No two simulations are ever identical!

WHAT THIS BOOK CONTAINS

Civilization II Strategies & Secrets is intended to be your guide as you invent or rewrite history. The original *Civilization Strategies & Secrets* book was published by Sybex in 1993, shortly after the first version of the DOS-based *Civilization* game was released by MicroProse. The book was later revised, and a Second Edition was published to include information about the Windows-based version of the game.

Civilization II Strategies & Secrets contains information about the *Civ II* main commands and game screens you'll be using as you experience simulations. This book also offers strategies and provides answers to frequently asked questions about *Civ II*, plus gives information on how to communicate on-line with other fans of this game. For aficionados of the *CivNet* game, which is a cross between the original Windows-based *Civilization* game and *Civilization II* (and includes the ability to experience multiplayer games), information about this version of the game is also featured in this strategy guide.

You can use this book as an ongoing reference, as well. The charts within it will guide you through the prerequisites to obtaining Knowledge Advances that lead to your civilization's ability to build Wonders of the World, create City Improvements, and establish more advanced Military Units.

WHO SHOULD READ THIS BOOK?

If you have purchased the *Civilization II* game from MicroProse and plan to play this game on your PC-based computer, then you're the person for whom this strategy guide was written. Likewise, if you're interested in learning about playing *CivNet*, then you'll want to check out Chapter 10, *CivNet and Multiplayer Simulations*, which provides a comprehensive discussion of its features.

AN INTRODUCTION TO THE *CIVILIZATION II* EXPERIENCE

Have you ever gotten so involved in a game of Monopoly that it seemed almost real? Monopoly is hardly realistic, but it is easy to become engrossed in the excitement of wheeling and dealing while you buy and sell real estate—and lose your shirt—and go directly to jail—for hours.

In terms of computer entertainment, few games offer the same level of ongoing excitement and challenges that the *Civilization* game series does. Games like *SimCity 2000* (by Maxis) allows you to build and then manage a city, though there is no military strategy element. *Civilization II*, the sequel to the best-selling *Civilization* and *CivNet* games from MicroProse, will capture your imagination. Instead of buying and selling real estate, your goal in *Civilization II* (also referred to throughout this book as *Civ II*) is to take a small, nomadic tribe of people and do whatever is necessary to help them develop into a thriving, technologically advanced, and ultimately space-traveling society.

Civ II is not a flashy, action-packed game, nor is it a military shoot 'em-up game (though you *will* be forced to protect your people and perhaps enter small battles or all-out wars). Rather, *Civ II* is a graphics-based, role-playing strategy game—one that's extremely realistic and highly detailed.

Your Role in Building a Civilization

From the moment a game begins, you will be asked to make decisions that will have ramifications years later. As in real life, everything in *Civ II* is somehow connected and actions and results have a cause-and-effect relationship. For example, your tribe of settlers must discover the alphabet and learn language skills before they can become literate. Once the population is literate, your people can learn about astronomy, the first step on the path toward space exploration. Literacy also allows for the opportunity to build a great library and opens the door to developing dozens of other City Improvements (these will be discussed in detail in Chapter 8, *The Benefits of City Improvements and Wonders of the World*).

In *Civ II* you must build and control your empire as it comes into contact with other civilizations, including small tribes of Barbarians. You could find yourself at war with Alexander the Great or signing a critical treaty with Napoleon or Julius Caesar. Perhaps you will trade knowledge with Ramses of Egypt. The packaging for the original *Civilization* game had a teaser line that said, "Build an empire to stand the test of time. The action is simulated, but the excitement is real!" With the many improvements made to the *Civ II* game, this statement is more accurate then ever.

From the time your civilization is created (4000 B.C.), you are the ruler and decision maker; although you will have advisors offering you suggestions and counsel. In fact, *Civ II* contains a new, multimedia-based feature that allows you to hold Town Council meetings. This new feature lets you see and hear your advisors, and argue them down in person—not just read their text-based reports and recommendations.

In the early stages of the game, your job is relatively straightforward. The decisions to be made will be obvious. However, once your civilization expands, you must push for the technological developments and City Improvements, maintain your military, feed your people, and manage the government affairs at home and abroad. In *Civ II,* the relationship you develop with rival empires is extremely advanced. There are many levels of peace and numerous opportunities for war. These are just a few of the responsibilities requiring you to make choices that will have a direct impact on your civilization's evolution. The key to your civilization's survival is to successfully manage your cities, keep your people happy (or at least relatively content), and make decisions that will benefit them in both the long term and the short.

Civilization II Simulations Are Historical Events (Sort Of)

Civilization II is a simulation—but what exactly *is* a simulation? In this case, a simulation is a computer-generated scenario that takes into account a vast amount of fact-based historical information to mirror reality (somewhat). A computer simulation is interactive and open-ended, which means there is no right or wrong direction in which to proceed. There are also very few set rules.

In an arcade game, you must beat one skill level before proceeding to the next, but a simulation has a much less predetermined structure. A simulation is a model—a representation or replication of something. Pilots and astronauts use flight simulations to accurately replicate flying airplanes or orbiting the globe in a space shuttle, just as the military uses computer simulations for training in battle. In *Civ II*, the computer is used to simulate world history. The computer is programmed with an extensive list of cause-and-effect scenarios. Depending on how you proceed and the decisions you make, the programming will automatically adapt to your game experience.

This ability to adapt is called artificial intelligence (AI), and in *Civ II*, the AI of the game has been greatly improved over previous versions of *Civilization*. In fact, the *Civ II* compact disc comes with several predefined scenarios that are quite close to simulating major events in world history. As you proceed in a simulation, however, your actions may cause your civilization to evolve in different directions than real-life history did, which could lead your empire to extreme prosperity and universal peace— or total destruction and cultural devastation.

Is This Game Only for History Buffs?

Although *Civ II* is based on history, you don't need to be a history buff to really enjoy the game. In fact, even if you were bored to death in history class, hated reading the textbook, and dreaded those documentary films about long-ago rulers and peoples, you *might* become obsessed with this game once the civilization you create and manage starts to take shape. Of course, anything you remember from those history classes could come in handy, but historical information vital to playing *Civ II* is provided both in the game itself and within this book—presumably in a more exciting fashion than in your high school or college history textbook. After all, this is a game—so have fun!

THE LOOK AND FEEL OF *CIVILIZATION II*

Civ II is primarily a graphics-based game; however, there is little on-screen action (meaning animated graphics). Rather, the simulation in *Civ II* is made up of several main information and map screens that allow you to control the *action* using simple keyboard or mouse commands. For this version of the game, MicroProse has made many improvements to the game's graphics and sound effects, so everything that you control on the screen actually looks like what it's supposed to represent.

In earlier versions of *Civilization*, the various types of Military Units, for example, were depicted on the Main Game screen as square icons with small, nondetailed pictures within them. These same units in *Civ II* appear in a 3D form and seem far more realistic. Airplanes look like the type of plane they represent, and you can actually see the weapons being held by Riflemen Units. The cities look like huts when a simulation begins, and then they evolve as they become more advanced.

Civ II also now contains multimedia features. These added animated sequences are not required when playing the game, though they add an element of realism. If you want to experience all the graphics and sound that have been incorporated into this version of the game, you must keep the *Civ II* Program CD inserted into your computer's CD-ROM drive when playing the game.

It will probably take you an hour or two to become fully aquainted with *Civ II* and to understand exactly what's happening as you take each turn. A *turn* represents the passing of years during a simulation. Playing the game and experiencing a single simulation can take between five minutes and fifteen hours, or more, depending on how well-defined and organized are your decisions. So make yourself comfortable at the keyboard, think about your place in history, and get ready to take on the responsibilities of a ruler.

Establishing Goals and Customizing Features

Early in a simulation, you must choose to pursue one of two ultimate goals: to help your empire thrive from the standpoint of technology and knowledge and eventually to colonize space, *or* to focus on building up your military in order to conquer the entire planet before the year A.D. 2020 when a simulation automatically comes to an end.

As you proceed, one important key to success is to always look at the big picture. For example, if you're concentrating on allocating the right resources to defeat attacking Barbarians, you must also continue to maintain your civilization through each turn and make the necessary advancements by planning for the future. Thus, you're going to have to accomplish multiple tasks at once, or you will probably fail in the long run.

Before an actual simulation begins, you will have to make a variety of decisions that allow you to customize many elements of the actual game-play experience. Once you've become familiar with this game, you'll want to check out the MapEditor program that allows you to create from scratch the world(s) upon which your simulation(s) will take place. See Appendix A, *Creating Worlds with the Civilization II MapEditor*, for a detailed discussion of this new feature for customizing your simulations. Also, be sure to read Chapter 1, *The New Civilization Environment*, which describes the many new features that *Civ II* offers.

HAVE A WINNING REIGN!

As you play *Civ II*, you will be experiencing one of the best simulation games the computer software industry has to offer. Your imagination, along with your ability to keep in mind the bigger picture, will play a key role in your success as the ruler of your civilization. Enjoy your reign, don't let the power of having a military force at your disposal go to your head, and good luck!

1

The New Civilization Environment

icroProse's *Civilization* game series has been on

the market for several years and has undergone several revisions. Since the original

DOS version was released, *Civilization* has, like civilization itself, continued to evolve

and build up a vast number of dedicated followers. The DOS version of *Civilization*

offered PC gamers a superior approach to their strategy gaming; but let's face it, the

game had extremely dull graphics and sound. Next came the Windows edition, which

included some enhancements to the overall game play and a number of improvements

to the game's graphics and sound. The evolution of *Civilization* continued with a

Macintosh version as well as a Super Nintendo Entertainment System version.

In late 1995, MicroProse released *CivNet*, a total revision of the original *Civilization*
game that introduced many new features, including multiplayer gaming. The features
of *CivNet*, along with some game-play strategies in a multiplayer environment, are discussed in Chapter 10, *CivNet and Multiplayer Simulations*.

As computer technology evolved and the demands and expectations of consumers
increased, MicroProse set out to create yet another new version of *Civilization* that
would take advantage of multimedia graphics and sound for a new look and enhanced
game play. The result of this effort is *Civilization II*, which was released in April 1996.
Civ II is designed to run under the Microsoft Windows 3.1 and Windows 95 operating
environments. While the overall look of the game is new, the gaming aspects that have
set *Civilization* apart from all other computer games remains top-notch.

This chapter describes many of the new features and enhancements that make up *Civ II*. If you're new to the *Civilization* game series, and *Civ II* is your first exposure to this type of game, these enhancements promise you an enjoyable game experience. If, however, you're one of the thousands of gamers who have gotten hooked on one of the original versions of the game, then you're in for a major treat when you experience *Civ II* on your PC—making history on your own desktop, probably in your sweatpants or muumuu!

CIVILIZATION II
OFFERS A NEW LOOK

The most obvious difference between *Civ II* and its predecessors is its overall look. High-resolution graphics are used to create eyecatching icons that replace the basic (and boring) icons that used to make up the entire game. The Main Game screen's map offers an isometric grid instead of the square grid found in previous versions of the game. This means that your viewing perspective is from an angle, and the on-screen graphics appear 3D, as shown in Figure 1.1.

To make it easier to manage your population, which extends out of its Home City to eventually cover large amounts of the game screen, the Civilization game series divides your people into different types of individual units (graphic representations of citizens or military), each of which has its own responsibilities and capabilities. Another major enhancement made to *Civ II* is that all the game's units now carry shields, which appear on the Main Map. The shields provide important information about the unit, as shown in Figure 1.2. Each shield's color helps you immediately determine which empire each unit belongs to (Barbarians are—no surprise here—red). At the top of each shield is an energy bar for that unit, which will be reduced as that unit enters into battles. A green energy bar represents a healthy unit. As a unit participates in battles, its energy bar turns yellow and then red while, at the same time, begins shrinking. When the energy bar is totally depleted, that unit dies. If a unit survives a battle yet has an energy bar that is almost gone (with only a small amount of red showing), you must order that unit to rest over a period of several turns—or return that unit to a friendly city to regroup and revitalize its energy. The energy bar and

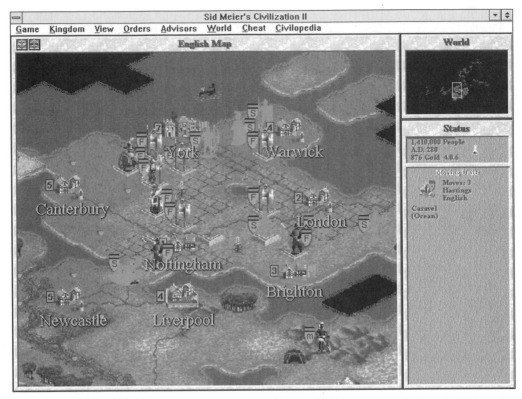

FIGURE 1.1: Check out the new and improved *Civ II* Main Game screen, featuring 3D graphics and a new viewing perspective.

shield for each unit greatly enhance the unit-to-unit battle sequences, which are also supported by fascinating graphic animation and far more realistic sounds.

UNITS NOW HAVE HIT POINTS AND FIREPOWER

In addition to giving units a new look and an energy meter, the enhanced *Civ II* game has also changed how these units fight. Units now contain hit points and contain firepower, which are new game-play concepts in *Civ II*. Hit points are shown graphically by the color of the energy meter within the unit's shield. Both the length of the energy meter and its color help you to instantly ascertain the relative strength of a unit. When a unit participates in a battle and is inflicted with injuries, its hit points decrease (its energy meter changes from green to yellow to red and shrinks). Hit points represent a unit's durability in battles. In the early stages of a simulation, units have 10 hit points each. Units with firearms have 20 hit points, and units with steel armor have 30 hit points—thus, they have stronger defenses. Battleships are heavily armored and have 40 hit points. Each time a unit is hit during a battle, it loses one hit point. Thus, a basic unit can survive 10 direct hits before getting killed.

FIGURE 1.2: The units in *Civ II* have been redesigned to look like what they actually represent—such as this Settler Unit from *Civ II*, which has a shield containing an energy meter.

Firepower refers to the damage a unit can cause on an enemy unit each time it inflicts a hit. Different units have various firepower strengths, which are described in detail in Chapter 6, *Civilization II Units*, which describes each type of unit in the game.

Now that units have both hit points and firepower, you must take this information into account before launching attacks. It is now possible to determine how your unit will measure up to the enemy unit *before* an attack. If your unit has fewer hit points than the enemy, it will not be able to keep up a strong defense, so you must be sure that your unit at least has superior firepower before initiating an attack. This is just one way that strategy plays an even bigger role in combat situations when you're experiencing *Civ II*. In this version of the game, units can also be Fortified and obtain Veteran Status, which increases their hit points and firepower.

In previous versions of *Civilization*, a unit either won and survived—or lost and perished after a battle. Now, units can exit a battle having been injured and weakened, which means they are alive and still in the game, though extremely vulnerable to future enemy attacks. At the conclusion of a battle, if a unit has received injuries (that is, its energy bar is either yellow or red and is somewhat depleted), that unit must be given ample opportunity to recuperate and regain its strength.

An injured unit can replenish some of its energy by skipping a turn (press the spacebar or select the No Orders command on the Orders pull-down menu). Units will heal faster if they return to a friendly city and remain there over a period of several turns. Cities that contain certain improvements, such as a port facility for rebuilding naval units or an airport to repair air-based units, will allow injured units to heal even more quickly—often after a single turn.

THREE TYPES OF MILITARY UNITS

Military Units in *Civ II* are now divided into three categories:

- All-Purpose Infantry
- Fast Moving Cavalry
- Heavy Weapon Artillery

There is also a larger selection of Military Units than in previous versions of the game, so you now can choose from several different types of ground based units, air-based units, and water-based units. Each type of unit will have different strengths, weaknesses, hit points, firepower, movement abilities, and costs. With this larger selection of Military Units comes the need to spend more time developing your fighting strategy to make the best use of the units at your disposal. Knowing when and how to build specific types of Military Units will mean the difference between conquering the world and being defeated (and having future historians make cruel jokes about your parental legitimacy).

OTHER SPECIALIZED UNITS

Especially in the later stages of a simulation, there are very specialized types of units that you can create. These specialized units include: Settler, Engineer, Diplomat, Spy, Caravan, and Transport Units.

Civ II offers the ability to create Settler Units early in a simulation. Settler Units can found cities as well as build roads, irrigation systems, and mines. They can also perform several other functions, many of which take multiple turns to accomplish. In the middle and later stages of a simulation, Engineer Units can be created. Engineer Units are more advanced than Settler Units and can accomplish tasks, such as building Terrain Improvements (roads, irrigation systems, mines, fortresses, railroads, airbases,and the like) much faster. Likewise, Diplomat Units that are available early in a simulation can later be replaced by Spy Units, which have more capabilities. Spy Units can do everything a Diplomat Unit can, plus they can poison enemy water supplies and plant nuclear devices. Caravan Units, used for establishing trade routes and helping other friendly cities build Wonders of the World, can be replaced by Transport Units in later stages of a simulation. Transport Units can move more rapidly (greater distances per turn), and offer greater economic benefits when trade routes are established.

A NEW LOOK FOR CITIES IN *CIV II*

The appearance of cities on the Main Map has also been greatly improved in *Civ II*. At the start of a simulation, you can choose the style of architecture you want your cities to resemble, and then as the game progresses, you'll see actual graphic representations of your cities that are far more detailed than those boring squares with numbers found in previous versions of the game. As a city grows, the graphic of that city on the Main Map also grows, and when your civilization reaches the industrial

NOTE
Experienced *Civilization* players should carefully study Chapter 6, *The Civilization II Units*, which provides detailed specifications for each type of unit. Understanding what each new type of unit offers is important, because many of the powers and capabilities of units that appeared in older versions of this game have changed.

era, you'll be amazed to see the architecture reflecting the changing times. Cities in *Civ II* still contain numbers, as you can see in Figure 1.3, which represent the size and strength of the city. Terrain Improvements (an enhanced feature of *Civ II*) also look rather different in this version of the game.

Corruption Now Plays a Bigger Role in a Simulation

In other versions of *Civilization*, when empires expanded and spread out over large areas and even multiple continents, corruption took place in cities located far away from an empire's capital city, especially if certain City Improvements were not built in those far-off cities. Trade was also affected by corruption and the distance between cities in which a trade route was established. These concepts still hold true in *Civ II*,

FIGURE 1.3: In *Civ II*, cities are represented with high-resolution graphics that are extremely detailed, expand and evolve as each city grows, and reflect architecture changes as the simulation evolves into more modern eras.

though the impact of corruption has been expanded. The shield production (productivity) of a city is also impacted by its distance from the capital city. In cities located far away from the capital city, you should expect some reduction in productivity. City Improvements, such as police stations, can be used to help control corruption (though, like death and taxes, it will always be with us).

Changing Production Can Cost You

In all versions of *Civilization*, a city can produce units, City Improvements, or Wonders of the World. In previous versions of the game, you could instantly switch from building a Catapult Unit, for example, to building City Walls, with no negative impact to your empire. In *Civ II*, however, if you decide to change what a city is building in mid-production, you may be penalized for it by a stiff fine. If you're building a unit and you want to switch what type of unit a city is producing in mid-production, that's OK. But, if you choose to switch from producing a unit to a City Improvement or Wonder of the World in mid-production, then you'll be fined by 50 percent of the number of shields that have already been produced and allocated toward the development of whatever the city is building. Once a city has built whatever it's producing, you are welcome to change what those items of production are (unit, improvement, or wonder) with no penalty.

New City Improvements Add New Elements of Strategy

Each City Improvement that you can build within each of your empire's cities offers some type of specific benefit to that city. Several of the new City Improvements that you can build in *Civ II* are used to assist in helping injured units rejuvenate their energy meters after battles.

Adding a Port Facility in a city (located near a river or ocean) allows water-based units to regain energy quickly after a battle. Airports are used to restore the energy to air-based units (aircraft), and Barracks now have the ability to restore energy to ground units. (Barracks also allow a city to produce ground-based Veteran Units.) For this to work, an injured unit must return to a friendly city and spend at least one turn there.

To boost revenue generated by trade, you should build the new Superhighway Improvement within cities. Now, citizens working within a city radius will be 50 percent more productive, plus irrigated land surrounding a city containing a Superhighway Improvement will create 50 percent more food per turn. Meanwhile, creating Railroads on a terrain square (a Terrain Improvement created by Settler and Engineer Units) increases workers' shield production in the underlying terrain.

Some City Improvements from the original *Civilization* game now have new benefits. A Coliseum is capable of making four unhappy citizens content in each city in which it is built (once your empire has acquired the Electronics Scientific Advance). Cathedrals now make 3 citizens per city go from being unhappy to content (once your empire has discovered Communism). Courthouses make 1 content person happy when an empire is ruled as a Democracy. If an empire is ruled under another form of government, a Courthouse Improvement makes it more difficult for enemies to bribe your people.

Additional strategy changes that involve City Improvements are that City Walls built within a city are now cheaper to build and have no maintenance cost per turn associated with them. In *Civ II*, if you want a city to grow beyond the size of eight, it's now necessary to build an Aqueduct. A Sewer System (City Improvement) is required for a city to grow beyond the size of 12.

After your empire has discovered the knowledge of Radio, both Settler and Engineer Units can build Airbases in any terrain square where they could normally build Fortresses. An Airbase is a City Improvement that allows air-based units to land and refuel.

Terrain Improvements Also Offer Benefits

When you build a City Improvement within a city, that city receives some type of benefit. In *Civ II*, when you instruct your Settler or Engineer Units to build Terrain Improvements, the nearby city will receive benefits as well. Terrain Improvements in *Civ II* include irrigation facilities, roads, railroads, fortresses, airbases, and mineral mines. All roads created in your empire will automatically be upgraded to railroads when the Railroad Scientific Advance is acquired by your empire. Engineer Units, with the appropriate knowledge, can build Terrain Improvements twice as fast as Settler Units. Once the knowledge of Refrigeration is acquired, Settler and Engineer Units have the ability to change terrain squares into farmland, which allows for vastly improved production. In addition to building Terrain Improvements, *Civ II* offers new terrain types that also offer benefits to cities.

New Government Types and Changes in Government Rule

Feudalism is a new form of government through which you can choose to rule your empire. Additional Government types available in *Civ II* include Monarchy, Communism, Republic, Anarchy, and Democracy. Detailed descriptions, along with information about the benefits and drawbacks to each type of government, are presented in Chapter 9, *Civilization II Governments and Types of Terrain*. Be sure to read that chapter because significant changes have been made to what you can and cannot do when ruling your empire under each form of government.

USING DIPLOMACY TO CONQUER THE WORLD

Diplomacy has also been enhanced in *Civ II*. Now, computer-controlled rival civilizations will remember your actions and learn from their past dealings with you. As a result, you as the leader of your empire will develop a reputation—for good or ill—over time. To learn what your reputation is among rival leaders, check out the Foreign Minister's report and use the Reputation feature.

Now, when you make contact with rival civilizations, your relationship with them is no longer cut and dry. In other versions of *Civilization*, either you were at war with rival empires, or your empire would engage in a treaty with them. In *Civ II*, once you make contact with a rival empire, you can contact the ruler of that empire at any time by accessing your Foreign Minister's report and activating the Send Emissary option. Unlike with previous versions of the game, it is no longer a requirement to first establish an embassy within a rival empire before negotiating treaties or developing trade routes.

Keep in mind, the game's built-in artificial intelligence (AI) programming carefully monitors your actions when you empire comes into contact with rival civilizations that are computer controlled. What this means is that if you constantly make treaties and then break them, the computer will remember this and act accordingly in the future. As the ruler of your empire, over time you will develop a reputation among rival civilizations. Breaking treaties has penalties that will impact you over the course of the simulation—that is, unless you have a good reason for breaking a treaty. What constitutes a good reason? If a rival Diplomat Unit steals a Scientific Advance (technology) from you, then you will be justified in breaking a treaty (there will be no long-term penalties).

It is also possible for a rival's patience to wear thin, making it tougher to deal with. To help keep your reputation untarnished, *don't* make treaties with rival empires that you do not plan to uphold. As alternatives to participating in all-out peace treaties, refuse to sign peace treaties or to participate in temporary cease-fires. Other than the military repercussions from rivals, there is no penalty for refusing a treaty or breaking a cease-fire.

Civ II offers you the opportunity to develop a relationship with a rival on any one of several levels. In other versions of the game, your empire could either be at peace or be at war with another empire. Now, you can experience a temporary cease-fire, neutrality, an alliance, or a strong peace treaty, or you can be at war with your rivals. Cease-fire agreements are temporary ways to keep rival empires out of your way while you focus on other aspects of building your empire. A cease-fire will last approximately sixteen turns, and then dissolve automatically, unless you extend it by offering some form of financial incentive to the rival civilization.

At the start of a simulation, your empire will have a neutral relationship with all other empires that exist. This neutrality will remain in effect until you actually encounter another empire and choose to decline an offer for a peace treaty. Another way to break the neutrality is to launch an attack on another empire.

In *Civ II*, a relationship can be established between two empires that is actually stronger than a standard peace treaty. An alliance gives you the ability to ignore your ally empire's areas of control and lets you build cities (and place units) near other cities that are part of the empire with which you have an alliance. As well, peace treaties allow you to coexist with other empires (without raging war); however, if any of your units violate the other empire's terrain, you run the risk that the peace treaty will be broken, with all the subsequent repercussions.

In the later stages of a simulation, pay careful attention to the benefits and draw-backs of ruling your empire under the various types of governments. Under Democracy, for example, you will *not* be permitted to break treaties.

USING DIPLOMAT AND SPY UNITS

In addition to their regular tasks, Diplomat and Spy Units can be ordered to take part in counterespionage activities (see Figure 1.4). A Diplomat or Spy Unit that is stationed in a friendly city has the ability to stop a rival empire from stealing technology from you. If you have experienced other versions of *Civilization*, you know that Diplomats can open up lines of communication with rival empires. In *Civ II*, a Diplomat Unit's job is to develop and maintain contact with other empires and report major develop-ments to you. Diplomat Units can also engage in sabotage and disrupt production in enemy cities or steal technologies outright. Diplomat Units have become a much more powerful tool in this version of the game.

FIGURE 1.4: When you send a spy into a foreign city, it can establish an embassy, steal a technology, investigate a city, perform sabotage, or poison the city's water supply.

New to *Civ II* are Spy Units, which have even more capabilities than Diplomat Units. Spies can provide you with all sorts of information about rival empires that they infiltrate—and at the same time, they can attempt to win over an enemy unit or city, then get it to defect to your empire. Stealing technology, sabotage, and counterintelligence are all part of a Spy Unit's job description, as shown in Figure 1.5.

NEW WONDERS OF THE WORLD

Wonders of the World all provide your empire with specific benefits once you obtain them. *Civ II* offers most of the wonders available in other versions of the game, but many of them have new capabilities. Plus, there are seven all-new wonders that can now be obtained during the Renaissance and Industrial eras of a *Civ II* simulation.

Here are some of the new Wonders of the World benefits of which you should be aware. See Chapter 8, *The Benefits of City Improvements and Wonders of the World*, for a complete list of each wonder and what it can do for your empire.

 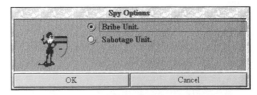

FIGURE 1.5: Spy Units are a new type of Military Unit in *Civ II* that can perform several extremely useful tasks. If a Spy Unit meets up with an enemy unit, the Spy Unit can either sabotage the enemy unit or attempt to bribe it so that it joins your empire.

The Pyramids   This wonder still has all its old capabilities, but now it also acts as a Granary. Its impact benefits all cities within your empire, not just a single city.

The Lighthouse   Triremes (ships with three banks of oars) can now move around in the open ocean without fear of sinking, once this wonder has been acquired. Additionally, all ships built begin at the Veteran status level, making them 50 percent stronger.

The Great Wall   This wonder now doubles the combat strength of units when fighting against Barbarians. Additionally, anytime you encounter a rival empire, they will be forced to offer you a peace treaty. The final benefit of The Great Wall is that all your cities will advance from the effects of having the City Walls City Improvement built within them, even if this improvement hasn't been built. The Great Wall's benefits will become obsolete when your empire discovers Metallurgy.

Magellan's Expedition   All ships can now move across two extra terrain (ocean) squares per turn.

Michelangleo's Chapel   This wonder offers the benefit of a Cathedral in every one of your cities, once you have acquired it. Thus, by both building a Cathedral City Improvement in each city and acquiring the Michaelengelo's Chapel Wonder of the World, you stand a much better chance of keeping your population happy (or at least content) on a long-term basis.

The United Nations   As soon as this wonder is built, your empire will benefit from having an embassy in every rival city that exists within the simulation. Additionally, if you're ruling your empire under a Democracy, you have a 50 percent better chance of being able to overrule your senate's decisions when it comes time to launching attacks and initiating wars. You'll also have more control in foreign policy negotiations when ruling under a Democratic form of government.

SETI Program   Acquiring this wonder instantly gives you the benefit of having the equivalent of a Research Lab Improvement in every one of your cities.

- **Colossus**   The impact of this wonder remains the same as in other versions of the game; however, its benefits will become obsolete once your empire discovers the Flight Scientific Advance.

- **The Great Library**   This wonder's benefits will also become obsolete when your empire makes the Electronics Scientific Advance.

- **J.S. Bach's Cathedral**   Again, this wonder's benefits will become obsolete after your empire experiences the Theology Scientific Advance.

GETTING READY TO RULE YOUR OWN EMPIRE

This chapter outlined many of *Civ II*'s major additions and game-play modifications made to the *Civilization* game. If you are already familiar with other versions of *Civilization*, as you experience this game you're bound to discover many other exciting minor changes, additions, and improvements that have been made. However, whether you're a new or experienced player, now is a good time to review the next three chapters to get acquainted with selecting pre-game options, *Civ II*'s Main Game and City screens, and the commands available to you on *Civ II*'s Menu Bar. Then you can check out Chapter 5, *Your First Civilization II Simulation*, for a guided walk-through of a real simulation experience—or can jump right in and begin experiencing your own simulation.

In addition to providing an overview of the commands and overall game play of *Civ II*, this strategy guide contains tactics and tips and maneuvers throughout that you can follow to help you conquer the world or colonize space. Use these strategies as a reference once you actually begin playing *Civilization II*.

2

Getting a
Simulation Started

Before a simulation actually begins, *Civilization II* offers an abundance of pregame options that allow you to customize your overall game-play experience. This chapter outlines the pregame options available to you when you first start *Civ II*.

THE PREGAME OPTIONS

When you first start the game, the very first option you encounter is what language you wish to experience the game in. The available options include English, French, and Dutch. Using the mouse, click on the language of your choice, and then click on the OK button.

Within a few moments, *Civ II*'s opening animation will appear. Press any key on the keyboard to stop this animation and proceed. At this point, the computer will check to see if the *Civ II* compact disc has been inserted in your computer's CD-ROM drive. Unless you have done a complete installation of the *Civ II* game, and all the game's files have been placed on your computer's hard disk, it will be necessary for the game to periodically access the *Civ II* CD, if you want to view the game's animation features. If the *Civ II* CD is not in the CD-ROM drive, a window will appear asking if you wish to place the disc in the drive or continue without the CD inserted. (Unless the CD is inserted into your computer's CD-ROM drive, you won't be able to view the game's new animation features.)

The *Civilization II* window with a list of pregame options will now appear, as shown in Figure 2.1. This menu offers you the following options:

⊕ **Start a New Game** This option allows you to begin playing a new simulation.

Start on Premade World   Experience a new simulation on a world that has already been created. The *Civ II* game comes with several premade worlds bundled on the program CD.

Customize World   Instead of experiencing a *Civ II* simulation on a random, computer-generated world, this option allows you to customize the world on which your simulation will take place.

Begin Scenario   Bundled onto the *Civ II* CD-ROM are several scenarios that attempt to re-create historical events. You can play one of these scenarios by choosing this option.

Load a Game   Use this option to load a simulation that you previously saved. At any time during a simulation, you can save your game using the Save Game command on the Game pull-down menu (or you can press Ctrl + S). You can also load a simulation and terminate the one you're currently experiencing. Use this option if you make a serious mistake from a strategy standpoint and need to backtrack by loading an earlier edition of your current simulation.

View Hall of Fame   Once a simulation comes to an end—say you conquer the world, colonize space, or retire, or your empire itself gets conquered—your score and simulation information will be saved. The Hall of Fame is where you can view your previous game scores and gloat over your achievements.

View Credits   Have you ever stopped to think about how many people were involved in the creation of *Civilization II*? Well, here's your chance to see the names of the people responsible and raise a toast to their talents.

FIGURE 2.1: The *Civilization II* window with its list of pregame options appears after you select a language option for the simulation and the computer has checked for the presence of the *Civ II* CD.

START A NEW GAME

Using the mouse, select the Start a New Game option and then click on the OK button. You will be asked to select the size of the world on which you want your simulation to take place, as shown in Figure 2.2. The options available to you are as follows:

- Small (40×50 squares, quick game)
- Normal (50×80 squares)
- Large (75×120 squares, long game)

The larger the world, the longer the simulation will take to complete because you'll have a greater area of land to explore and conquer. From the Select Size of World window, you can also choose the Custom button and have total control over the size of the world. The default option for this window is the Normal world size. At any time, you can return to the previous pregame option window by clicking on the Cancel button.

Select a Difficulty Level

Next, you will be asked to select an overall level of difficulty for the game. The options available to you in the Select Difficulty Level window, as shown in Figure 2.3, are as follows:

- Chieftain (easiest)
- Warlord
- Prince
- King
- Emperor
- Deity (toughest)

The level of difficulty you select will affect the overall game in several ways. For example, it will determine the starting and ending year of the simulation, the aggressiveness of rival empires, and how easy it will be to keep your people happy. If you're

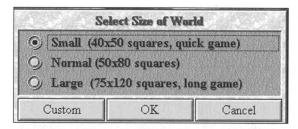

FIGURE 2.2: The Select Size of World window contains three options for the size of your simulation world, which also affects the duration of play.

new to *Civ II*, you'll want to experience your first several simulations on the Chieftain level and work your way toward more difficult challenges. Unless you're an absolute expert at this game, the chances of beating the game at the Deity level are practically nonexistent. (Even gods have to go through training school first.)

Select Rival Empires

The next pregame option allows you to determine the number of rival empires that will exist at the start of the simulation. You can choose between three and seven rival empires. The more rivals you choose, the earlier in the simulation you will encounter them—and the bigger chance you will have of being forced to fight multiple battles at once as the simulation progresses. From the Select Level of Competition window, you can also choose the Random option, which forces the computer to determine how

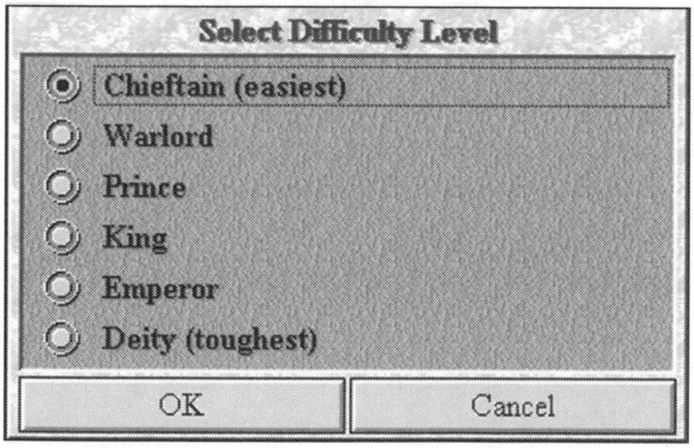

FIGURE 2.3: The Select Difficulty Level window offers six different levels of difficulty from which to choose.

many rival civilizations will exist at the start of your simulation. Keep in mind, no matter how many rival civilizations you choose from this window, you'll still have to deal with Barbarians throughout the simulation.

Speaking of those nasty Barbarians, these are computer-controlled enemies that will appear from time to time just to cause trouble. Each civilization in a simulation has a color associated with it, so you can easily identify each empire's units and cities. Barbarians are always red. (Barbarians have red units and cities.) The next pregame option allows you to determine how often and where Barbarians will appear. Unfortunately, there is no way to totally abolish these enemies from the game. From the Select Level of Barbarian Activity window, you can choose:

- Villages Only
- Roving Bands
- Restless Tribes
- Ranging Hordes

By choosing the Villages Only option, Barbarians can only appear randomly when one of your units investigates a hut that is located on the Main Map. These huts can contain Barbarians, or bonuses such as money, Scientific Advances, extra units, or even a small tribe that wants to join your empire. The remaining options under the Select Level of Barbarian Activity window determine how often Barbarians will appear and how big and strong their forces will be when they do randomly appear.

Custom Rules Options

Next, you must choose to play *Civ II* using the Standard Rules or using Custom Rules. Make your selection and then click on the OK button. By choosing the Custom Rules option from this window, another window, titled Select Custom Features, will appear. Using the mouse, click on any of the following options that you want to activate, and then click on the OK button to continue.

- Simplified Combat
- Flat World

⊕ Select Computer Opponents

⊕ Accelerated Start Up

⊕ Bloodlust (No Spaceships Allowed—this is a game about conquering the world)

⊕ Don't Restart Eliminated Players

The next pregame question is an easy one—your sex. Your options are Male or Female (duh!). Choose one from the Select Gender window, and click on the OK button. Now, you'll have to choose your tribe, as shown in Figure 2.4. There are twenty-one different tribes to choose from, or you can select the Custom button and enter the name of any real or fictitious tribe you choose. Make your selection, and then click on the OK button to continue.

What's the difference between playing a game using Standard Rules and Custom Rules?

You can choose between playing a game under the Standard *Civ II* Rules (default option), or Custom Rules. If you choose the Custom Rules option, you can adjust the following options that will alter your game-play experience:

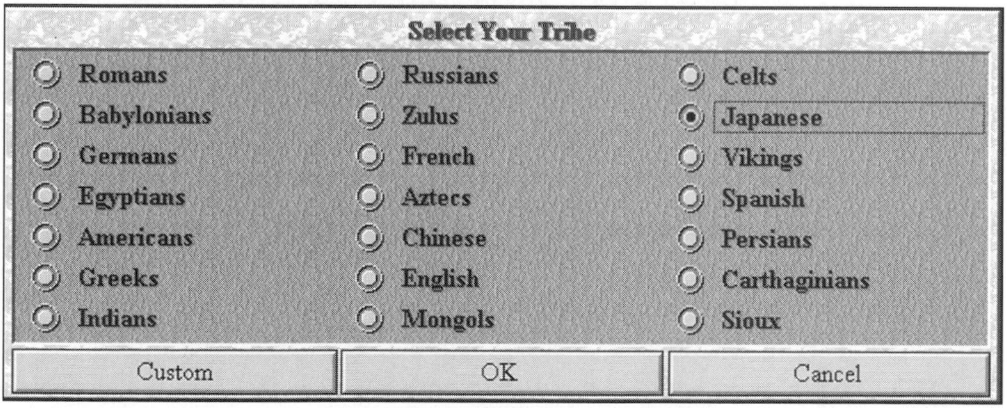

Select Your Tribe

○ Romans	○ Russians	○ Celts
○ Babylonians	○ Zulus	⊙ Japanese
○ Germans	○ French	○ Vikings
○ Egyptians	○ Aztecs	○ Spanish
○ Americans	○ Chinese	○ Persians
○ Greeks	○ English	○ Carthaginians
○ Indians	○ Mongols	○ Sioux

Custom	OK	Cancel

FIGURE 2.4: The Select Your Tribe window allows you to choose the name (and nationality) of your tribe from among twenty-one options, or you can create your own tribe by clicking the Custom button.

⊕ **Simplified Combat**   When you remove the check-mark from this menu option, your units will no longer have Hit Points and Firepower. As a result, when they fight a battle, either they will be victorious and survive, or they'll lose the battle and wind up dead. Using the Simplified Combat option causes the units in *Civ II* to act like units in the original *Civilization* game. This will allow you to incorporate strategies that you developed for the original game into your simulations when playing *Civ II*.

⊕ **Flat World**   By selecting the Flat World option, units will not be able to proceed once they reach the boundaries of the world (the edge of the map). To reach the opposite end of the world, they'll have to turn around and travel in the opposite direction. When a Round World option is selected, the world is a circle, which means the map will scroll. If a unit travels off the end of the map, it will automatically wind up on the opposite end.

⊕ **Select Computer Opponents**   Before a simulation, you can select which computer-controlled civilizations you will be competing against and determine the starting locations for your rival empires.

⊕ **Accelerated Startup**   You can skip over the early stages of a simulation and begin toward the middle of one using this command. Before the simulation begins, the computer will establish cities for you, build units, and acquire Knowledge Advances on your behalf. Thus, when the simulation actually begins, you'll be the ruler of an established empire.

⊕ **Bloodlust**   When you experience this type of simulation, there is only one ultimate goal in the game—to become the world's strongest military and conquer the world. You will not be allowed to build spaceships.

⊕ **Don't Restart Eliminated Players**   During a simulation, if you conquer an empire, the computer might automatically create additional Settler Units for the conquered empire, allowing it to resurrect itself. When this command is active, once a rival empire has been conquered, it's gone forever (at least until the simulation ends).

By choosing the Custom button in the Select Your Tribe window, you can use the keyboard to enter your name for the Leader's Name, your tribe's name, and how you want your tribe to be referred to (for example, , people from Japan are Japanese) in the Customize Your Tribe window, as shown in Figure 2.5.

Each form of government under which your empire can be ruled allows you to have a different title, such as Ms. Ruler, Mr. Visionary, Emperor, Prime Minister, Lord of All I Survey, Leader for Life, Supreme Ruler, and so on. You can click on the Titles button in the Customize Your Tribe window to set the official titles for you, the leader, under each form of government, as shown in Figure 2.6. Then click on the OK button to continue.

If you select one of the twenty-one tribe choices, within the Please Enter Your Name window a default name for you (the leader) will appear. This default name is from real-life history; however, you can type in your own name or any name you choose. This is the name by which your advisors will refer to you. Enter a name for yourself and then click on the OK button.

Now that you've named your tribe and have selected a name for yourself, it's time to choose the type of architecture that will be used to build your cities. From the Select Your City Style window shown in Figure 2.7, you can choose one of the following options:

- ⊕ Bronze Age Monolith
- ⊕ Classical Forum
- ⊕ Far East Pavilion
- ⊕ Medieval Castle

The architectural style you choose will not impact your game, though it *will* determine how your empire will appear on screen, once your simulation gets underway. A white box will appear around your selection. When you're ready to proceed, click on the OK button.

Well, that's it. You've made all the pregame decisions necessary, assuming you originally selected the Start a New Game option. The computer will now generate the world in which your simulation will take place, and within a few moments, an In The Beginning . . . information window will appear. This window tells you briefly about the birth of your tribe and is the last thing you'll see before the simulation officially begins. For the final time, click on the OK button, and your date with history will start.

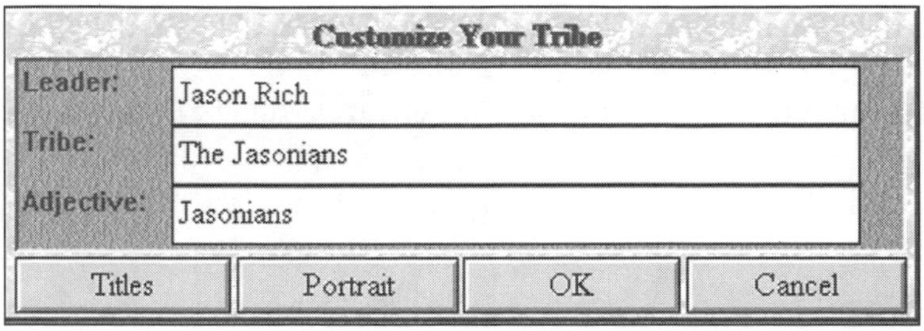

FIGURE 2.5: In addition to naming your leader, your tribe, and how they will be referred to, you can determine what you, the leader, will look like by clicking on the Portrait button at the bottom of this window.

STARTING A SIMULATION ON A PREMADE WORLD

The Start on Premade World option you begin a simulation on a premade world. On choosing this option (and clicking on the OK button), a Select Map To Load dialog box will appear on the screen, as shown in Figure 2.8. The *Civ II* game comes with a few premade maps. Maps are saved with a .mp extension.

On choosing a map, another window will appear, asking "Do you wish to randomize this world's villages and resource squares? Yes or No." Next, you'll be asked

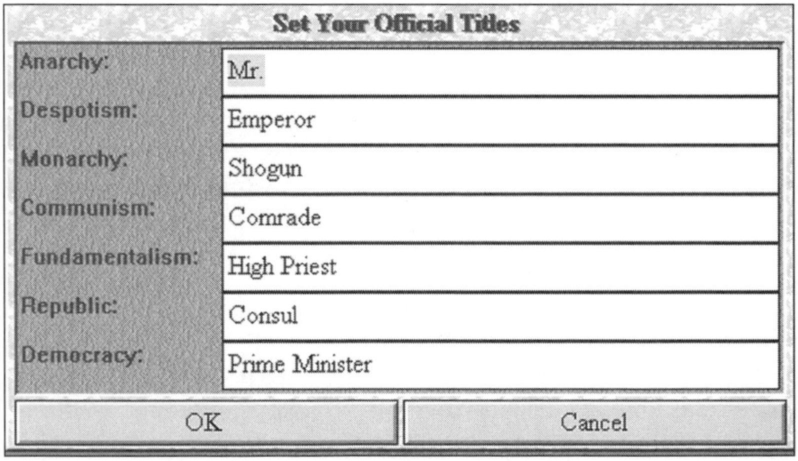

FIGURE 2.6: When you select the Titles button at the bottom of the Customize Your Tribe window, you can type in the titles you want to be referred to under each form of government.

Select Your City Style
Bronze Age Monolith
Classical Forum
Far East Pavilion
Medieval Castle
OK
Cancel

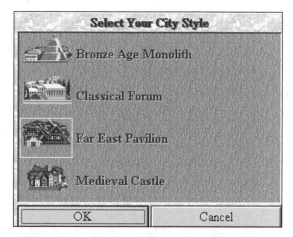

FIGURE 2.7: Choose an architectural style for your cities from this window. This will determine how your empire looks on screen.

if you wish to randomize the player starting locations (Yes or No). This will be followed by additional pregame menus, allowing you to select the difficulty, competition, and Barbarian activity levels; game rules (Standard or Custom); the leader's gender; your tribe; your name; and the architectural style for cities. The simulation will then begin on the premade world you selected.

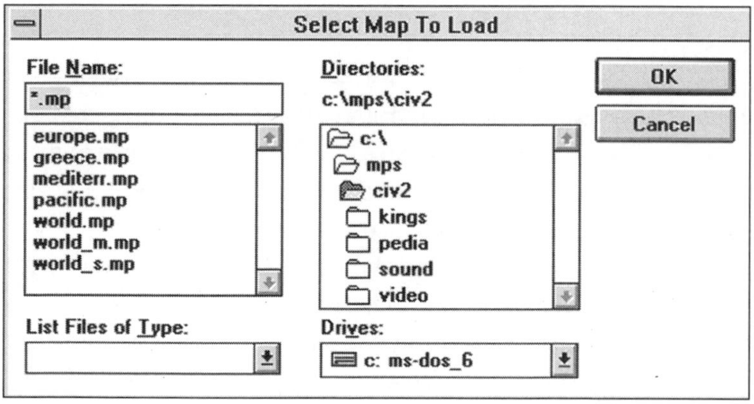

Select Map To Load
File Name:
*.mp
europe.mp
greece.mp
mediterr.mp
pacific.mp
world.mp
world_m.mp
world_s.mp
List Files of Type:
Directories:
c:\mps\civ2
c:\
mps
civ2
kings
pedia
sound
video
Drives:
c: ms-dos_6
OK
Cancel

FIGURE 2.8: Load a map file to select a premade world on which to experience your simulation.

CUSTOMIZING A WORLD

The Customize World pregame option allows you to customize the world on which your simulation will takes place. When you select this option, you'll be given an assortment of decisions to make that will ultimately determine the size, climate, and details of the world.

Begin by choosing the World Size (Small, Normal, or Large) option and clicking on the OK button to proceed to the next customization window. For any of these options, you can click on the Random button, and then let the computer make the decision on your behalf. Next, you can customize the size of the individual land masses in the world (Small, Normal, or Large). This will be followed by another window, asking you to determine the Land Form type (Archipelago, Varied, or Continents). Moving right along, you'll have to set the climate for your world (Arid, Normal, or Wet), followed by the Temperature (Cool, Temperate, or Warm).

The age of your world will also have to be selected (three, four, or five billion years old). The remainder of the customization options are the same as if you selected the Start a New Game pregame option.

All of the decisions you make—about the overall world size, land mass size, land form type, climate, and temperature—will impact the long-term growth of your empire. Smaller land masses don't leave too much room for multiple civilizations to coexist, so battles will take place more often and earlier in the game. Meanwhile, if the climate is too wet or too dry, building productive cities will be more challenging.

BEGINNING A SCENARIO

The *Civ II* CD-ROM comes with several scenarios that the programmers have created. These scenarios are loosely based on real-life historical events, as you can see in Figures 2.9 and 2.10, and begin with your empire already established. Each scenario has predefined goals that you must attempt to achieve by a certain year.

Choose the Begin Scenario pregame option and the Select Scenario To Load window will appear, listing files with a .scn extension. These files indicate presaved *scenarios* as opposed to presaved *simulations*. Choose the scenario of your choice, and click on the OK button. A new window, containing a description of the scenario and your objectives, will be displayed. You will then have the opportunity to select which empire you wish to lead and then the overall level of difficulty of the game. The scenario simulation will then begin. Remember, when a scenario begins, your empire will be well established (as will your competition). Begin by determining the current situation(s)

World War II – Europe

Length: June 1940 to Dec 1947

The date is June, 1940. German Panzers are poised to strike through the Ardennes, disembowelling the Allied defenses and driving on to Paris in an astounding six week blitzkrieg. Can Churchill rally his troops in time, or will England likewise succumb to the Axis juggernaut? Meanwhile, in the east, the Russian Bear sleeps. Has the Molotov-Ribbentrop pact assured Germany's eastern flank? Or will the Axis seek its lebensraum on the Russian steppes?

OK

FIGURE 2.9: At the start of a scenario, a special text-based window will appear, offering you background information and outlining your objectives.

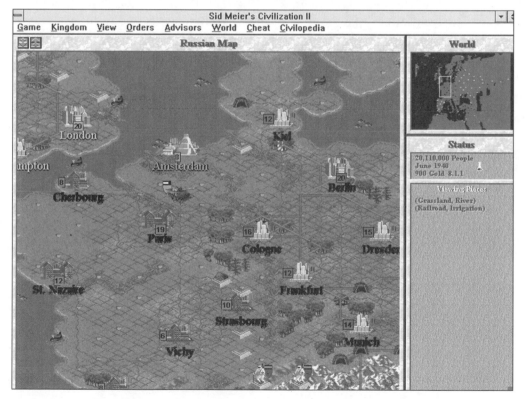

FIGURE 2.10: This game screen shows the World War II scenario right at the beginning. Notice the year is 1940 and the population is over 20 million. Depending on which empire you choose to rule, your objectives will be different.

you face, learn the lay of the land, consult with your advisors, fight for your visions, and then proceed to develop your strategies. To succeed in completing the objectives of a scenario, you must quickly obtain a good understanding of what your empire is facing and what its military and financial resources include.

LOADING A SAVED GAME

Simulations in *Civ II* are designed to take many hours to experience from start to finish. So, unless you have absolutely no life, chances are you'll want to take breaks and continue a simulation at a later time. This can be done by first saving your game data, and then reloading that game using the Load a Game pregame option. This displays the Select Game To Load dialog box shown in Figure 2.11. If during a simulation you make what turns out to be a serious error in strategy, you can use this option to reload your simulation from an earlier point, before the mistake was made.

> **TIP**
>
> Another time when you'll use the Load a Game option is right after the *Civ II* game crashes and you need to restart a simulation. If you find that the game crashes often, be sure to activate the Save Game After Every Turn option on the Game Options menu. See Chapter 4, *The Civilization II Menu Bar*, for a complete discussion of the game menus. Also, as a general rule, you'll want to save your game data often as you experience a simulation.

On choosing the Load a Game option, a Select Game To Load dialog box will appear, which contains a list of simulation files that have already been saved, as shown in Figure 2.11. Saved games have a .sav file extension. If you use the default file names to save a simulation, the first few letters of each filename will represent the leaders name. The second part of a saved game's filename will represent the year in which the simulation was saved (a simulation takes place over the course of many years). Choose the filename that represents the simulation you want to load, and then click on the OK button. The simulation will now pick up where you left off when it was last saved.

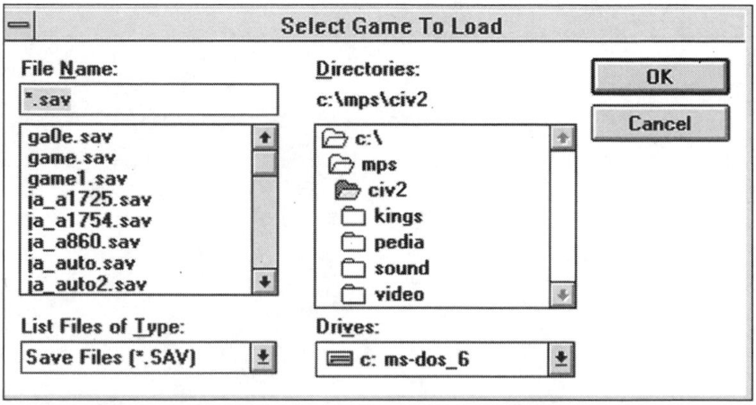

Select Game To Load

File **N**ame:	**D**irectories:	
*.sav	c:\mps\civ2	**OK**
		Cancel

File Name list:
ga0e.sav
game.sav
game1.sav
ja_a1725.sav
ja_a1754.sav
ja_a860.sav
ja_auto.sav
ja_auto2.sav

Directories list:
c:\
mps
civ2
kings
pedia
sound
video

List Files of **T**ype:
Save Files (*.SAV)

Dri**v**es:
c: ms-dos_6

FIGURE 2.11: The Load a Game option allows you to determine which file, containing a saved simulation, you wish to load. Saved games can be loaded from your computer's hard disk or a floppy disk. All saved game files have a .sav extension.

YOU'VE SELECTED PREGAME OPTIONS, NOW WHAT?

As soon as you've selected the type of game you'll be playing using the pregame options and your simulation actually begins, you'll be forced to start making decisions as you establish your tribe and start building it into a world-dominating empire. If you're new to *Civ II*, be sure to read Chapter 5, *Your First Civilization II Simulation*, which offers a guided walk-through of managing your empire in the early stages of a simulation. Good luck as you proceed to make history.

Rome 6

Tarracina 3

Neopolis 5

Hera 3

3

The *Civilization II* Game Screens

C iv II is composed of two primary game screens. It is from these screens that you'll create, build up, and manage your empire as you work your way toward colonizing space or becoming a world dominator. This section of *Civilization II Strategies & Secrets* offers details about all the command and game-play options available to you from the Main Game screen and the City screen. Once you have a good comprehension of what's available to you from these primary game screens, you'll be well on your way to understanding the *Civ II* game.

THE MAIN GAME SCREEN

In several ways, *Civ II*'s Main Game screen, shown in Figure 3.1, is easier to understand than the Main Game screen of *Civilization* or *CivNet*. One of the most obvious changes in *Civ II* is the viewing perspective of the Main Map. Perhaps you have already noticed that *Civ II* features high-resolution graphics and all of the units, cities, and other graphics have been redesigned. The graphics are now extremely detailed and often appear three-dimensional. The Main Map area on *Civ II*'s Main Game screen takes advantage of an isometric grid instead of the square grid you may already be familiar with from past versions of the game. Now, each terrain square is diamond shaped instead of square because you're viewing the terrain from an angle, looking proudly down on your empire.

The Main Game screen offers a close-up graphical overview of the terrain in the Main Map, a Menu Bar with a series of pull-down menu options at the top of the screen,

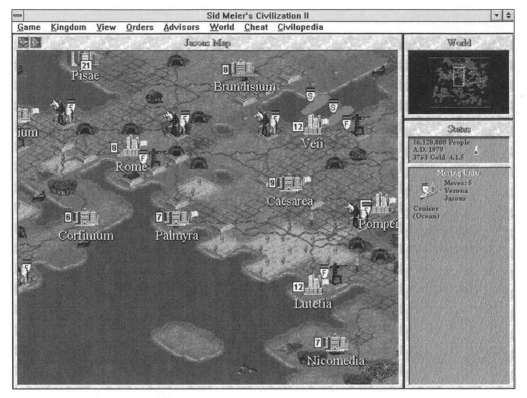

FIGURE 3.1: The Main Game screen contains a Menu Bar, a Main Map window, and a window displaying vital information.

a small map of the entire (explored) world, plus a data window that contains vital information about each terrain square, city, and active unit.

The Main Game screen's Menu Bar consists of the following eight pull-down menus:

- Game menu
- Kingdom menu
- View menu
- Orders menu
- Advisors menu
- World menu

⊕ Cheat menu

⊕ Civilopedia menu

To activate any of these pull-down menus, you can hold down the keyboard's Alt key and press the key for the first (underlined) letter in the menu's name—<u>G</u>ame, <u>K</u>ingdom, <u>V</u>iew, <u>O</u>rders, <u>A</u>dvisors, <u>W</u>orld, <u>C</u>heat, or <u>C</u>ivilopedia—on the Menu Bar (for example, press Alt + G for the Game Menu, Alt + K for the Kingdom menu, and so on). To select the Civilopedia menu, you must press Alt + C twice. If you're using a mouse, you can point the mouse pointer at the appropriate choice on the Menu Bar and click the left mouse button to select that choice.

With each pull-down menu comes a variety of commands, some of which you will use often during a simulation. Others you'll use less frequently—but when you do use them, they will come in extremely handy. All of the Menu Bar's pull-down menu options are described in detail in Chapter 4, *The Civilization II Menu Bar*.

NOTE The Civilopedia is an on-screen encyclopedia of *Civilization* information, It contains detailed descriptions of commands and game screens that you'll need to understand the game. After reading this strategy guide, you probably won't need to access the Civilopedia too often. Still, it's nice to know it is waiting for you should you need it during a simulation.

THE MAIN GAME SCREEN'S WINDOWS AND MAPS

A vast amount of information can be gleaned from using the options found under the various pull-down menus; however, there is also a substantial amount of information constantly available to you on the Main Game screen's maps and windows.

The World Map Window

Located in the upper-right corner of the Main Game screen is a small map of the entire explored world on which each simulation takes place (see Figure 3.2). All terrain on the planet will eventually be viewable from this map, unlike the larger Main Map, which at any given time only displays a portion of the overall world.

At the start of a simulation, the World Map will appear almost entirely black because you have not yet begun exploring. As you move your various units around on the Main Map, however, more and more of the world's terrain will be revealed.

FIGURE 3.2: This window shows you a close-up view of the world map.

The World Map window is separate from the Main Map and the Status windows. Using the mouse, it is possible to reposition it anywhere on the game screen, at any time. By placing the mouse pointer at one of the World map window's corners, you can resize this window (just as you can do with any window within the Microsoft Windows 3.1x or Windows 95 operating system).

Located within the World Map window is a white box. This white box represents the area of the world that is visible on the larger Main Map. Using the mouse, you can move this white cursor anywhere within the World Map, and the Main Map will automatically reposition itself around the area you selected. This makes jumping around and seeing the entire world easier.

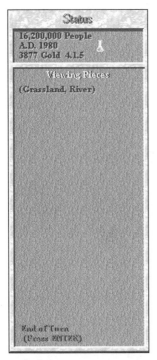

FIGURE 3.3: The Status window displays your empire's current population, the current year, the amount of money in your empire's treasury, and the tax rate.

The Status Window

Just below the World Map window, along the right side of the screen, is the Status window, as shown in Figure 3.3. This window is divided into two main areas. At the top of the Status window the current population of your empire is displayed. Just below the population is the current year, and below that is the amount of money in your empire's treasury, along with the tax rates that you have set.

The top portion of this screen will keep you informed about the funds available to you, as well as the Tax, Luxury, and Scientific Rates you have selected. The small icon to the right that looks like a beaker to the right of this financial information provides a graphic representation of the scientific work that is being done by your empire's scientists during each turn. The brighter yellow the light bulb appears, the more active your scientists are.

Most of the information within this Status window can and will change constantly as each turn takes place. Use this window to track how quickly your population and finances are growing (or shrinking!), and at what intervals time is passing.

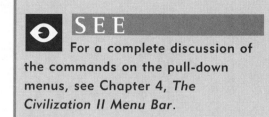

SEE For a complete discussion of the commands on the pull-down menus, see Chapter 4, *The Civilization II Menu Bar*.

You'll notice that nowhere in the Status window is there a graphic representation of your Throne Room/Palace, which was a feature found in the *Civilization* and *CivNet* games. If you want to view your Throne Room, select the View Throne Room command on the Kingdom pull-down menu.

Working your way down to the lower portion of the Status window, this is where you can view information about the active unit and the terrain that the Active Unit is currently on. A graphic representation of the active unit will appear in the middle of the status window, along with text-based information describing the number of terrain squares that the active unit can cross during a turn. Information about the unit's home city and empire will also be displayed, along with the type of terrain the Active Unit is standing on. If any Terrain Improvements have been made to the terrain that the active unit is standing on, such as roads, irrigation systems, and the like, this information will also be displayed within the Status window. Often, multiple units will be occupying the same terrain square, so if the active unit is standing on a terrain square with multiple units on it, this information will also be displayed within the Status window.

The lower portion of the Status window is used to inform you about trade routes, pollution, and other information that's pertinent to the current turn. At the completion of a turn, the message "End of Turn (Press Enter)" will appear at the bottom of the Status window.

The Main Map Window

Basically, everything that happens in *Civ II* is seen taking place on the Main Map, as shown in Figure 3.4. You can view cities and units in great detail, along with a graphic representation of the terrain. If roads, mines, irrigation facilities and/or any other Terrain Improvements have been made, they are visible from the Main Map. This Map also shows the types of terrain that make up each continent. The Main Map is where

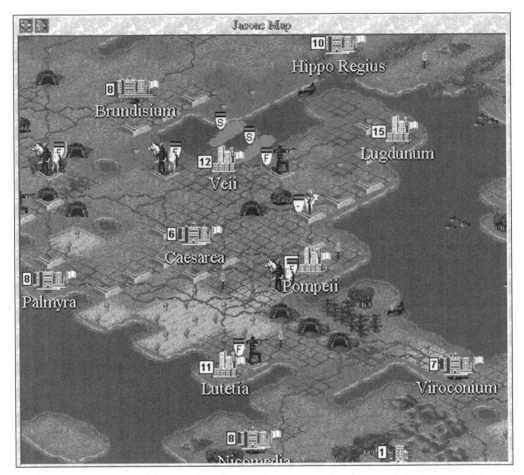

FIGURE 3.4: You will see much of what takes place in *Civ II* on the Main Map window.

you move around your units, build your cities, and conquer your enemies in battle (or are obliterated by them).

During each turn, you will move one unit at a time. The active unit will be the one flashing on the Main Map. To make an alternate unit active during a turn, use the mouse to click on that unit, and then use any of the commands on the Orders pull-down menu to determine what actions, if any, the now active unit will take.

On the Main Map, each type of unit looks different. Using the commands available to you on the Orders pull-down menu (with the mouse or their direct keyboard equivalents), you can place a unit in Sleep mode. When you do this, that unit will change to a solid gray color on the Main Map, and the letter "S" (for Sleep) will appear within that unit's shield.

Simply by looking at the Main Map, you can tell if a unit has been Fortified because that unit will be standing still and the letter "F" (for Fortified) will appear within that the unit's shield. A stone-line base will form around the Fortified Unit as well. Units that have been commanded to travel from one location to

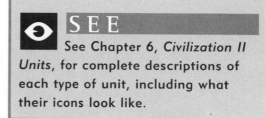

SEE
See Chapter 6, *Civilization II Units*, for complete descriptions of each type of unit, including what their icons look like.

another using the GoTo command will display a "G" (for GoTo) within their shields.

Keeping tabs of what your Settler and Engineer Units are doing is also easy when you know what to look for on the Main Map. Settler and Engineer Units that are building roads will have the letter "R" on their shields, while Settler Units working on irrigation systems will have the letter "I" within their shields. The Settler Unit you see here displays an "M" in its shield because it is in the process of building a mine.

Using the other visual clues found on the Main Map, you can quickly analyze each city, simply by looking at its size and the strength value (a number), which appears next to each city on the map. Roads, irrigation systems, railroads, mines, and all other Terrain Improvements are all graphically depicted on the Main Map. If a city has City Walls built around it for protection, this too will be displayed graphically. Irrigation is graphically depicted on the Main Map as blue water trails in a small grid-like shape. Roads, on the other hand, appear on the Main Map as solid tan lines.

It is important to learn how each unit, city, terrain type, Terrain Improvement, and other types of icons are graphically depicted on the Main Map if you want to have a good understanding of this game, which is more graphically oriented than the original *Civilization* or *CivNet* games.

Controlling the Main Map Window's View

The Main Map is the largest portion of the Main Game screen. This map area represents a small portion of the World Map; however, using two different sets of controls, you can determine the size of the area of terrain you're viewing at any given time. Located in the upper-left corner of the Main Map window are two small icons. If you click on the left icon, you can zoom in, which means the area of terrain you can see will decrease, but the size of each icon and unit will become larger. By clicking on the right icon, you can zoom out, which means that the area of terrain you view will increase but the size of the icons, units and the detail of the map will diminish.

To give you additional control over the size of terrain area you view in the Main Map window, take advantage of the commands available on the View pull-down menu. These commands are:

⊕ Zoom In

⊕ Zoom Out

⊕ Max Zoom In

⊕ Standard Zoom

⊕ Medium Zoom Out

⊕ Max Zoom Out

These commands are described in Chapter 4, *The Civilization II Menu Bar*, which follows this chapter. Figure 3.5 shows you the Main Map window in Standard Zoom view, while Figures 3.6 and 3.7 display the Main Map window as viewed with the Max Zoom In and Max Zoom Out commands, respectively.

THE CITY SCREEN

The second most important game screen in *Civ II* is the City Screen. Every city within a simulation has a City screen, which graphically depicts just about everything you need to know about a specific city within your civilization. Each city you build will have its own City screen. This screen is divided into multiple sections. You'll have to become acquainted with the meaning of each graphic icon to fully understand what's happening within each city.

A City screen will automatically appear when a city is initially founded, and then again when the city has completed the production of a unit, City Improvement, or

FIGURE 3.5: The Main Map window in Standard Zoom view.

Wonder of the World. You can also gain access to this screen at any time (during a turn), by clicking the mouse on the city that's displayed on the Main Map. A city on the Main Map looks like a building, or series of buildings, which is accompanied by a number that represents the overall strength and size of the city. Unless it is covered by nearby units or Terrain Improvements, the name of each city will also be displayed on the Main Map. You'll notice that, like your units, all the cities within your empire are color-coded based on the color that's associated with your empire. Each empire has a color associated with it, so you can differentiate between friendly and enemy cities and units.

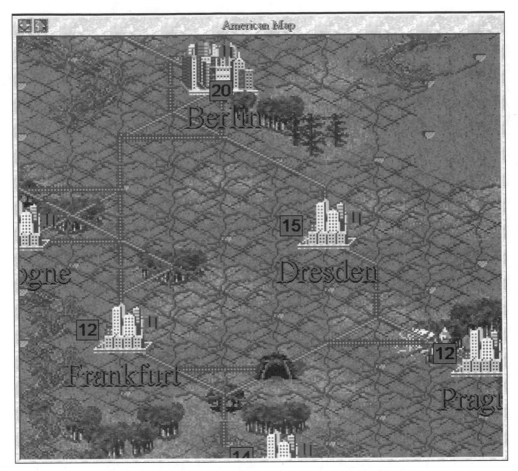

FIGURE 3.6: The Max Zoom In command changes the view of the Main Map window to show an extreme close-up of its detail.

From the City screen, you can expect to obtain information about the city's location, population, resources, food storage, current production, and obtained improvements or wonders. You'll notice that each of these windows contain special graphic icons—for example, the population roster in the upper-left corner of the City screen depicts several different types of citizens.

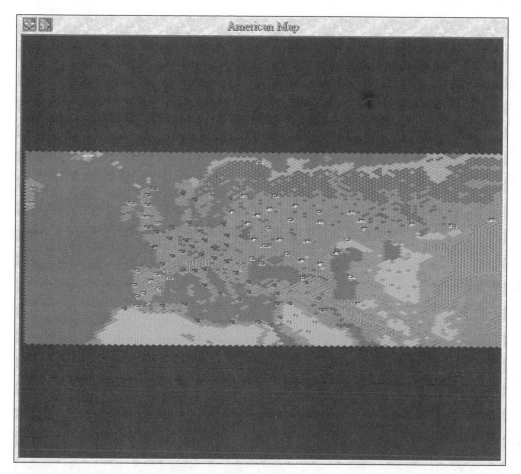

FIGURE 3.7: The Max Zoom Out command changes the view of the Main Map window to show a bird's-eye view of the terrain.

CREATING CITIZENS AND ASSIGNING THEIR ROLES

It is from the City screen that you order your citizens to produce (or purchase) City Improvements. The City screen also gives you the ability to create Specialists—Taxmen, Scientists, and Entertainers. You can see the size of your population, represented both graphically and numerically, by checking the very top of the City screen window and studying the population roster located below it.

As you can see from the graphic depiction of your citizens in the upper-left corner of the City screen, there are two primary types of people in your population—

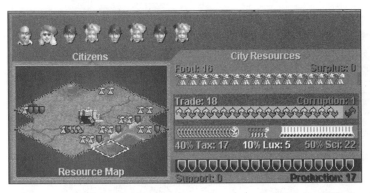

FIGURE 3.8: This population roster shows normal citizens (Workers).

Workers and Specialists. The Workers in your population can be happy, content, or unhappy with your leadership abilities. (See Figure 3.8.) Their attitude will have a major impact on your empire's overall productivity and growth, so your population's happiness is something you'll have to watch closely and keep control of throughout each simulation.

Specialists (those who have been made into Taxmen, Scientists, and Entertainers) have much more power in the city. They help to build units, improvements, and wonders, plus they raise money for your empire by collecting taxes and better managing finances in each of the cities in which they work. Creating Specialists results in decreased food production for the city because a Worker has to be taken out of the workforce to be converted into the Specialist's position. With fewer Workers, less food is produced by the city.

Taxmen, Scientists, and Entertainers look different than they did in previous versions of *Civilization*. In *Civ II*, you will see heads in the population roster, as shown in Figures 3.9 and 3.10. Taxmen look like business people. Scientists look like little Albert Einsteins, and Entertainers look like Elvis Presleys. As soon as you transform a normal citizen into a

TIP

In *Civilization*, you get more points if your population is a happy one. Your population can also be merely content, which isn't worth as many points, but it's much better than having an unhappy population. To keep a city from entering into a state of civil disorder, you'll want to ensure that it maintains more happy people than unhappy people.

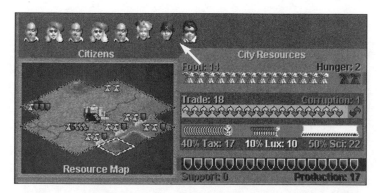

FIGURE 3.9: This population roster shows one Entertainer mixed in with the general population of the city. As your empire evolves and becomes more modernized, the look of the population in this roster will change, although what the icons represent remains the same.

Specialist, you'll see that the food, trade, and production capabilities of that city change. This information is depicted graphically near the center of the City screen (to the left of the Food Storage window).

Entertainers are meant to keep the population happy (or at least content). As your city grows and becomes productive, you'll want Taxmen to boost a city's efficiency and to generate more tax revenues. Taxmen allow each city to better manage finances and tax collection. With Taxmen, tax dollars can be stretched, so you can keep the Tax Rates lower, which in turn will keep your population happier in the long run. Scientists increase the creation and discovery of Knowledge Advances.

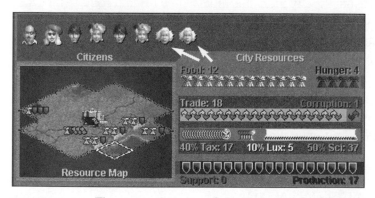

FIGURE 3.10: This roster shows two Scientists mingled with the general population of the city.

TIP
Don't create Specialists until the city becomes productive and can maintain an adequate storage of food. Also, keep in mind that the use of Entertainers is only a quick and temporary fix for changing the attitude of the city's population.
Building specific improvements (such as Temples and Cathedrals) and wonders provides a long-term way of keeping your population happy.

Creating Specialists

You create Specialists from within the City screen. Just below the population roster is a map of that city, plus a series of colored icons that represent how that city's workforce is being allocated. Yellow icons on the map represent food production. The small blue shield icons represent the development of resources (such as improvements and wonders), while the orange icons on the small map represent trade. The larger diamond in the center of the map is the heart of the city itself. Using the mouse, click on the icons on the small map to transform the people the icons represent into Specialists. You can also move the colored icons around the outskirts of the city, so that they can cultivate the best terrain. The first time you create a Specialist, the person on the right-most side of the population roster will be transformed into an Entertainer. If you do it again, a second Specialist will be created.

You may notice that the chart located next to the small map, which depicts how the energies of the population are divided, changes as an Entertainer is created. Food production for that city is reduced, and production goes up. Now, to transform the Entertainer you just created into a Taxman, click on the Entertainer's head (on the population roster). Notice that the city's income, represented by gold coins in the chart next to the small map, increases. Now, to transform a Taxman into a Scientist and boost knowledge production, click once again on the Taxman's head (on the population roster).

It is all too easy to create too many Taxmen, Entertainers, and Scientists within a city, resulting in serious problems for that city. One of your most important tasks in managing a city is keeping a safe balance. You want each city to be as productive as possible, while at the same time generating as much scientific knowledge and revenue as possible.

THE FOOD STORAGE WINDOW

In the upper-right corner of the City screen is the Food Storage window. After one of your cities creates enough food to keep the population alive, any surplus food is placed in storage. Building a Granary helps to increase the storage capacity for a city's food supply. How much food surplus a city creates is represented by the number of wheat icons found in the Food Storage window of the City screen.

CREATING CITY IMPROVEMENTS AND WONDERS

FIGURE 3.11: The City screen's Production window allows you to allocate a city's resources toward building units, improvements, and wonders.

Below the Food Storage window is the City screen's Production window, as shown in Figure 3.11. It is from this window that you determine what each city will allocate its production resources to build. Every city within your empire can build units, City Improvements, or Wonders of the World; however, each city can only build *one* thing at a time, and each thing takes multiple turns to complete. Knowing what to create in each city and when to create it is one of the ongoing strategy elements of the game.

In the top-center of the Production window is the name and icon of the unit, improvement, or wonder being built within that city. This listing is a graphic depiction of how far along is production. Anytime you access the City screen, you can choose to change what the city is producing by clicking on the Change button located at the top of the Production window. Instead of waiting for the city to finish building the unit, improvement, or wonder (over the course of multiple turns), you can choose to spend money from your empire's treasury and buy whatever it is that the city is building. By clicking on the Buy button, you can purchase the unit, improvement, or wonder instantly, so that it will be available to you on your next turn.

Should you decide to change what is being built and you click on the Change button, another window will appear on the screen. This *What shall we build in (town name)?* Window, shown in Figure 3.12, contains a list of units, improvements, and wonders that your empire currently has the scientific knowledge to build. This list includes the names of each unit, improvement, and wonder, its icon, and the number of turns it will take to complete building the item. If you're going to build a Military Unit, additional information about that type of unit's movement capabilities, attack strength, defensive strength, and hit points will be displayed.

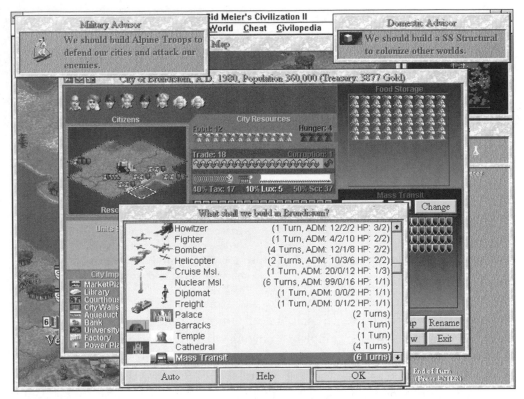

FIGURE 3.12: The City screen's *What shall we build in (town name)?* window is where you can select what it is you want your city to build.

On the right of this window is a scroll bar that allows you to move up or down to view the entire list of units, improvements, and wonders that can be built. When you're ready to make your selection, use the mouse to highlight and select the menu option, and then click on the OK button located at the bottom of the window. Two smaller Advisor windows will appear at the top of the City screen simultaneously. Your Military Advisor will recommend what type(s) of Military Units you should build, while your Domestic Advisor will tell you via a text-based massage which Improvements a city requires in order to continue growing.

When you look at the City screen's Production window, what you selected will now appear, showing you that the city is currently building the selected unit, improvement, or wonder.

Civilization II's Auto Build Feature

Once you've built up many cities within your empire, spending the time returning to each city's City screen after each city builds whatever you allocated it to build would become far too time-consuming. However, notice that at the bottom of the *What shall we build in (town name)?* window are three command buttons—Auto, Help, and OK, as shown in Figure 3.13. The new Auto Production feature can be activated, by clicking on the Auto (for Automatic) button. This activates Auto Production mode. (This Auto option stands for automatic production of units and improvements, and has nothing to do with an automobile production plant that builds cars.) Instead of having you determine what unit or improvement will be built within a city, Auto Production mode lets the computer make the determination for you. The Auto Production feature will not build Wonders of the World, but it will choose the best units or improvements to produce on your behalf.

When you click on the Auto Production button, another window appears, asking you to decide if you want the computer to allocate the city's resources toward building up your empire's military or if peaceful expansion is more important. When the *Who will control production?* window appears, you must choose to allow your Military Advisor, Domestic Advisor, or both advisors to take control over production and automatically determine what units or improvements will be built within a city set on Auto Production mode.

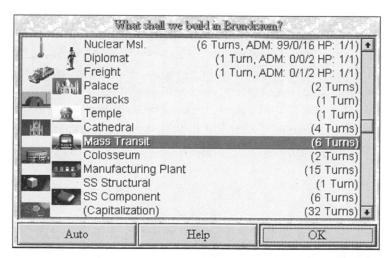

FIGURE 3.13: The *What shall we build in (town name)?* window's Auto button lets you activate Auto Production mode, in which the computer automatically determines what unit or improvement the active city will build.

FIGURE 3.14: The City screen's City
Improvement roster shows the improvements
and wonders (if any) that have already been
built within that city.

The City Improvement Roster

In the lower-left corner of the City screen
is a window that contains a list of City
Improvements and Wonders of the
World that a city has already built. As
each city purchases or produces a City
Improvement, the icon representing the
improvement will appear within this
City Improvement roster, as shown in
Figure 3.14. The gold coins to the right
of the listed items in the City Improvement roster indicate those improvements that
can be sold to raise money, if it becomes necessary. At the start of the game, the only
item listed within the City Improvement roster for your capital city will be a Palace,
which is automatically built when the capital city is founded. You can use this window to quickly determine what resources a city has and what still must be built to help
it sustain itself and continue to grow.

Some improvements, such as Granaries, are necessary to maintain the city's
growth and population, while Wonders of the World, such as the Apollo Program, are
necessary to progress in the game. Some improvements also help to keep your population happy, while others are needed to reduce corruption, improve productivity, or
generate or store more food.

Notice the a scroll bar on the right side of the City Improvements roster. Using the
mouse, you can scroll up or down the city's list of improvements and wonders. Because
the improvements made to each city are worth money, it is possible to sell a City
Improvement, if you find that your finances are running low; however, you won't want
to sell something the city requires to maintain its population. For example, a Granary
is important for storing surplus food to feed a growing population. If you decide to sell
a city's Granary, the city could experience a famine shortly thereafter, resulting in a
population reduction—and people thirsty for your blood.

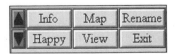

FIGURE 3.15: The City screen's command
buttons provide access to valuable information about your empire's cities.

A CITY'S MILITARY LINE-UP

The City screen can also be used to help you determine the number and types of Military Units that a city has built (and currently has in operation on the Main Map). You can do this by looking at the graphic representation above the City Improvement roster. If a blue shield is located near one or more of these units, it represents the cost per turn that is associated with keeping that unit operating away from its home city.

THE CITY SCREEN'S COMMAND BUTTONS

In the lower-right corner of the City screen are eight command buttons that provide you with additional information about each of your cities. These buttons are shown in Figure 3.15. These command buttons do the following:

- **Up and Down Arrows** Use these arrow buttons to scroll through all of your cities' City screens quickly. Instead of returning to the Main Game screen, and then clicking on a different city in order to access its City screen, you can flip through and view each of your cities' City screens easily and quickly with these buttons.

- **Info** The Info button displays text-based information about the selected city within the area located directly to the left of the command buttons. The display includes information about trade routes, what resources the city needs, and any resources of which it has a surplus.

- **Map** By clicking on the Map button, a small map appears that is similar to the Main Map. However, this map contains no detail whatsoever.

- **Rename** If you choose to rename a city, click on this command button and then type a new name for the city.

- **Happy** This command button causes an expanded Population roster to appear. This detailed (graphic-based) roster will tell you about the happy, unhappy, and content people living within that city.

- **View** Click on this button to see a graphic representation of the city, including graphic depictions of each improvement and wonder within that city.

Exit   Click on this button to make the City screen disappear, allowing you to return to the Main Game screen.

RESIZING THE CITY SCREEN

If you look in the upper-left corner of the City screen, there are three buttons. Clicking on the button marked with an "x" allows you to close the City screen and return to the Main Game screen. The middle button allows you to shrink the size of the City screen. This allows you to view it in conjunction with the Main Game screen. If you shrink the City screen, you can fit multiple City screens on the computer screen at the same time to get a bigger picture of what's happening within your empire. The next button to the left in the City screen's upper-left corner resizes its window to the default size, which is about two-thirds of the total screen area.

TIP

There are two other ways you can exit a City screen. You can set this function for the Enter key on the Game pull-down menu. Pressing Enter then clears the City screen and returns you to the Main Game screen. Alternatively you can click on the upper-left corner of the City screen window.

Now that you have a basic understanding of the information available to you on the *Civ II* game screens, go on to Chapter 4, *The Civilization II Menu Bar*, for a closer look at each of the commands and options available to you on the game's pull-down menus. The statement, "you've got the whole world in your hands" takes on a new meaning once you understand the commands available to you from the game's pull-down menus. It is with these commands that you'll be able to take control over your empire and determine its fate as a simulation progresses.

4

The *Civilization II* Menu Bar

The *Civilization II* Menu Bar offers you complete control over the game, just as it did in the original *Civilization* and *CivNet* games. *Civ II*, however, offers several new commands that enhance your game-play experience. This chapter describes the purpose of each command that is available to you on the Menu Bar's eight pull-down menus.

You can use either the mouse or the keyboard to access any of the pull-down menus. To open a menu with the mouse, simply click on its name. When using the keyboard, press the Alt key in conjunction with the first (underlined) letter in the menu's name. With a menu fully displayed, you can just point to the command you want and click on it, or you can use the keyboard equivalent, which is listed beside the command. The keyboard equivalent for each command is shown with the command in the following discussion.

THE GAME
PULL-DOWN MENU (ALT+G)

The Game pull-down menu shown in Figure 4.1 gives you the ability to save your game data, customize the overall game-play experience, or end your simulation before achieving one of the game's two primary objectives: world domination, or space exploration and colonization. Several of the commands available on the Game pull-down menu display a submenu of additional options.

GAME OPTIONS (CTRL+O)

When you select this command, a window containing a variety of game options appears, as shown in Figure 4.2 appears on the screen. This window contains ten

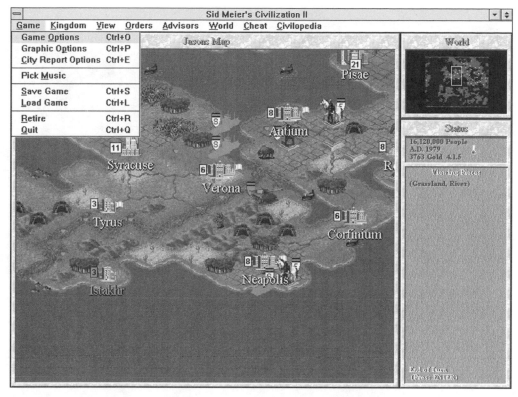

FIGURE 4.1: The Game pull-down menu contains several commands that help you control the game environment, including saving your simulations.

game-play features that can be turned on or off by placing a check mark in or removing it from the appropriate box next to each option. When a check mark is visible, that feature is activated. Use the mouse to place a check mark in the boxes next to the menu options you want active during a simulation. Similarly, remove any check marks for those options that you want to deactivate. These options can be changed at almost any time during a simulation.

- **Sound Effects** Turn the game's sound effects on or off.

- **Music** Turn the game's background music on or off.

- **Always wait at end of turn** You will be prompted to press the Enter key at the conclusion of each turn.

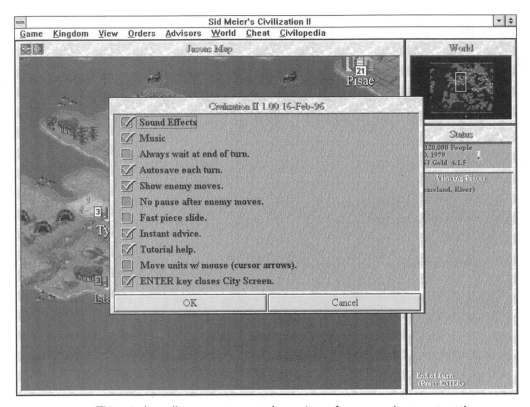

FIGURE 4.2: This window allows you to control a variety of game environment settings.

⊕ **Autosave each turn** This feature saves your entire simulation after each turn. This allows you to reload a simulation easily, should the game crash or hang up for some reason. It is highly recommended that you keep this function active. Your game data will automatically be stored in a file called ??_auto.sav, where the first two letters represent the first two letters of the leader's name.

⊕ **Show enemy moves** This option allows you to see the enemy's units moving around the explored portion of the Main Game screen. This slows down the game a bit but helps you see what your human or computer controlled opponents are doing.

⊕ **No pause after enemy moves** Activating this feature will speed up the game a bit.

⊕ **Fast piece slide**   The individual units move around the Main Game screen faster when this option is active, though the animation and the units' movements are less detailed.

⊕ **Instant advice**   Small advice windows will appear throughout a simulation, offering you game-play tips and strategies. This feature should be activated if you're new to this game.

⊕ **Tutorial help**   When activated, this feature causes additional help windows to appear. These windows contain game-play advice and strategy suggestions, plus details on short-cuts you can use.

⊕ **Move units w/ mouse (cursor arrows)**   The on-screen units can be moved using the mouse (if this option is activated) or the directional arrows on the keyboard.

⊕ **ENTER key closes City Screen**   In addition to clicking the button labeled "X" in the upper-left corner of the City screen's window to close it, you can simply press the Enter key to close it when this option is activate.

GRAPHIC OPTIONS (CTRL+P)

Similar to the Game Options command, the Graphic Options command displays the Select Graphic Options window, as shown in Figure 4.3. Place check marks in the boxes next to the options you want to be active during the simulation. These options allow you to view various types of animation that are built into the game. By placing a check mark next to any or all these options, you will see animated sequences at the appropriate times throughout the game. When you are viewing these animated features (which have no impact on the actual game), it takes up time and thus slows down the game. Unless you did a full installation of the *Civ II* game when you installed it onto your computer, the *Civ II* CD must be placed in your computer's CD-ROM drive to view some of these animation and video sequences, such as the High Council Meeting or the Wonders of the World videos.

⊕ **Throne Room**   View your Throne Room to see how its features progress as your empire grows.

⊕ **Diplomacy Screen**   View the Diplomacy screen.

⊕ **Animated Heralds**   View the celebration animation features.

Select Graphic Options

- ☑ Throne Room
- ☑ Diplomacy Screen
- ☑ Animated Heralds (Requires 16 megabytes RAM)
- ☑ Civilopedia for Advances
- ☑ Town Council
- ☑ Wonder Movies

OK	Cancel

FIGURE 4.3: From this Select Graphic Options window, you determine if you want to view the game's various animated sequences during the game.

- **Civilopedia for Advances**   When you create a Knowledge Advance, this command provides information about the advice from the Civilopedia automatically.

- **High Council (a.k.a. Town Council)**   View the High Council screen, which shows graphic illustrations of your advisors and displays text-based advice from each of them.

- **Wonder Movies**   See special animated sequences each time your empire develops a Wonder of the World. Each wonder's animated sequence is different.

CITY REPORT OPTIONS (CTRL+E)

To obtain information about what is happening within each of your cities, you must consult with your advisors. By activating the options shown in Figure 4.4, you can have the advisors offer you text-based warnings, even if you do not choose to access their reports. Activating these submenu options allows you to easily keep closer tabs on your empire. Use the mouse to place a check mark in the boxes next to the menu commands you want to be active during the simulation.

- **Warn when city growth halted (Aqueduct/Sewer System)**   A warning will appear when something needs to be done within a given city to

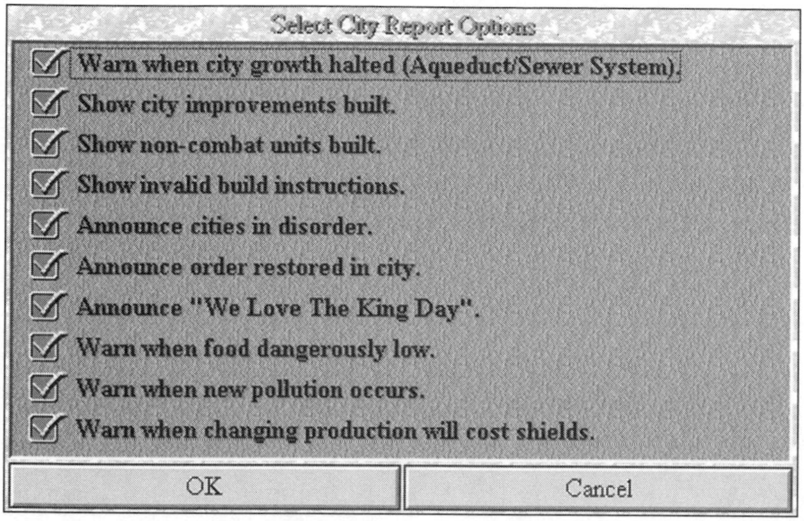

FIGURE 4.4: The Select City Report Options window provides you with various options for getting text-based reports from your advisors periodically during a simulation.

ensure its continued growth and prosperity. Once a city reaches a certain size, you must take specific steps, such as building an Aqueduct City Improvement, to ensure ongoing growth.

Show city improvements built   When you examine a city, you will see the City Improvements that have already been built.

Show non-combat units built   When you examine a city, you will be able to see how many Settler, Diplomat, and other types of nonmilitary units that city has built.

Show invalid build instructions   You will be notified if you have ordered a city to build an improvement or wonder that cannot be built at that time. For example, you will be warned if you try to build a Wonder of the World that has already been built or if you have a city set to build City Improvements in Auto Production mode, while there are no new improvements that *can* be built within that city. Because only one of each type of improvement can be built within each city of your empire, you will also be warned if your building efforts are being unnecessarily duplicated.

- **Announce cities in disorder** If too many members of a city's population become unhappy (which can happen for many different reasons), a city will go into a state of disorder. If this feature is activated, when you're viewing the Main Game screen, a special icon will appear within the city square of the city that is in a state of disorder. A special text-based warning message will also be displayed.

- **Announce order restored in city** Once you have taken the appropriate actions to restore order to a city that is in a state of disorder, if this feature is activated, the disorder icon that appeared at the time of disorder will disappear, and a text message will be displayed announcing that the city is no longer in trouble.

- **Announce "We Love The King Day"** Every so often, if you're doing a good job keeping your population happy, they will celebrate your good leadership by allowing you to build an expansion onto your throne room. This feature has no impact on the overall game play, but it does go a long way toward boosting the ego of the player. Unlike in the original *Civilization* or *CivNet* games, a graphic representation of your castle/throne is not constantly displayed on the Main Game screen.

- **Warn when food is dangerously low** If you're in the process of starving a city's population, this can cause a drastic population reduction in a city. By activating this feature, you will be warned when a city's food supply is running low. This will give you ample time to take the appropriate actions.

- **Warn when new pollution occurs** In the later stages of a simulation, building certain City Improvements, such as Factories, will create pollution. If pollution isn't kept under control, it will begin to have a negative impact first on individual cities and then on your empire as a whole. Activating this feature will cause warnings to appear when new pollution is being created, so you can take the appropriate steps to control it before its too late.

- **Warn when changing production will cost shields** Making sudden changes in what a city is producing can sometimes cost you. This feature, if activated, will warn you when you are about to be charged for making a change in a city's production.

PICK MUSIC (ALT+M)

This command allows you to select the background music you hear during the game. The game's CD must be placed in the computer's CD-ROM drive to listen to the background music.

SAVE GAME (CTRL+S)

You can manually save your game data anytime by selecting this command. When you choose to save your game, a Select File Name For Saved Game window appears. In this window select a file name for your saved game, along with a location to save the game data. A default file name will always be created that is based on the first few letters of the leader's name and the year the simulation is currently in. You can choose where on your computers hard disk (or floppy disk) to save your game data, by selecting the drive letter and a folder or directory, if necessary. Click on the OK button when a you have named the file and selected its location. During a simulation, use the Ctrl + S command often to save your game data. If you find the game hangs frequently, make sure you activate the AutoSave each turn option in the Select Game Options window.

LOAD GAME (CTRL+L)

At any time before or during a simulation, you can choose to load a previously saved game, using this feature. This command can be handy if you ever find you've made too many less-than-satisfactory decisions and you decide you want to cancel the current simulation. Instead of starting the simulation all over again, you can simply load a previously saved version and continue with the simulation.

RETIRE (CTRL+R)

In *Civ II*, a simulation ends when you have colonized space, when your empire has conquered the entire planet, or when your empire has been defeated by a rival civilization. If you wish to end a simulation before one of these events is achieved, you can choose to retire. On selecting this option, your *Civ II* score will be calculated and displayed before the game actually ends.

QUIT (CTRL+Q)

This is the fastest way to end the *Civ II* game and return to the Windows Program Manager or Windows 95 desktop. When you select this command, you will be asked if you wish to save your game data first. As a general rule, you should save your game data before exiting, so that you can continue experiencing that simulation later on.

THE KINGDOM PULL-DOWN MENU (ALT+K)

From the Kingdom pull-down menu shown in Figure 4.5, you can take control over your empire's finances by adjusting the Tax Rate. In addition, you are given the option to foment a Revolution, resulting in a change in government type. At any time, you can check out your Throne Room or instantly locate one of the cities in your empire, using commands found under this menu. While the commands under this pull-down menu aren't used often, they do provide you, the supreme ruler of your empire, with additional power and control.

TAX RATE (SHIFT+T)

During a simulation you can adjust the Tax Rate by choosing this command. Activating this feature causes the *How shall we distribute the wealth?* window to appear. This window contains three scroll bars that you can adjust to determine how the tax revenue generated by your empire will be distributed. Each of these scroll bars—Taxes, Science, and Luxuries—can be adjusted between 0 and 100 percent (based on the type of government under which you are ruling your empire). Located just above these scroll bars is a text message that tells you how much total income is being generated, the total cost of keeping your empire running, and the number of turns it currently takes to make new Scientific Discoveries.

VIEW THRONE ROOM (SHIFT+H)

At any time during a simulation (not just during a We Love The King Day), you can view the full-screen graphic representation of your palace. A nice, ego-boosting moment.

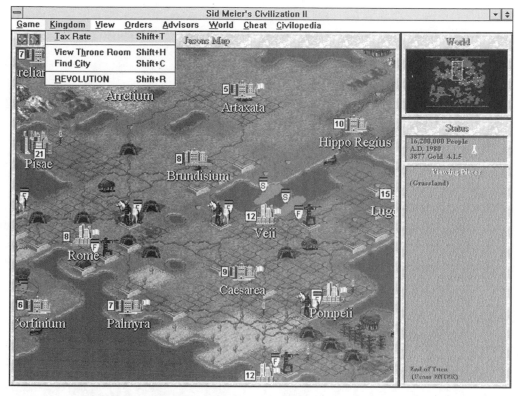

FIGURE 4.5: The Kingdom pull-down menu contains a variety of commands that help you control specific aspects of your empire, such as restructuring its tax rate or changing its form of government.

FIND CITY (SHIFT+C)

Once your empire grows, it will consist of many different cities that will be located throughout the world. To instantly locate a city, use this feature. A *Where the heck is . . .* window will appear with a list of cities. Highlight the city you want to view, and the Main City screen will then frame that city. You can then click on the City button (on the Main Game screen) to view that city's City screen.

REVOLUTION (SHIFT+R)

When you are ready to change the form of government your empire is being ruled under, choose this option. Types of governments available in *Civ II* include: Anarchy, Despotism, Monarchy, Communism, Fundamentalism, Republic, and Democracy. Each form of government has specific benefits and drawbacks that are outlined in Chapter 9, *Civilization II Governments and Types of Terrain*. When you cause a

Revolution, be prepared for your empire to enter into a temporary state of Anarchy (unless you have first acquired the appropriate Wonders of the World).

THE VIEW PULL-DOWN MENU (ALT+V)

Because *Civ II* is a Windows-based game, the graphics have been greatly improved. As a result, you can view the Main Map of the Main Game screen from multiple perspectives, depending on how much terrain and the level of detail you want to see at any given time. If you're fighting a battle, you might want to zoom in to see a large amount of detail. Or, in times of peace, you might want to zoom out a bit (see less detail), but view a larger area of terrain. The commands found under the View pull-down menu shown in Figure 4.6 allow you to customize how you view the Main Map area.

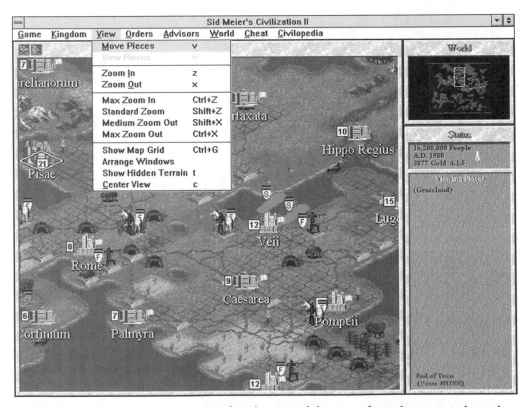

FIGURE 4.6: You can adjust the size of each unit and the area of terrain you can view using the View pull-down menu's commands.

⊕ **Move Pieces (v)**   During a turn, you can select which unit(s) you want to activate, using this command. A white square will appear that you can move around the Main Game screen. When you center this white square cursor on a unit, you can then activate that unit. This comes in handy if a unit has been Fortified or put into Sleep mode and you want to revive it, or when multiple units are located on the same terrain square and you must differentiate between them.

⊕ **View Pieces (V)**   Use this option to view all the units located on a single terrain square that you select. This option will only become active when multiple units are located on the same terrain square as the active unit. Unless you use this command, only the active unit will be visible on the Main Map, even if several other non-active units are located below it.

⊕ **Zoom In (Z)**   From the Main Game screen, you can zoom in on the action. This command gives you a closer viewing perspective for a specific area. While the unit and icons on the Main Map will appear larger, the actual area of terrain you can see will be smaller.

⊕ **Zoom Out (X)**   From the Main Game screen, zooming out allows you to see a larger area of terrain, though each of the units and icons on the map will appear smaller.

⊕ **Max Zoom In (Ctrl + Z)**   For the closest possible view of a specific area of the Main Game screen, you can use this command. All icons and units will appear extra-large, but you will only be able to view a small area of terrain.

⊕ **Standard Zoom (Shift + Z)**   This is the default viewing perspective. Use this command to instantly switch back to this perspective.

⊕ **Medium Zoom Out (Shift + X)**   View the map from a perspective that is about halfway between what the Max Zoom In and Max Zoom Out commands provide. The icons and units appear smaller than the Standard Zoom mode.

⊕ **Max Zoom Out (Ctrl + X)**   To instantly obtain a bird's-eye view of the Main Game screen, use this command. All the icons and units will appear tiny; however, you will be able to see a large area of the world map.

⊕ **Show Map Grid (Ctrl + G)**   This command causes black gridlines to appear on the map, outlining each of the terrain squares. The grid that appears will remain on the screen until this feature is deactivated. With the new viewing perspective *Civ II* offers, this feature allows you to easily calculate the distance and direction a unit will have to travel to get from one location to another.

⊕ **Arrange Windows**   The Main Game screen is made up of multiple windows, including the Map, World, and Status windows. Using this command, you can move these windows around on the screen.

⊕ **Show Hidden Terrain (T)**   If several units are piled up on one terrain square, and you want to view the terrain itself, use this command to hide the units temporarily. A Hidden Terrain window will appear in the lower-right corner of the screen, instructing you to click on the OK button when you are finished viewing.

⊕ **Center View (C)**   This command focuses the Map on a specific unit, city square icon, or terrain square.

THE ORDERS
PULL-DOWN MENU (ALT+O)

The commands on the Orders pull-down menu, shown in Figure 4.7, are used frequently throughout a simulation to control your units. Keep in mind, not all these commands are used for all types of units. Some can only be used to control Settler and Engineer Units, while others are specifically for certain Military Units, such as ships.

⊕ **Build New City (B)**   Use this command to order Settler Units to create and found a new city at a specific location on the map.

⊕ **Build Road (R)**   This command is only available for Settler Units (and, later in a simulation, Engineer Units) when you want them to build roads that link two or more cities.

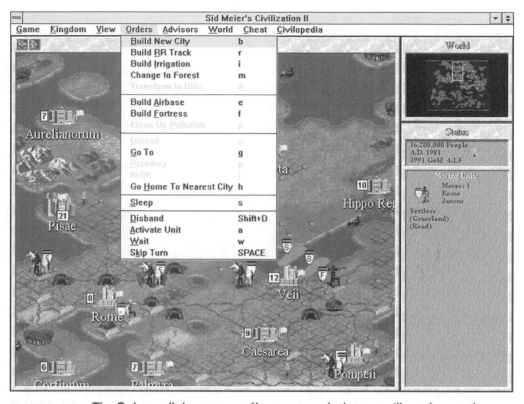

FIGURE 4.7: The Orders pull-down menu offers commands that you will use frequently throughout every simulation to control each of your units. Depending on the type of unit that is active, the commands available for selection on this menu will change.

- **Build Irrigation (I)**   You can access this command only when you want Settler Units (and Engineer Units) to build irrigation systems around cities to help each city grow. Irrigation can only be built on terrain squares that are adjacent to water (oceans, rivers, or other irrigated terrain squares).

- **Change to Forest (M)**   Settler Units can be used to change a terrain square into a forest.

- **Clean Up Pollution (P)**   One of the important tasks that only a Settler Unit can accomplish is cleaning up pollution that your cities create.

Unload (U) When you have units traveling on some type of ship, and the ship approaches land, use this command to unload the units from the ship onto the land.

GoTo (G) If you want a specific unit to travel from one location to another over the course of multiple turns, use the GoTo command to instruct that unit to travel to a specific city without your having to manually move it during each turn. When this command is used, the Unit will automatically take the best route possible to the destination that you select. Units can be ordered to travel to a friendly or rival city, by selecting the appropriate city name from the GoTo command window that appears.

Set Home City (H) Instead of using the GoTo command to move a unit to a specific location over a period of several turns, this command causes the active unit to automatically return to the nearest friendly city.

Sleep (S) This command places an active unit in sleep mode. If an enemy unit approaches, the unit that's in Sleep mode will instantly and automatically become active.

Disband (Shift + D) This command causes the active unit to be demobilized. It will disappear and no longer be available to you.

Activate Unit (A) If a unit is in Sleep or Fortified mode, you can reactivate it using this command.

Wait (W) During a single turn, if you want to move a specific unit before you move the unit that is currently active, use this command. The current active unit will once again become active later in that turn.

Skip Turn (spacebar) Allows the current Unit to do nothing during a specific turn.

Pillage (Shift + P) A Military Unit can be ordered to destroy all Terrain Improvements (irrigation systems, mines, railroads, and the like) located on the enemy square that they're currently on. This command will only be displayed if the active unit is capable of executing this order.

⊕ **Paradrop (P)**   This command is used to launch an attack with the Paratrooper Military Units. This command will only be displayed if the active unit is capable of executing this order.

⊕ **Airlift (L)**   This command is used to transport Military Units using Aircraft Units. This command will only be displayed if the active unit is capable of executing this order.

⊕ **Fortify (F)**   Instead of placing a unit in Sleep mode when you plan on keeping them in the same location over multiple turns, you can Fortify a unit, which greatly enhances its defensive capabilities should that unit (or the city its protecting) be attacked by an enemy. The only drawback to Fortifying a unit is that you must manually place it back on active duty (using the Activate command) if you want to move it or make the unit fight. This command will only be displayed if the active unit is capable of executing this order.

THE ADVISORS PULL-DOWN MENU (ALT+A)

The High Council option offers video animation and audio advice (you will actually hear and see your advisors), while the other options on the Advisors pull-down menu shown in Figure 4.8 allow you to see informative text and graphics-based reports.

⊕ **Consult High Council (Ctrl + T)**   This command runs a new multimedia feature that allows you to meet with and hear reports from your top advisors. A High Council window will appear on the screen, and video images of your Military, Science, Trade, Foreign, and Attitude Advisors will be displayed. Below each advisor is a button labeled with the name of the advisor. Click on the button for the Advisor you want to hear from, and a video report from that advisor will be displayed. When you want to end the High Council meeting, click on the Cancel button at the bottom of the window. The advice given to you will often be in the form

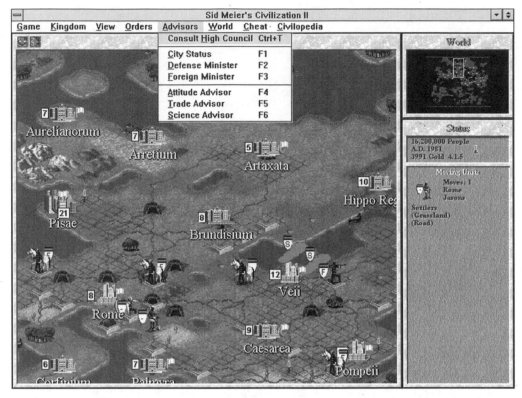

FIGURE 4.8: This pull-down menu lets you keep tabs on your empire by paying attention to the information offered to you by your advisors.

of strategic hints that will help your empire grow. Obviously, you can choose to follow this advice, or you can ignore it entirely. You will notice that during a High Council meeting, the Main Game screen is still visible (although it's partially covered up), but that it turns black and white until the High Council Meeting is over.

⊕ **City Status (F1)**   The City Status report is a text-based window that lists the Tax, Science, and Luxuries for each of the cities in your empire, along with the number of turns it will take to complete the unit, improvement or wonder that each city is working on.

⊕ **Defense Minister (F2)**   This advisor offers you information on your military's status. You will see a graphic representation of each unit that is available to you. By clicking on the Casualties button at the bottom of the Defense Minster's display, you will see a list of the units that have been lost in battle. Click on the Close icon to dismiss the Defense Minster and return to the simulation.

- **Foreign Minister (F3)** Your Foreign Minister provides you with details about rival empires. You can view information about each rival empire, and determine what scientific knowledge that civilization has acquired (by checking its Intelligence report). You can also choose to send an Emissary to a rival empire.

- **Attitude Advisor (F4)** Do a quick check on the overall happiness of your population by reading the report of your Attitude Advisor. This report lists each of the cities in your empire, and displays the number of happy, content, and unhappy citizens in each city.

- **Trade Advisor (F5)** This command allows you to see a list of how each of your empire's cities are benefiting from trade routes that have been established.

- **Science Advisor (F6)** This advisor provides a summary of the scientific knowledge that your empire has already acquired, determines how long it will take to obtain the next advance, and displays flow charts to help you determine what knowledge and technological strategies you should pursue to meet your long-terms goals.

THE WORLD PULL-DOWN MENU (ALT+W)

The commands found on the World pull-down menu shown in Figure 4.9 are primarily used to access information pertaining to various elements of your simulation, such as the Wonders of the World that your empire has acquired, the Top 5 largest cities in the simulation, your current game score, or the demographics of your empire. The Spaceships command, however, will become critical and used often near the final stages of a simulation, if the goal you choose to pursue is to colonize space.

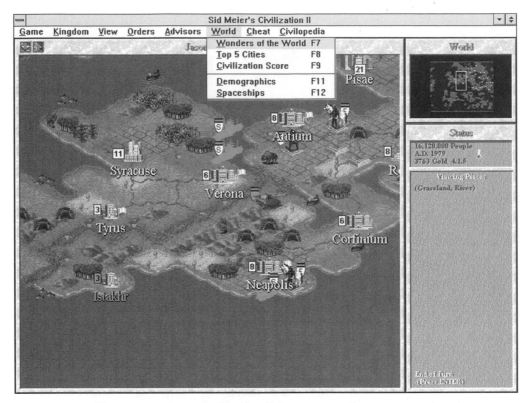

FIGURE 4.9: The commands on the World pull-down menu allow you to monitor the status of several global aspects of your empire.

- **Wonders of the World (F7)** This command allows you to view a list of the Wonders of the World that your empire has already acquired.

- **Top 5 Cities (F8)** This command allows you to view a list of the five most powerful empires that exist as part of the simulation. This is a listing of the largest and most productive cities that currently exist in the world. Thus, cities from rival simulations could very well be listed.

- **Civilization Score (F9)** This command provides a graph that depicts the prosperity of all empires to date and allows you to view your current point score.

Demographics (F11)   This command displays a chart that gives you a quick summary of your empire's population and includes your Approval Rating, Population (size), GNP ($), Mfg. Goods (Mtons), Land Area (size), Literacy Rate, Pollution, Life Expectancy, Family Size, Military Service, Annual Income ($ per capita), and Productivity. For each of these categories, you will also be ranked (first, second, third, and so forth) within the other empires that exist in the simulation. You can use this screen to determine how your empire compares to rival empires. None of these categories have much meaning or impact on the simulation itself. Rather, they are provided to help you get a bigger picture of what's happening within your empire as compared to rival empires. If your ranking in the various categories is low, then you have a lot of work to accomplish to ensure that you catch up with the rival empires.

Spaceships (F12)   Late in the simulation, when one or more empires begins developing spaceships, this command allows you to check your progress in the race to colonize space.

THE CHEAT PULL-DOWN MENU (ALT+C)

Sometimes, the easiest way to make progress in a simulation is to cheat. Of course, a true test of a good player is being able to complete a simulation *without* cheating, but if you're the impatient type, then go ahead and cheat to your hearts content. You can also use these Cheat features to experiment with your strategies during a simulation, but as soon as you activate Cheat mode, your point score will be affected. The Cheat pull-down menu is shown in Figure 4.10.

Toggle Cheat Mode (Ctrl + K)   Before you can being cheating, you must turn on the Cheat mode feature. When you do this, you will see this message: "If you enable cheat mode, this will be recorded in your game score. Do you really want to enable cheat mode?" The message appears along with a Yes and No button. By selecting the Yes button, and then

FIGURE 4.10: The Cheat pull-down menu provides several commands that give you a great deal of control to influence a simulation.

clicking on the OK button, all the following cheat options will be made available to you, starting with your next turn.

⊕ **Create Unit (Shift + F1)** On selecting this command, you can create any unit that is currently within your empire's technological know-how, or you can choose the Advanced option that allows you to instantly create any type of unit. You can also create a unit that is within the technological knowledge of a rival empire by choosing the Foreign option on the Create Unit submenu. Select the Veteran option to make a unit a Veteran. These submenu commands appear at the bottom of the Select Unit To Create window that appears when you select the Create Unit command. The unit you create using this cheat method will appear in the same spot as the unit that is currently active during the turn. There is no financial cost associated with using this cheat feature to quickly build units, and the home city for the newly created unit will be the same city that contains the current active unit.

- **Reveal Map (Shift + F2)**   Instantly view the entire World Map, including all unexplored terrain, with this command. You can also choose to reveal the locations of all cities within a single rival empire, or you can reveal the locations of all cities by selecting the corresponding buttons found on the Select Map View window that appears when you select the Reveal Map cheat command. Once you choose which rival cities you want to see, click on the OK button at the bottom of the Select Map View window to see the total World Map.

- **Set Human Player (Shift + F3)**   You can choose to have a Human Player take control over any rival civilization that is currently being controlled by the computer. When you choose this command, the Select Human Player window will appear. Within this window will be a complete list of all empires that exist in the current simulation. Select which empire you want the human player to take control over, and then click on the OK button to continue the game.

- **Set Game Year (Shift + F4)**   With the completion of each turn during a simulation, a predefined number of years pass. Using this cheat command, you can alter the current year by changing the number of turns that have elapsed thus far. If you reset the counter to 1, the year of the simulation will instantly change back to 4000 B.C. Since every simulation ends at a predetermined year (which depends on the skill level you're playing on), you can add extra years (and turns) to any simulation using this cheat option.

- **Kill Civilization (Shift + F5)**   Use this command to instantly kill off and conquer a rival civilization. When you select this feature, a window will appear asking you to choose which civilization you would like to destroy. Highlight your choice and click on the OK button. Your Military Advisor will then report that the civilization you selected has been conquered. Keep in mind that if that civilization had any active Settler Units, those units can still found new cities, so the rival empire will not be totally destroyed until any left-over Setter Units are defeated.

⊕ **Technology Advance (Shift + F6)**   Instead of waiting for your empire's scientists to discover a specific scientific advance, you can use this command. You will be asked to choose which civilization you wish to obtain the new advance, and then whatever knowledge that empire was working to discover will be acquired instantly. The *Which discovery should our wise men pursue, sire?* window will appear asking you which advance you wish to discover next.

⊕ **Edit Technologies (Ctrl + Shift + F6)**   Using this cheat feature, you can instantly give and take away technologies. By clicking on the Give/Take All button, you can give your empire all the technologies, and then take away technologies from rival empires.

⊕ **Force Government (Shift + F7)**   Instantly switch government types without going through a period of Anarchy (unless you choose Anarchy as the form of government you want to rule your empire under).

⊕ **Change Terrain At Cursor (Shift + F8)**   Using the mouse or the keyboard, place the white square cursor anywhere on the Main Game screen's Main Map, and then choose this cheat command to add features that Settler or Engineer Units would normally have to build over a period of several turns. A Select Terrain Feature window will appear, allowing you to instantly build an irrigation system, a mine, a road, a railroad, a fortress, or an airbase on the selected terrain square. You can also add pollution to the selected terrain square. Using the mouse, you can select multiple features to build, and then click on the OK button to actually build those terrain features and continue.

⊕ **Destroy All Units At Cursor (Ctrl + Shift + D)**   If an enemy has positioned one or more units on a single terrain square, you can position the white square cursor on that terrain square and instantly destroy all the units on it, whether they are active, in sleep mode, on sentry duty, or fortified.

⊕ **Change Money (Shift + F9)**   Choose which civilization's treasury you want to add money to and then from the Change Treasury window that appears, type in any amount you wish. The maximum amount you can enter each time you use this cheat command is $9,999.

⊕ **Edit Unit (Ctrl + Shift + U)**   You can edit the active unit using the Edit Unit window that appears when you select this cheat feature. Options available from this window include: Toggle Veteran Status (On/Off), Clear Movement Allowance, Set Hit Points, Set Home City, Fortify/Unfortify, and Change Caravan Commodity (for Caravan Units).

⊕ **Edit City (Ctrl + Shift + C)**   You can fully customize one of your empire's cities using this command. The following options become available from the window that appears when you select this cheat feature: Change Size, Delete All Wonders, Clear Disorder & We Love King, Copy Another City's Improvements, Set Shield Progress, and Toggle City Objective. The great thing about this feature is that you can alter your own empire's cities to make them stronger, plus you can also tamper with individual rival cities and make them weaker. The Change Size command allows you to change the size of a city. Every city's size is given a numerical value, and with this command, you can increase or decrease that value. With the Delete All Wonders command, you can remove from that city any Wonders of the World that have been build within that city. If a city is currently experiencing civil disorder or a "We Love Our King" celebration, you can cancel out either of these events using the Clear Disorder & We Love King command. If one city in your empire seems to have the right mix of City Improvements to make it superior, using the Copy Another City's Improvements command, you can duplicate what the successful city has. With the Set Shield Progress command, you determine how quickly a city can produce new units, improvements or wonders. Finally, with the Toggle City Objective command, you can determine what the city's resources are being used for.

⊕ **Edit King (Ctrl + Shift + K)**   Use this option to edit the various attributes of your king. When the Editing (Kings Game) window appears, you can edit the following options: Edit Treaties, Set Last Contact, Set Attitude, Set Reputation, Clear Patience, Clear All Last Contact, Set Research Goal, Clear Research Goal, Edit Name, Copy Another King's Tech, and Toggle Female Flag. Click on the options you wish to alter. In most cases, a window of submenu options will appear allowing you to customize the option you selected.

⊕ **Scenario Parameters (Ctrl + Shift + P)**   If you have chosen to experience one of *Civ II*'s built-in scenarios, this cheat feature allows you to win more easily, by adjusting the following features: Tech Paradigm (10/10), Turn Year Increment, Starting Year, Maximum Turns, Wipe All Goody Boxes, Restore All Goody Boxes, Reveal Whole Map, Cover Whole Map, Set Scenario Name, Toggle Tutorial War Flag, Edit Victory Conditions, and Edit Special Rules. On choosing one of these options, a window of submenu options will appear that allows you to modify the option of your choice.

⊕ **Save As Scenario (Ctrl + Shift + S)**   Instead of saving your current simulation as a standard game file, you can save it as a scenario using this command.

THE CIVILOPEDIA PULL-DOWN MENU (ALT+C TWICE)

The Civilopedia is a reference manual that is built into the *Civ II* game. You can find information by selecting the commands available on the Civilopedia pull-down menu shown in Figure 4.11. This reference tool allows you to look up details about every aspect of the game. For example, if you select the Civilization Advances option, you will see a complete listing of all scientific advances that your empire can obtain during a simulation, plus you will see the benefits of each advance.

To make finding information in the Civilopedia easier, everything is divided into the following categories that help you find information faster. For example, if you want to look up information about a Musketeer Unit, you'd select the Military Units command from the Main Civilopedia menu, amd then choose the unit type you're interested in learning about. The categories available to you from the Civilopedia are:

⊕ **Civilization Advances**   Review information about each of the scientific advances available during a simulation.

⊕ **City Improvements**   Find out about the benefits, drawbacks, and costs associated with each type of City Improvement.

⊕ **Wonders of the World**   Learn about the benefits that each Wonder of the World offers to your empire.

⊕ **Military Units**   Discover the costs, benefits, and drawbacks associated with each type of Military Unit. This information will help you build the best possible military force.

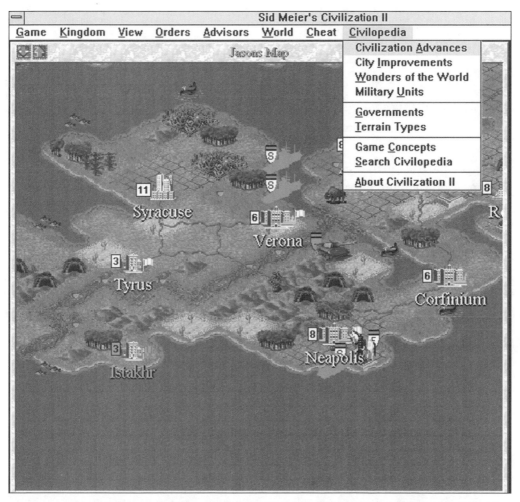

FIGURE 4.11: *Civ II* has a built-in storehouse of information called the Civilopedia. From this reference tool, you can learn about the various aspects of the *Civ II* game.

⊕ **Governments**   Obtain information about each form of government that you can rule your empire under, and learn about the potential benefits and drawbacks of each form of government.

⊕ **Terrain Types**—Learn about the types of terrain on which you can build your empire. Some terrain types are better than others for founding cities, so the more you know about the terrain, the better off you will be.

⊕ **Game Concepts**   Read about some of the overall game concepts and rules pertaining to general game play.

⊕ **Search Civilopedia**   Search the entire Civilopedia based on a keyword that you enter.

⊕ **About *Civilization II***   View general information about *Civ II* and review the opening animation of the game.

If you have taken the time to get familiar with the pregame options, the *Civ II* game screens, and the pull-down menu commands, you're ready to kick off a simulation and experience this game for yourself. Chapter 5, *Your First Civilization II Simulation*, provides a guided walk-through for your first *Civ II* simulation.

5

Your First
Civilization II Simulation

A re you ready to establish an empire and set out to conquer the world? Perhaps you want to eventually colonize space? Now that you've reviewed the basics, it's time to put your knowledge to the test and get a simulation underway. This chapter provides a guided tour through the first batch of turns in a simulation.

CUSTOMIZING THE GAME ENVIRONMENT

When you start *Civilization II*, you need to make some pregame decisions to set up the game environment. Before launching this simulation example, the following pregame options were selected:

- Start A New Game (to begin a simulation from scratch)
- Normal World Size (50×80 terrain squares)
- Chieftain level of difficulty
- Level of Competition was set to 3
- Barbarians were set to appear in villages (huts) only
- Standard Rules
- Male Gender
- Japanese nationality

- Jason as the leader's name
- Far East Pavilion architecture style

Note that even if you attempt to duplicate the exact commands and decisions described in this section, the simulation you experience on your own computer will be different—

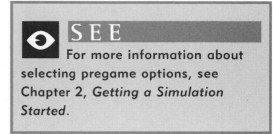

SEE For more information about selecting pregame options, see Chapter 2, *Getting a Simulation Started*.

because that's the nature of the game. *Civilization*, like civilization itself, is ever-changing, unpredictable, maddening, and thrilling.

STARTING THE SIMULATION

Within moments after the final pregame option is selected, the computer generates the world on which the simulation will take place, and the In the Beginning . . . information window appears on the screen, as shown in Figure 5.1. When you click on this window's OK button, the Main Game screen appears on the computer screen, and the simulation is off and running.

VIEWING TUTORIAL HELP

A Civ Tutorial window appears at the top of the screen, offering advice on founding a first city, as shown in Figure 5.2. At the start of your first turn, this window tells you the options available to your Settler Unit. To turn the Tutorial Help option off, access the Game Options window from the Game pull-down menu.

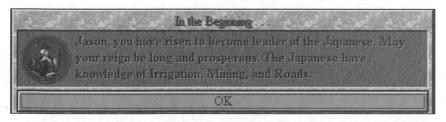

In the Beginning . . .

Jason, you have risen to become leader of the Japanese. May your reign be long and prosperous. The Japanese have knowledge of Irrigation, Mining, and Roads.

OK

FIGURE 5.1: The *In the Beginning* . . . information window appears at the very start of a simulation, after you have made all the pregame decisions.

On the Main Map a small area of actual terrain is exposed, and a Settler Unit is active—the only unit that has been created thus far. Notice that the Japanese empire now has a population of 10,000, the year is 4000 B.C., and there is a grand total of $50 in the treasury. The default Tax Rates are in effect (40 percent for Taxes, 0 percent for Luxuries, and 60 percent for Science). This information is available to you throughout the game in the Status window on the right side of the Main Game screen.

FOUNDING A CAPITAL CITY

An ideal location for a capital city is near water (so that irrigation can be created), but *not* along a major coastline where ship-based enemies can launch attacks from the water. By moving the Settler Unit across several terrain squares (which happens over the course of a few turns), you will discover a good location for a capital city.

Place the Settler Unit on the terrain square where you want the city to be built. Next, select the Found New City command on the Orders pull-down menu (or press B). A window titled *What shall we name this city?* appears on the Main Game screen. In this sample simulation, the default city is Kyoto, the ancient capital of Japan; however, you can change it to any city name you'd like. When you click on the window's OK button, your capital city (for the Japanese empire) will be built on the Main Map.

Once the capital city is built, a City screen for Kyoto automatically appears on the screen. From this screen, you must determine what will be the first unit, improvement, or wonder that your new city will build. An excellent strategy is to begin building several Warrior Units (Military Units) to protect your capital city and explore the surrounding terrain.

In the City screen's Production window shown in Figure 5.3, the default option is to create a Warrior Unit. After three or four Warrior Units have been created over the course of the next few turns, you will want to switch to building Settler Units to begin

FIGURE 5.2: Assuming you have the Tutorial Help option turned on (which is the default selection), you will periodically receive advice on how to proceed in a simulation.

expanding your empire. Right now, however, exit the City screen, by clicking on the Exit button.

Observing Time Passage at the End of a Turn

Because you have reached the end of the current turn, a message stating "End of turn (Press Enter)" appears in the lower-right corner of the Main Game screen. Each time a turn comes to an end, time (represented in years) passes. As you press Enter several times, while your first Warrior Unit is in production, watch the Main Game screen's Status window and see how time passes (right now, because the game is set on Chieftain level, time is moving in increments of 20 years).

Every turn has three key elements—Production, Human Movement, and Computer Movement. During the Production portion of every turn, the computer determines how much progress (in terms of what's being built within each city) will take place during that turn, based on all of the elements in the game, such as how many Scientists exists and what the Tax Rates have been set to. The Human Movement portion of the turn is when you can issue orders to each of your units, one at a time. Finally, the Computer Movement portion of a turn is when the computer takes control of all of the other civilizations (and Barbarians) in the game, and chooses what they will do during each turn.

ESTABLISHING A KNOWLEDGE ADVANCE

In the year 3960 B.C., while you were waiting for your first Warrior Unit to be created, the Japanese Scientists requested the leader (that's you) to decide what Knowledge Advance they should strive to acquire, as shown in Figure 5.4. Notice that an information window from the Science Advisor appears, recommending that the empire discover Bronze Working (Scientific Advance) next, so that it will be able to build both a Phalanx (Military Unit) and the Colossus (a Wonder of the World). Take the Science Advisor's advice and assign the Scientists to discover

FIGURE 5.3: This Production window shows a Warrior being created.

Bronze Working, by highlighting the option and clicking the OK button at the bottom of the *What discovery shall our wise men pursue?* window.

As you will see in Figure 5.5, each time your Scientists discover a new Knowledge Advance, an information screen will appear, telling you what units, improvements, or wonders this new knowledge allows your empire to create.

Within a few additional turns, your Scientists will report back that they have acquired the knowledge of Bronze Working, and once again the *What discovery shall our wise men pursue?* window will appear, along with another recommendation from your Science Advisor. Once more, follow the advice of this wise advisor, and choose Ceremonial Burial. This enables you to build a Temple (City Improvement).

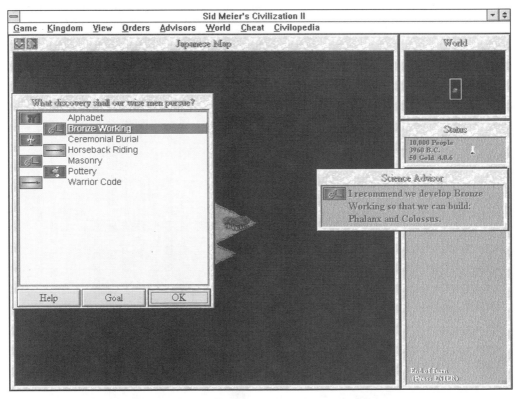

FIGURE 5.4: The *What discovery shall our wise men pursue?* window appears, along with a text-based information window containing a report from the Science Advisor.

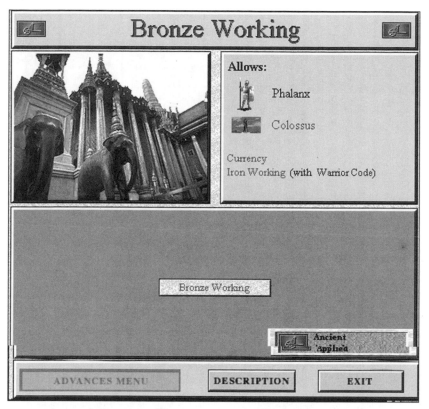

FIGURE 5.5: This information screen tells you that Bronze Working enables Phalanx Units and the Colossus (Wonder of the World) to be created by your cities, should you assign your cities to produce them.

What Steps Can Be Taken to Boost Scientific Knowledge?

Sir Francis Bacon once said, "*Knowledge itself is power.*" In *Civ II*, the knowledge you acquire in the form of Knowledge Advances gives you the power to build more advanced units, City Improvements, and Wonders of the World, which in turn allows you to become a stronger military force and ultimately travel to the stars more rapidly.

Throughout every simulation, you'll always want to keep your scientific development moving forward so that your empire is constantly developing and maintaining a technological

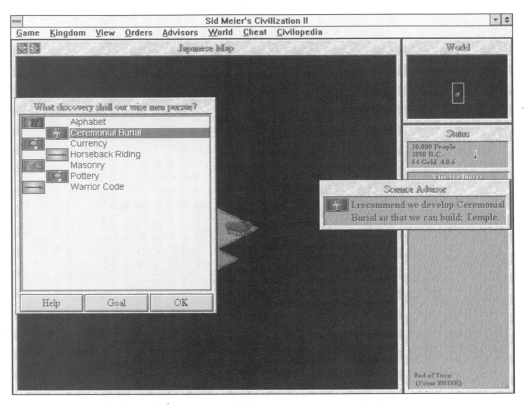

FIGURE 5.6: This time, when your Science Advisor asks what knowledge the Japanese Scientists should pursue, choose Ceremonial Burial.

edge over the competition, especially when it comes to Wonders of the World. Once a wonder is acquired by a civilization, it is no longer available to other empires *unless* it's taken by force (that is, by the empires' conquering the city in which the wonder was built).

By combining Scientists (Specialists), City Improvements, Wonders of the World, and a good Scientific Rate (this is done by adjusting the Tax Rate), you can maximize your Scientists' ability to generate new Knowledge Advances.

Let's begin with Scientists. By creating one or more Scientists (Specialists) from the City screen of a given city, you are taking away from the workforce of that city, yet at the same time increasing that city's ability to generate scientific knowledge without your having to build anything within a city. Creating Scientists is an easy way to quickly boost the scientific knowledge being developed. Scientists can only be built in cities that contain more than five people in the population roster (on the City screen).

Building one or more of the City Improvements—University, Library, or Research Lab—will also boost the amount of scientific knowledge being developed within a city. Keep in mind that building several of these improvements within each city will dramatically boost its scientific development. To reach maximum levels, you will want to build the following specific Wonders of the World in cities that already contain some or all of these City Improvements.

- Copernicus' Observatory (Wonder of the World) should be built in a city that already contains a University, Library, and Research Lab. To double the rate of science being developed within a city that already contains these City Improvements or Copernicus' Observatory, be sure to build Isaac Newton's College (Wonder of the World).

- Building the SETI Program (Wonder of the World) will double your empire's science output, because it offers the equivalent of building a Research Lab (City Improvement) within every city in your empire.

- The Great Library (Wonder of the World) is also a powerful knowledge tool, because it automatically gives you all the Knowledge Advances that at least two other rival empires have already acquired. Use this wonder if you're falling behind, from a technological standpoint.

Building the City Improvements and Wonders of the World to boost science output is a long-term strategy that works on an ongoing basis. Obviously, the more cities you equip with these City Improvements, the faster you can acquire new Knowledge Advances that will benefit your entire empire.

Moving and Fortifying a Unit

In the year 3860 B.C., a first Warrior Unit is created. The unit appears (flashing) in the same terrain square as Kyoto. Now that this unit is active, you can use the directional arrows on the keyboard to move it around on the Main Map. Each turn, a Warrior Unit can move one terrain square in any direction. Over the next few turns, have this unit begin exploring, while Kyoto builds additional Warrior Units. By the year 3760 B.C., a second Warrior Unit will be created. Meanwhile, the original Warrior Unit has begun exploring the nearby terrain around Kyoto.

Now you have two units under your command. The newly created unit can move one terrain square so that it is standing next to Kyoto, and then can be fortified to help protect the city against enemy attacks. As an alternative, this unit could be Fortified inside Kyoto. To Fortify an active unit, wait until it is standing on (or near) the terrain square you want it to guard. From the Orders pull-down menu, choose the Fortify command (or press F). Within the unit's shield, the letter "F" will appear, and within one or two turns a stone base around the unit will also appear on the Main Map, signifying that it has been Fortified.

During this same turn, your Scientists report back that the knowledge of Ceremonial Burial has been acquired as an element in developing ancestral respect in the Japanese empire. The Scientists are ordered to pursue Horseback Riding next. One benefit to acquiring Horseback Riding is that it allows for highly mobile Chariot Units to be created. One of the strategy elements of this  game involves choosing which Military Units you'd like to create in the long-term, and then making sure that your empire's Scientists pursue the right Knowledge Advances, in the correct order, to allow the units, improvements, or wonders of your choice to be built as early in the simulation as possible.

EXPLORING

Now, the year is 3680 B.C. and you have one Warrior Unit guarding Kyoto, another exploring the nearby terrain, and a third Warrior Unit newly created, as shown in Figure 5.7. Use this new unit to explore in an opposite direction from the other Warrior Units, so that you can uncover as much territory as possible in the shortest amount of time.

If you look at the World Map, in the upper-right corner of the Main Game screen, you'll see the area of terrain that the units are uncovering. As they explore new territory, the black area (representing unexplored terrain) on the World Map and on the Main Map is reduced. As you have your units explore early in a simulation, it's a good idea to have them locate the coastline and then explore along that coastline. This allows you to determine the size and shape of the continent on which you'll initially be building your empire. Rule of thumb: survey first, conquer next, settle and grow later.

EXPLORING A HUT

As the year 3580 B.C. rolls around, yet another Warrior Unit is created. Once again, use this unit to explore. Within two turns, this new Warrior Unit encounters a hut, which in *Civ II* represents a small, unexplored village. Throughout the simulation, as you explore the terrain, you will find many of these huts randomly placed on the map. By moving a unit onto the same terrain square as the hut, you can explore it. Within the hut could be some type of bonus—or a horde of angry Barbarians! As shown in Figure 5.8, your Military Unit discovers a friendly tribe of skilled mercenaries.

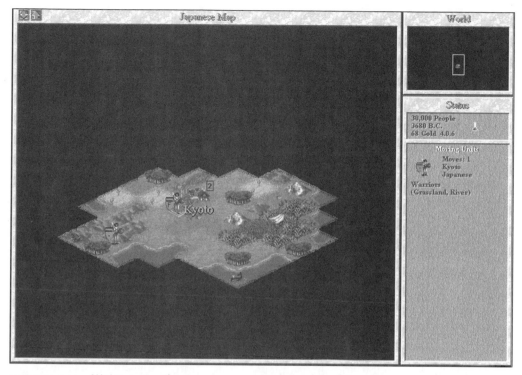

FIGURE 5.7: Within just a few turns, you are already controlling an army composed of three Warrior Units. Two are being used to explore new territory, while the third unit guards your capital city.

The Horsemen Unit has the ability to travel across multiple terrain squares per turn, which makes it excellent for exploration—so order one of your Warrior Units to return to Kyoto to help guard the city. As you do this, the Japanese Scientists report that their work has permitted them to acquire the knowledge of Horseback Riding.

FIGURE 5.8: After discovering a tribe of friendly mercenaries, a Horsemen Unit joins your empire. Now five units are under your control.

This time, the Science Advisor suggests that you pursue the Warrior Code, to heighten your military sensibilities, but just to show that you're the supreme ruler, order the Scientists instead to first pursue The Wheel. The Wheel will give you the ability to create Chariot Units (Military Units).

Time passes. The year is now 3440 B.C. You have two units protecting Kyoto, and one of your exploring Warrior Units has uncovered yet another hut. This time, upon exploring the hut, a text-based message window appears, stating, "Weeds grow in empty ruins. This village has been abandoned." At least there were no Barbarians were waiting to attack. As a result, the Warrior Unit that discovered the hut will continue exploring nearby terrain.

CHANGING UNIT PRODUCTION

Because you have multiple units that are under your control, access Kyoto's City screen and change what the city is producing. For your empire to expand, it's critical that you begin building Settler Units, which can be used to establish new cities and expand your power and influence. Using the mouse, click on the Kyoto City icon found on the Main Map, and Kyoto's City screen appears. By clicking on the Change button in the Production window (found in the lower-right corner of the City screen), the *What shall we build in Kyoto?* window appears, along with suggestions from several of your trusty advisors, as shown in Figure 5.9. You can see in the window that, based on the knowledge your empire has acquired thus far, you can build Settler Units, Warrior Units, Phalanx Units, Horsemen Units, Barracks (City Improvement), or a Temple (City Improvement). You can also start building the Colossus (Wonder of the World). However, your goal right now, as you can see in Figure 5.10, is to build Settler Units in Kyoto, so that you can extend your empire by founding more cities. Highlight the Settler Unit option and click on the OK button to continue.

Over the course of the next several turns, the units you've been using to explore have uncovered a nice chunk of terrain, and they've even gotten quite lucky. They have discovered six huts, and, as a result, earned $50 worth of gold. They've also induced five tribes of wandering mercenaries to set down roots and join your growing empire. The result of this exploration is that one Archer Unit, two Chariot Units, and two more Horsemen Units have been added to your army. Your Scientists have also discovered The Wheel and were ordered finally to develop The Warrior Code, which is exactly what the Scientific Advisor had initially recommended.

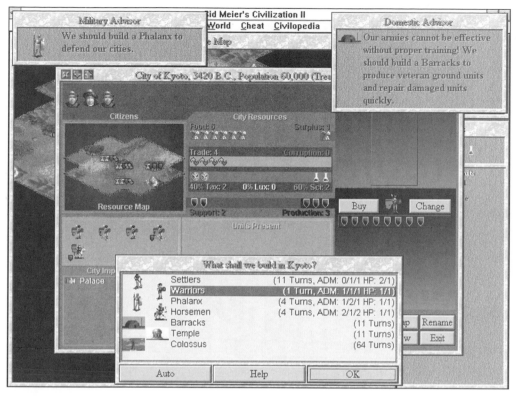

FIGURE 5.9: From the *What shall we build in Kyoto?* window, you can see that it will take 11 turns for Kyoto to create a Settler Unit.

HOLDING A HIGH COUNCIL MEETING

Periodically, during a simulation, you will be asked if you wish to hold a High Council Meeting, as shown in Figure 5.11. You can select the Consult High Council option to initiate a meeting. At any time during a simulation, however, if you're stymied and need a little guidance or consensus-building, you can choose to hold such a meeting. Simply select the High Council option found under the Advisors pull-down menu. A High Council Meeting gives you a chance to hear and see what all your advisors think about how your empire is doing. When a High Council Meeting

NOTE

In some menus in this game, the High Council meeting is referred to as a Town Council Meeting. They're the same thing, so don't get confused.

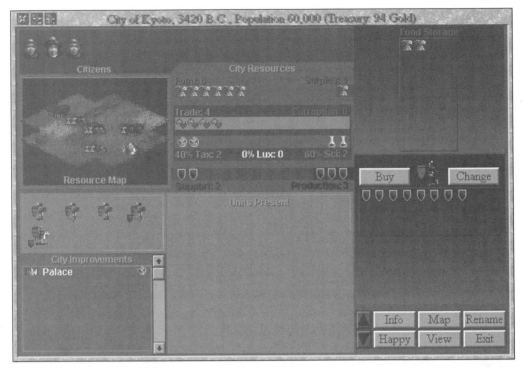

FIGURE 5.10: The Settler Unit icon in the Production window (in the lower-right corner of the City screen) represents what's now being built.

begins, the Main Game screen will change from color to black-and-white, and the High Council window will appear on the screen. To use this feature, the *Civ II* CD must be inserted into your computer's CD-ROM drive. This feature takes advantage of the multimedia capabilities of your computer.

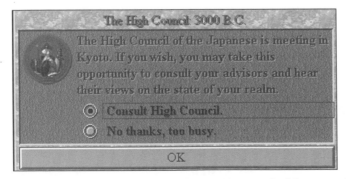

FIGURE 5.11: In the year 3000 B.C. you are asked by your advisors if you wish to hold a High Council meeting.

Below each picture of an advisor is a button labeled with the name of the advisor. Click on each of these buttons, one at a time, to see and hear the respective advisor's report. These reports will often contain strategies and game-play tips that will help your empire prosper, as shown in Figure 5.12. In this example of a High Council meeting, the Military Advisor suggests that your empire build Barracks to maintain your military. Meanwhile, your Trade Advisor recommends that the Japanese Scientists pursue the knowledge of Currency.

ENCOUNTERING A RIVAL EMPIRE

Just after the High Council Meeting adjourned (2800 B.C.), one of your Military Units encountered a unit from a rival empire. When one of your Military Units comes into contact with an enemy empire—in this case, the English empire—a text-based window appears on the screen, asking how this first contact should be handled. As the leader

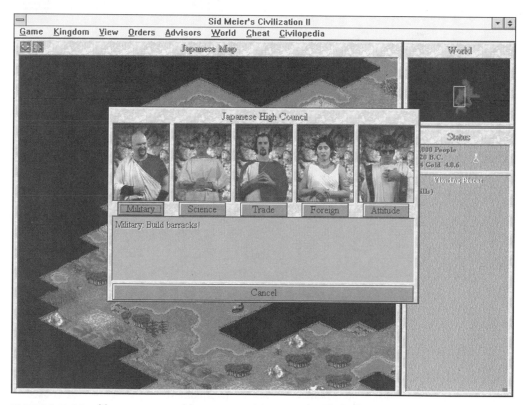

FIGURE 5.12: You can see and hear your advisors in the High Council window.

Can Holding a High Council Meeting Help My Empire?

At any time during a simulation, you can see text-based reports from your various advisors by accessing the Advisors pull-down menu. The High Council Meeting, however, offers live-action video footage (multimedia) of your advisors and allows you to see and hear what advice they have for you. Even if you choose *not* to review the text-based reports from your advisors on a periodic basis, it's an excellent strategy to hold a High Council Meeting every so often, to obtain advice on how to proceed in the future. Your advisors (during a High Council Meeting) will recommend strategies that can benefit your empire's pursuit of its goal.

To hold a High Council Meeting, access the Advisors pull-down menu and select the High Council command. Next, click on each of the buttons associated with your advisors to hear and see their reports.

of the Japanese empire, you have the option to grant an audience to the English leader and hold a conversation, *or* you can send away the English emissary, as shown in Figure 5.13. In this sample simulation, the *No, send her away* option was selected. You have better things to do.

As a result of your refusing to meet with the English leader, the English empire launches a sneak attack on your Military Unit just outside the English city of York. A battle ensues in which your Chariot Unit is victorious. As a result, your Chariot Unit earns Veteran Status, which makes it 50 percent stronger (Figure 5.14). Another English unit from York launches an attack against your Chariot Unit, and loses as well.

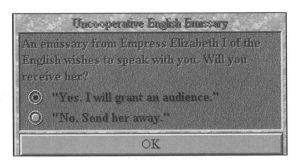

FIGURE 5.13: When one of your units encounters a rival empire, an Uncooperative Emissary window like this may appear, telling you that their leader requests an audience.

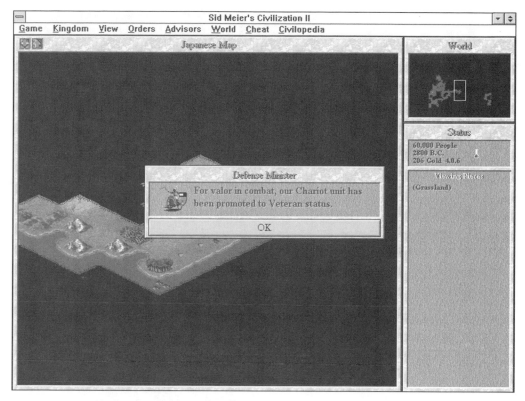

FIGURE 5.14: In battle a unit can be killed or injured. If it survives, it can earn Veteran status, becoming 50 percent stronger.

Although your Chariot Unit's energy has been somewhat reduced, you send it to invade the city of York. In Figure 5.15, you can see that your unit was successful in capturing the city. York now, to its surprise, becomes part of the Japanese empire. As a reward, you get to take one Scientific Knowledge away from the English. Pottery is selected, so that within your cities you'll be able to build Granaries (City Improvements), which in turn help to strengthen the people as they increase in number.

After you capture York, that city's City screen appears. From the Production window, you can assign this city to begin producing any type of unit, improvement, or wonder that you are able to create, based on the knowledge your empire has acquired thus far. Because your immediate goal is to build additional cities and expand, accept the default option in the Production window, which is to produce Settler Units.

Defense Minster

Japanese capture York. 32 gold pieces plundered.

OK

FIGURE 5.15: By launching an attack on a city and defeating any Military Units that are protecting that city, your army can march in and simply take it over.

Allowing a Unit to Recuperate

Normally, after a battle, if your unit survives, it will be weak because its energy meter will have been reduced. When this occurs, for the next several turns (until the unit recuperates), use the No Orders command on the Orders pull-down menu (or press the spacebar) each time the injured unit becomes active.

PLACE A NEW CITY IN AUTO PRODUCTION MODE

It's 2620 B.C., and one of your units explores yet another hut. This time it discovers a tribe of people who want to join your empire. The result is the founding of a new Japanese city, called Osaka. With this city comes a larger population plus $256 worth of gold for your treasury. When Osaka's City screen appears, you can get it ready for automatic production by setting it to Auto Production mode: just click on the Change button in the Production window and then select the Auto button at the bottom of the *What shall we build in Osaka?* window. For this city, turn the production responsibilities over to your trusty Military and Domestic Advisors, by selecting the Both button in the *Who will control production in Osaka?* window. Now that the city is set to Auto Production mode, it is building a Phalanx Unit. You can determine this by looking at the Production window of the Osaka City screen (Figure 5.16), and noting there is a Phalanx Unit displayed in that window. You can tell that the city is in Auto Production mode because the Change button that usually appears in the upper-right portion of the Production window is replaced by an Auto Off button. To protect Osaka, Fortify your Horsemen Unit, which discovered the hut next to what has become the city.

What's the Fastest Way to Help a Unit Regain Its Strength After a Battle?

You can do two things to help a damaged (injured) unit recuperate after a battle:

1. When the unit again becomes active, press the spacebar, or select the No Orders command, to let it rest for several turns. The drawback to this is that the unit remains weak. If another enemy moves in to attack, your injured unit is vulnerable. If you are keeping the injured unit in the field, however, always surround it with other friendly Military Units and Fortify the injured unit. It will take multiple turns for it to recuperate, so be patient and keep it inactive but protected.

2. Alternatively, after the battle, move the injured unit to a nearby home city and keep it there for several turns (until its energy meter returns to being a solid green bar). If possible, place an injured ground-based unit within a city that has a Barracks (City Improvement). This will cause the recuperation process to take only one turn. If you have an injured air-based unit, have it return to a friendly city that contains an Airport (City Improvement, not an Airbase Terrain Improvement). Injured ship-based units should return to a friendly city that contains a Port Facility (City Improvement) to experience a speedy recovery (one turn).

FOUNDING ADDITIONAL CITIES USING SETTLERS

Remember a while back when you ordered Kyoto to produce Settler Units? Well, the year is now 2580 B.C. Your empire's population has grown to 140,000 people, thanks to a lucky streak when you had your units explore huts. Now, however, Kyoto has produced its first Settler Unit, which means you can use this unit to found additional cities. Your goal for this Settler Unit is to find a suitable location to build another city. This city should be located somewhat close to Kyoto, but not *too* close, otherwise the two cities will eventually compete for the same resources from the surrounding land—and both cities would wind up with food production problems.

When the Settler Unit (or any new unit, improvement, or wonder) is created within a city, you have the option to continue the game, or to switch to the City screen and change what the city is producing. If the city is producing a unit, and you don't return to the City screen to alter its production, that city will continue producing additional units of the same type (in this case, Settler Units). If the city has been producing an improvement or wonder and completes the task, but you don't return to the City screen to change what the city *should* produce, during every turn a window will appear warning you that the city is producing something that already exists. The exception to this

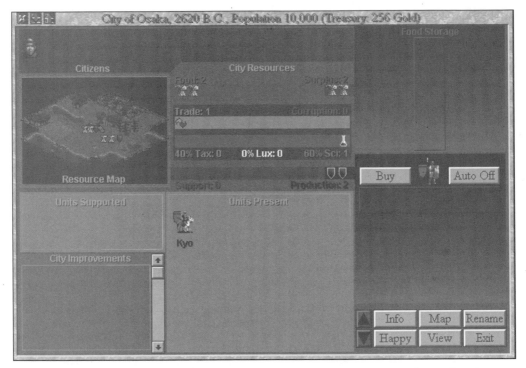

FIGURE 5.16: From the Osaka City screen, you can see that this city has been placed in Auto Production mode and that it is busy producing a Phalanx Unit.

rule is if you have the city set on Auto Production mode, which means the computer will automatically decide what that city should be producing.

Instead of having the new Settler Unit immediately go off and build a new city, you can have it irrigate the terrain near Kyoto, which will allow Kyoto to expand even more rapidly. You can also have the Settler Unit begin building a road to where the second city will ultimately be built. For now, spend a few extra turns to irrigate two terrain squares near Kyoto, and then send the Settler Unit off to create a new city. The existing Military Units will continue to explore the terrain.

CREATING ADDITIONAL CITIES

In subsequent turns, the captured city of York builds its first Settler Unit. Use the same strategy as you did with Kyoto and have this new Settler Unit irrigate two terrain squares adjacent to York before going off to found a new city. Remember, for a Settler

Unit to be able to irrigate a terrain square, the terrain square you want to irrigate must be adjacent to water (an ocean, river, lake, or other irrigated terrain square).

Meanwhile, your Settler Unit that was created by Kyoto has irrigated two nearby terrain squares and has moved off (about ten terrain squares away) to build a new city, as shown in Figure 5.17. In this simulation example, the city of Edo is founded by the Settler Unit, and from Edo's City screen, Auto Production mode was selected. The city is now producing a Phalanx Unit. When erecting your empire, don't build your cities too close together. This will help you to avoid food shortages and resource problems.

CHECKING THE EMPIRE'S STATUS

At this point, check out the empire's status by opening the Advisor pull-down menu and selecting to view the City Status screen, shown in Figure 5.18. The year is 2040 B.C. and the Japanese empire now has four cities within it—Kyoto, the former English

FIGURE 5.17: After irrigating two terrain squares around Kyoto, a Settler Unit moves about ten terrain squares away to found the city of Edo.

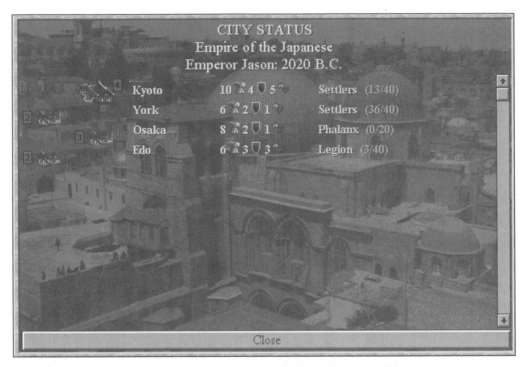

FIGURE 5.18: The City Status screen displays a report on your empire's cities.

city of York, Osaka, and Edo. This report informs you that two of your cities, Kyoto and York, are now building Settler Units, while Osaka is building a Phalanx Unit and Edo is building a Legion Unit. You can also see on this screen that it will take Kyoto and York a total of 40 turns to each produce another Settler Unit; however, Kyoto is already 13 turns into the production cycle, and York is 36 turns into the cycle.

By checking in with the Defense Minister (from the Advisors pull-down menu), you can see how many units you have in your empire and how many units (and of what types) are in production. Right now, as shown in Figure 5.19, there are one Settler Unit that's active (two in production), three Warrior Units active (none in production), two Phalanx Units active (one in production), one Legion Unit active (one in production), two Horsemen Units active (none in production), and two Chariot Units active (none in production).

GOING TO WAR

Living a quite peaceful existence is fine, even desirable, in real life—but this is a *military strategy* game, so go ahead and kick some butt. Do you recall capturing the city

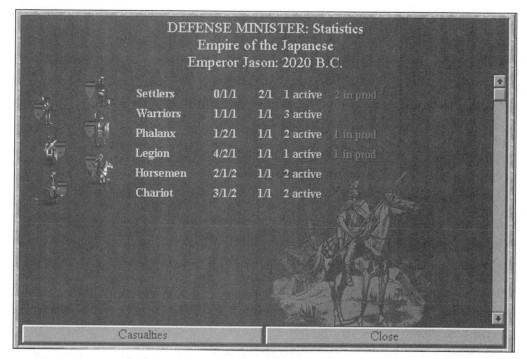

FIGURE 5.19: The Defense Minister screen provides vital statistics on the status of your empire's units.

of York from the English? Well, while exploring near York, your units discovered additional English cities. This time, when your units met up with the English, you agreed to a meeting between leaders (see Figure 5.20). It seems that the English aren't pleased with your military superiority and they want peace. Should you offer it? No way! Conquer them. As a result of your decision, you call the English cowards and reject their peace offering.

It seems the English want peace so badly, they're willing to offer you Scientific Knowledge in exchange for leaving them alone. Since this rival empire is weak, now is the best time to conquer it. Reject the peace offering. Next, the English offer you $250 to sign a cease-fire agreement. Forget it (Figure 5.21). Send in our military. This is war!

A battle begins. You send in one of your Legion Units to attack London, and after just two short but furious fights, you conquer the city and add it to your empire. Now mobilize your military and head for the nearby English city of Nottingham (see Figure 5.22). Victory there will be yours as well.

FIGURE 5.20: The Japanese agree to a meeting with the English, but you dismiss their peace offer.

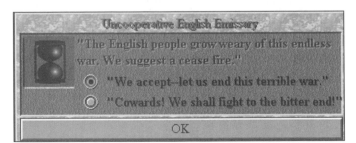

FIGURE 5.21: Refuse the English offer of knowledge in exchange for a cease-fire agreement. It's time to wage battle. To do this, you must select the "Cowards! We shall fight to the bitter end!" option. When you're meeting with rivals, the default options are always the peaceful ones.

FIGURE 5.22: Your powerful Japanese military has conquered York and London, and now you set your sights on Nottingham. Just two turns later (1720 B.C.) you invade Nottingham and conquer it as well.

VIEWING EXPLORED TERRAIN

At this point you can use the Max Zoom Out command on the View pull-down menu to take a look at the size and shape of the terrain your empire has explored thus far in the simulation, as shown in Figure 5.23.

Making Protection Improvements

As you build your empire, you'll want to consult frequently with your Science Advisor. Display the Science Advisor's report from the Advisors pull-down menu, to be brought up-to-date on all the Scientific Advances your empire has acquired. At the bottom of the Science Advisor report window is a Goal button. Click on it to see a list of all the Scientific Knowledge Advances available within the current game. Using the mouse, click on any of these advances, and another window will appear, telling you exactly what knowledge you must acquire to achieve the advance you selected.

Now check in with your Science Advisor (Figure 5.24), and you'll learn that your empire has acquired the knowledge of Masonry. So put this knowledge to use and begin building strong City Walls (City Improvements) within some of your larger cities, as shown in Figure 5.25. After all, you have already made contact with the English,

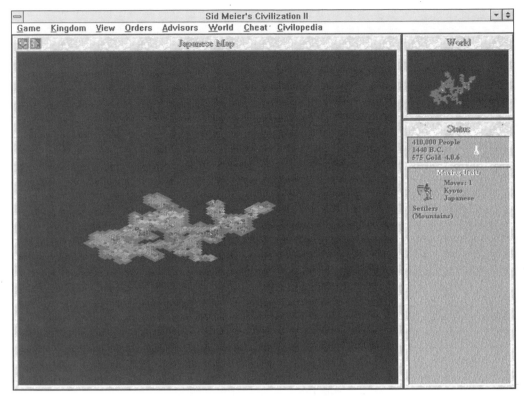

FIGURE 5.23: Use commands on the View pull-down menu to determine the amount of terrain you can see on the Map.

and it's only a matter of time before they'll be at your doorstep launching attacks. City Walls are an excellent defense for a city in the early stages of a simulation. Another good strategy is to build Barracks (City Improvement) within cities so that your empire's units can achieve Veteran status and become 50 percent stronger. Fortifying *any* type of Military Unit (with Veteran status) in or around cities adds a valuable element of defense.

CHECKING YOUR SCORE

At this point in the simulation, you can check your score in the current simulation by accessing the World pull-down menu and choosing the Civilization Score command (or pressing F9). The Civilization Score screen lists the current year in your Japanese empire, the Wonders of the World it has acquired, its current population, and the total score for your growing empire. Obviously, because you're still in the early stages of

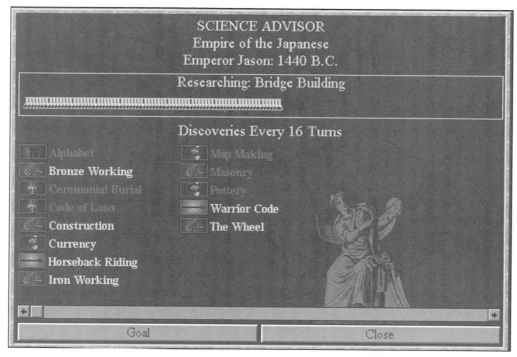

FIGURE 5.24: Click on the Goal button to determine the steps you must take to acquire the Knowledge Advances you desire. This is an excellent tool for developing long-term strategies.

this simulation, you'll observe that your score is relatively low. Notice, too, that you lost 50 points right from the start, for selecting (from the pregame options) an *easy* way to deal with Barbarians. But don't be discouraged, for you're just beginning your civilization and have barely flexed your power.

SUMMARIZING THIS SIMULATION

In this simulation, the objective selected was to become a dominant military force. Still, at the same time you attempted to build up the city domestically, by building City Improvements that would help each of your cities grow and prosper. In *Civ II*, it's important to keep a balance between military and internal growth—that is, unless you're planning to avoid military confrontations altogether by entering into peace treaties with all rivals, and then concentrating on Scientific Advances that will ultimately lead you to the colonization of space. It's *vitally* important that you define your long-term goals early in a simulation, and then work toward achieving those goals—by designing your military and empire accordingly.

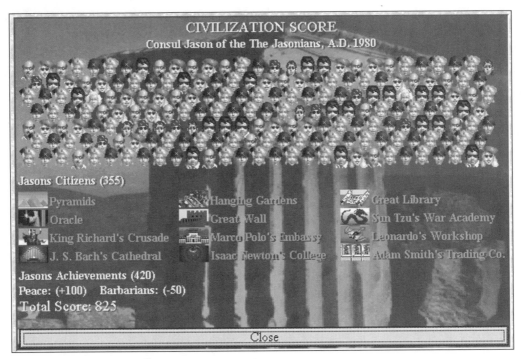

FIGURE 5.26: This typical Civilization Score screen summarizes an empire's progress.

With any luck, if you've followed along with this simulation walk-through, you now have a fairly good understanding of how you'll actually interact with the game and what types of challenges you can expect in the early stages of a simulation. Obviously, this simulation didn't demonstrate all the game's features, nor did it explore every possible situation you can encounter in your own simulations. Before you begin your own simulations, in which you assume the role of supreme ruler and set out to see first-hand why millions of computer gamers have become totally addicted to the *Civilization* game series, first take a look at the various ways *Civilization II* lets you measure your progress and score big points.

HIGH SCORIN' *CIVILIZATION* FUN

During a simulation, you can measure your progress in a number of ways—the total of funds in your treasury, your brilliant military conquests, the level of your scientific developments, or simply your total point score. At any time during a game, you can access the Civilization Score command on the World pull-down menu. The Civilization Score screen shows you the following information:

⊕ The total number of citizens in your empire

⊕ The Wonders of the World your empire has obtained

⊕ The number of bonus points you have received for each peaceful turn

⊕ The penalties assessed for causing pollution or choosing an easy Barbarian pregame option

⊕ The total Civilization Score you have earned thus far

The Civilization Score screen example shown in Figure 5.26 displays the year A.D. 1980, the empire's 12 acquired Wonders of the World, and its population of 355 citizens. At the bottom of this screen the total point score (thus far) appears.

CALCULATING YOUR *CIV II* SCORE

Your goal in *Civilization II,* you'll recall, is to colonize space or conquer the world. In achieving either of these ultimate goals, you also want to score at least 1,000 points by the end of a simulation. To do this, you have from the time a simulation begins (4000 B.C.) until the year A.D. 2020, when the simulation ends.

This *Civilization* score is made up of a number of components. The first component is a count of your civilization's entire population, combined with bonus points based on the status of each citizen. You can expect to receive 2 points for each happy citizen and 1 point for each content citizen. Next, the computer will evaluate the number of Wonders of the World your empire has acquired. You will receive 20 points for each Wonder of the World.

While *Civ II* is both a strategy game and a military simulation, you are actually awarded for *not* fighting. For each turn you experience without fighting either a battle or a war, you will receive 3 points.

Once your empire's Scientists have acquired all the possible Scientific Advances (which can happen near the very end of a simulation), they can begin creating an unlimited number of Future Technologies. For each Future Technology your empire creates, you will receive 5 bonus points.

At the very start of a simulation, a pregame option lets you adjust the Barbarian activity that will take place on the planet. From the Select Level of Barbarian Activity window (pregame option), you can choose one of the following options: Villages Only, Roving Bands, Restless Tribes, or Raging Hordes. When you make this selection, your *Civ II* score is affected. If you choose Villages Only, you'll receive a 50-point penalty (which means you start a simulation with –50 points) because this is the easiest option in terms of game play. Choosing Roving Bands results in a 25.point penalty. There is no penalty or bonus associated with selecting Restless Tribes, though if you're brave (or foolhardy) enough to choose the Raging Hordes option, you'll begin the game with a 50-point bonus.

Finally, at the conclusion of a simulation, the computer calculates the total number of terrain squares containing pollution, and penalizes you 5 points per polluted square. This can really add up if you're not careful. As the simulation is coming to an end, be sure to send out teams of Engineer (or Settler) Units to clean up polluted areas.

Bonus points are also awarded for achieving one of the game's main two objectives before the year A.D. 2020. If you reach your goal before that year, the computer will calculate your score based on the number of rival empires you have conquered plus the speed with which you defeated your enemies. You will earn 1,000 points for conquering a rival empire, and receive an added bonus based on how quickly this was achieved. There's also a point bonus for colonizing space before A.D. 2020. You will receive points for every 10,000 space colonists who successfully arrive at Alpha Centauri, plus earn an additional bonus based on how early in the simulation the colonists reach their destination.

THE THRONE ROOM— ANOTHER MEASURE OF YOUR SUCCESS

In the original *Civilization* game (and also in *CivNet*), one of the ways you could measure your success as a leader was by viewing the size and complexity of your Palace. Good leaders were rewarded by their loyal subjects, resulting in special additions being built onto their Palaces. *Civilization II* doesn't offer a Palace. Instead, this sequel rewards good leadership with attractive additions and designer-improvements to your Throne Room.

You can view your Throne Room at any time, by selecting the View Throne Room command from the Kingdom pull-down menu (or by pressing Shift + H). At the start of a simulation, your Throne Room is empty. By demonstrating good leadership skills, you will have the opportunity to make improvements to your throne room's walls, to its floor, and to the throne itself. Each element of the throne room has four different looks that you can achieve, one at a time. For example, you can choose to make four separate improvements to the actual throne chair (one each time you are awarded a Throne Room addition). Obviously, the mark of a great leader is someone with a Throne Room with most or *all* the possible add-ons and improvements.

The Throne Room has no impact on the overall *Civ II* game. It's simply built into the game so that you, the leader of your empire, can enjoy the benefits of your success. You can choose to totally ignore the Throne Room feature by accessing the Game pull-down menu and selecting the Graphics Options command. From its menu, you can deactivate the Throne Room graphics by removing the check mark from the Throne Room option in the Select Graphic Options window.

A SIMULATION COMES TO AN END

A simulation can end in any of the following ways:

- Your empire gets conquered by a rival.

- Your time runs out (in the year A.D. 2020) before you achieve your ultimate objective.

- Your empire colonizes space before the year A.D. 2020.

- Your empire conquers all rival empires, making you the leader of the world.

- You select the Retire command from the Game pull-down menu and in so doing end the simulation.

No matter what conditions bring your simulation to its conclusion, after your final turn a *Civilization* POWERgraph will be displayed, as shown in Figure 5.27. This POWERgraph offers you a graphical depiction of your empire's growth between the start of the simulation (4000 B.C.) and the end. Once you've viewed this graph, click on the OK button to continue.

After you review the Civilization POWERgraph, your final game score will be displayed on the Civilization Score screen. This is the same screen that you can view during the simulation, by selecting the Civilization Score command from the World pull-down menu; however, this display shows your final game score.

Now that your days as ruler have ended (at least for the current simulation), you will be ranked among the world's greatest leaders and given an overall rating. Finally, your score, ranking, and name will be posted (and saved on your hard disk) in the *Civilization* Hall of Fame.

In some circumstances, you can keep your simulation going, even *after* it has officially ended. For example, if your empire has colonized space, and you now want to conquer the world, this is possible, although your point score will not be affected. A window will appear on the screen asking if you want to continue the simulation or end the program. Well, you're the supreme leader—so *you* choose!

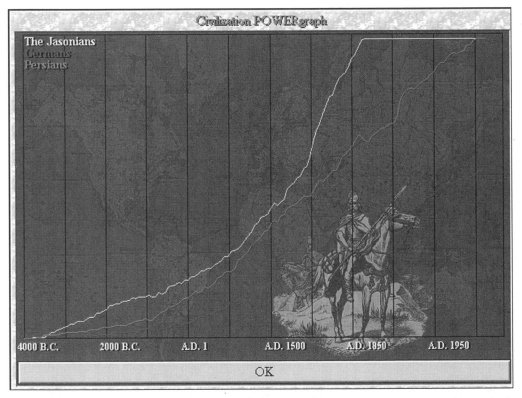

FIGURE 5.27: In this example of the Civilization POWERgraph, the Jasonian empire reached its growth and expansion peak around the year A.D. 1870 and then leveled off and remained constant until the year A.D. 2020.

6

The *Civilization II* Units

Like all the other *Civilization* games, the way you control your empire is by creating and then managing units, which represent types of military and nonmilitary forces that are under your leadership. *Civ II* offers many different types of units, each of which has unique capabilities. There is no limit to the number of each type of unit that you create within your empire. You're only bound by the production capabilities of your cities and the Scientific Advances (knowledge) that your scientists have acquired.

CREATING UNITS

Units are created within the Production window of the City screen of a given city, in exactly the same way as you would create a City Improvement or Wonder of the World. The units, however, represent the portion of your population which will venture out from cities to explore, conquer new territory, and fight battles. From the City screen, a list of available units that can be built will appear in the *What shall we build in (town name)?* window, as you can see in Figure 6.1. The units will be listed at the top of this display, followed by available City Improvements and then Wonders of the World. On the right side of this list will be how many turns (the cost) it will take to produce each type of unit.

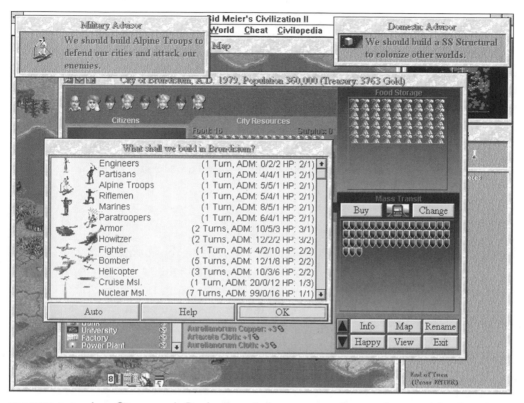

FIGURE 6.1: In a City screen's Production window, you can choose what type of unit a city should build, while the different types of units are listed in the *What shall we build in (town name)?* window.

BUYING UNITS

You can speed up the production process by choosing to spend cash from your empire's treasury and buying the unit you select for a city to produce. To buy a unit, first select it in the *What shall we build in (town name)?* window and then, in the Production window, click on the Buy button. The price of the unit will be displayed, as you see in Figure 6.2, and you will be asked whether you want to purchase the unit as opposed to waiting for the city to produce it. Unless you're experiencing some type of emergency where you *must* have a unit, it's always a better strategy to preserve the treasury and allow the cities to build the units over a number of turns.

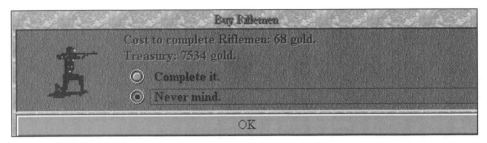

FIGURE 6.2: At any time, you can choose to spend some of your empire's money and buy a unit, rather than waiting for it to be built. If you buy a unit, it will be available to you at the start of your next turn.

CONTROLLING UNITS

During each turn in *Civ II*, you can control one unit at a time using the commands available to you on the Orders pull-down menu. The flashing unit on the Main Map is the active unit. Each unit occupies one terrain square on the Main Map. Depending on its type, a unit can move a predetermined number of terrain squares per turn. You determine the direction in which a unit will move, using your mouse or the arrow keys on the computer's keyboard (unless the GoTo option is activated.) With the GoTo option, all you have to do is select the destination for the active unit (any city), and the unit will automatically take the fastest route to that city over the course of multiple turns. A unit traveling under a GoTo command will have the letter "G" within its shield.

You can also choose to keep an active unit stationary while you move other units and then return to move the stationary unit. To do this, select the Wait command from the Orders pull-down menu (or press W). If you do not wish to return to the active unit during the current turn, press the spacebar, or select the No Orders command from the Orders pull-down menu.

It is possible for multiple units to share one terrain square on the Main Map. Some units, such as ships and planes, even require that other units share their space because the purpose of these units is to quickly transport other types of units.

GETTING INFORMATION FROM A UNIT'S SHIELD

In *Civ II*, units actually look somewhat like what they're supposed to represent. In addition, each unit carries a shield that serves multiple purposes. The color of the shield instantly tells you which empire that unit belongs to, because each empire is assigned a color at the start of a game.

Once a unit has received orders to accomplish a specific task, a letter representing that order will appear within its shield. For example, an "F" in a shield means the unit is Fortified, an "S"' represents Sleep (or Sentry) mode, and a "G" means the unit has been ordered to travel to a specific location with the GoTo command. A dash (–) means that the unit is not currently under any orders.

At the top of every unit's shield is an energy meter. When this meter is fully charged, it will be a solid green bar. This energy meter represents the current strength of the unit. If a unit gets attacked and receives a direct hit, the energy meter will change from green to yellow, and ultimately to red, and at the same time shrink in size. When an energy meter has turned totally red and then disappears, that unit will die.

RESTING INJURED UNITS

Unlike previous versions of the game, a unit that participates in a battle can survive and remain in the game. After a battle, however, the unit's energy meter will be diminished (which represents the extent of the unit's injuries). To replenish a unit's energy meter after battle, you have two options:

⊕ Allow the unit to rest for multiple turns. When the injured unit becomes active during each turn, select the No Orders command (or press the spacebar). You can begin using that unit again once after its energy meter is replenished. Unless you give a unit a rest after a battle, it will not be able to replenish its energy, and it will remain weak. A weak unit can easily be killed in a future attack.

⊕ The second alternative is to move the injured unit to any friendly city. A unit that returns to a friendly city will heal much faster. To speed up the healing process so that it takes only one turn, there are specific City Improvements you should build within your cities. Barracks will repair ground-based units in one turn, while Port Facilities will repair damaged ships. Airports will repair damaged air-based units.

REPLACING OLDER UNITS

As your scientific knowledge expands you'll be able to build more advanced types of Units. Thus, you'll want to replace older Units, so you don't have to deal with the expense of maintaining them. Old units that are no longer needed should be disbanded—use the Disband command on the Orders pull-down menu (or press Shift + D) when the unit you want to disband becomes active. If you have built the Leonardo's Workshop Wonder of the World, your Military Units will automatically be updated as new advances are acquired by your empire.

MILITARY UNITS

Every unit has an attack strength, which represents how strong it is when launching an attack on an enemy unit or city. Units also have a defense strength associated with them. If a unit is going to survive an enemy attack, its defense strength should be stronger than the attacking enemy's attack strength. It is your job to examine each type of unit's strengths and weaknesses to assign them to the tasks for which they are best suited. As a general rule, the more powerful a unit is, the longer it will take to produce, and the more money/resources it will cost.

What's the Best Way to Handle Out-of-Date Units and Keep Your Military as Current as Possible?

You can take any of several approaches to deal with out-of-date units that cost money and resources to maintain. You can simply use the Disband command (Shift+D), which cuts them from your army instantly. An alternative is to position them around key cities, Fortify them, and then use them as a line of defense against attacks. Another option is to use the older (out-of-date) units to fight your battles and be your first offensive wave when you attack a rival city. After all, you don't care if these units get killed because they're costing you money to maintain. If they're going to die, they may as well weaken the enemy in the process. When you use the older units for an attack, be sure you have stronger, more modern units ready to move in once the enemy is weakened.

After you develop the Leonardo's Workshop Wonder of the World, your Military units will automatically be updated as your scientists develop new knowledge and as more powerful and advanced types of units become possible to create.

The three primary jobs of a Military Unit are:

- **Exploration** Use units that have the ability to move across multiple terrain squares during each turn. This will allow them to cover more territory faster. Units used for exploration should be prepared to participate in surprise battles, but you should not necessarily use them to initiate attacks against enemy cities or units.

- **Protection/Guard Duty** Units with strong defensive capabilities should be stationed within or around your empire's cites to protect them from enemy invasion. To enhance a unit's strength when it's being used to protect a city, you can Fortify it, build Fortresses, or use units with Veteran status.

- **Invasion/Attack** The units that offer the highest attack strengths should be the ones you use to launch invasions and attacks. These units can be transported using aircraft, ships, or ground transports to get them to a specific location quickly. Keep in mind, aircraft and ships can launch their own attacks against other aircraft or ships, plus they can attack ground-based units and cities. To actually conquer an enemy city, however, it will ultimately be necessary for one of your ground-based units to enter into that city after it has been weakened by aircraft or ship attacks.

The following is a roundup of the types of units that you will be able to create and manage during a game. As your civilization expands, you could easily wind up creating and managing dozens, perhaps hundreds, of units. At the beginning of a simulation, the only type of Military Units that your empire will be able to build are Warrior Units. That is, until your scientists discover new Scientific Advances. In addition to providing you with each type of unit's Attack, Defense, Hit Points, Firepower, and Movement abilities, the required Scientific Advance your empire must first acquire before building each type of unit is also listed.

MILITARY UNIT SPECIFICATIONS

Military Units are divided into three categories, although some fall into two different categories. The categories for Military Units are as follows:

⊕ **Ground-Based Units** These are units that move on the ground and participate in ground-based battles. Table 6.1 lists the specifications for all of *Civilization II*'s ground units.

⊕ **Air-Based Units** Airplanes can participate in air-to-air battles, or air-to-ground battles, or they can even be used to transport ground troops from one location to another. Keep in mind, air-based units must stop for refueling or they'll crash. Refueling can be done at any friendly city or an airbase, which can be created on any ground-based terrain square by Settler or Engineer Units. Air Units can also land on Carrier Units (in the middle of oceans) to refuel. Table 6.2 lists the specifications for all of *Civilization II*'s air-based units.

⊕ **Naval Units** Ships can participate in ship-to-ship battles, or ship-to-ground battles, or they can be used to transport other types of units across oceans or along rivers. Table 6.3 lists the specifications for all of *Civilization II*'s naval units.

TABLE 6.1: GROUND-BASED MILITARY UNITS

UNIT	ICON	SCIENTIFIC ADVANCE REQUIREMENT	COST	ATTACK STRENGTH	DEFENSE STRENGTH	HIT POINTS	FIRE-POWER	MOVE-MENT
Archers		Warrior Code	30	3	2	1	1	1
Armor		Mobile Warfare	80	10	5	3	1	3
Artillery		Machine Tools	50	10	1	2	2	1

UNIT	ICON	SCIENTIFIC ADVANCE REQUIREMENT	COST	ATTACK STRENGTH	DEFENSE STRENGTH	HIT POINTS	FIRE-POWER	MOVE-MENT
Cannon		Metallurgy	40	8	1	2	1	1
Catapult		Mathematics	40	6	1	1	1	1
Cavalry		Tactics	60	8	3	2	1	2
Chariot		The Wheel	30	3	1	1	1	2
Crusaders		Monotheism	40	5	1	1	1	2
Dragoons		Leadership	50	5	2	2	1	2
Elephant		Polytheism	40	4	1	1	1	2
Fanatics[1]		Fundamentalism	20	4	4	2	1	1
Horsemen		Horseback Riding	20	2	1	1	1	2
Howitzer[2]		Robotics	70	12	2	3	2	2
Knights		Chivalry	40	4	2	1	1	2

(Continued on next page)

(Continued from previous page)

UNIT	ICON	SCIENTIFIC ADVANCE REQUIREMENT	COST	ATTACK STRENGTH	DEFENSE STRENGTH	HIT POINTS	FIRE-POWER	MOVE-MENT
Legion		Iron Working	40	4	2	1	1	1
Marines[3]		Amphibious Warfare	60	8	5	2	1	1
Mechanized		Labor Unions	50	6	6	3	1	3
Musketeers Infantry		Gunpowder	30	3	3	2	1	1
Partisans		Guerrilla Warfare	50	4	4	2	1	1
Phalanx		Bronze Working	20	1	2	1	1	1
Pikemen		Feudalism	20	1	2[4]	1	1	1
Riflemen		Conscription	40	5	4	2	1	1
Warriors		None	10	1	1	1	1	1

[1] This unit can only be built when an empire is being ruled under Fundamentalism.

[2] This unit is not hindered when attacking cities with City Walls.

[3] This unit can attack directly from a ship. Other types of ground-based Military Units must first exit the ship they are traveling on and then launch an attack from land.

[4] Defense strength when attacking mounted units.

What are the Best Ways to Protect a City Located In-Land?

Begin by fortifying several of your Military Units within the city and around it. Next, build City Walls (City Improvement) within the city. Then use Settler or Engineer Units to build Fortresses on the terrain squares surrounding the city (this really only needs to be done in later stages of a simulation when your cities have Wonders of the World and City Improvements that you want to protect). Building Barracks (City Improvement) allows the Military Units created from that city to obtain Veteran status, which makes them 50 percent stronger.

When air-based enemy Units become a concern, build the SAM Missile Battery (City Improvement) within cities you really need to protect. This improvement doubles the city's defensive capabilities against air-based attacks (in much the same way a Coastal Fortress protects a city against ship-based attacks). The SDI Defense (City Improvement) will help protect a city from a Nuclear Missile attack in the late stages of a simulation. The ability to build and use Nuclear Missiles happens when one of the civilizations obtains the Manhattan Project (Wonder of the World).

Creating the Great Wall (Wonder of the World) will instantly give all the cities in your empire the benefit of having City Walls (City Improvement) built within them. The Sun Tzus' War Academy (Wonder of the World) allows all Units created by your empire to be built with Veteran Status, so they'll be 50 percent stronger from the moment they're created.

TABLE 6.2: AIR-BASED MILITARY UNITS

UNIT	ICON	SCIENTIFIC ADVANCE REQUIREMENT	COST	ATTACK STRENGTH	DEFENSE STRENGTH	HIT POINTS	FIRE-POWER	MOVE-MENT
Bomber		Advanced Flight	120	12	1	2	2	8
Fighter		Flight	60	4	2	2	2	10

(Continued on next page)

(Continued from previous page)

UNIT	ICON	SCIENTIFIC ADVANCE REQUIREMENT	COST	ATTACK STRENGTH	DEFENSE STRENGTH	HIT POINTS	FIRE-POWER	MOVE-MENT
Helicopter[1]		Combined Arms	100	10	3	2	2	6
Stealth bomber		Stealth	160	14	3	2	2	12
Stealth fighter		Stealth	80	8	3	2	2	14

[1] This unit is not hindered by cities protected by City Walls, and will spot enemy submarines located in adjacent terrain squares (below).

TABLE 6.3: NAVAL MILITARY UNITS

UNIT	ICON	SCIENTIFIC ADVANCE REQUIREMENT	COST	ATTACK STRENGTH	DEFENSE STRENGTH	HIT POINTS	FIRE-POWER	MOVE-MENT
Aegis Cruiser		Rocketry	100	8	8	3	2	5
Battleship		Automobile	160	12	12	4	2	4
Caravel		Navigation	40	2	1	1	1	3
Carrier		Advanced Flight	160	1	9	4	2	5
Cruiser		Steel	80	6	6	3	2	5

UNIT	ICON	SCIENTIFIC ADVANCE REQUIREMENT	COST	ATTACK STRENGTH	DEFENSE STRENGTH	HIT POINTS	FIRE-POWER	MOVE-MENT
Destroyer		Electricity	40	4	4	3	1	6
Frigate		Magnetism	50	4	2	2	1	4
Galleon[1]		Magnetism	40	0	2	2	1	4
Ironclad		Steam Engine	60	4	2	1	1	2
Submarine		Combustion	60	10	2	3	2	3
Transport		Industrialization	50	0	3	3	1	5
Trireme[2]		Map Making	50	0	3	3	1	5

[1] Galleons are used exclusively for transporting ground units across oceans.

[2] Without the proper Scientific Advances, Triremes get lost at sea easily. Try to stay as close to land as possible, or at least end a turn near land.

What Are the Best Ways to Protect a City Along a Coast?

There are many strategies you can use to defend cities located along coastlines. These cities must protect themselves from land-based attacks as well as attack from enemy naval units. Thus, you'll want to begin by fortifying several of your own Military Units (preferably those with high defense strengths) within and around each of your cities. Next, you can have your Settler or Engineer Units build Fortresses on terrain squares surrounding the land-based areas of the city, and then fortify Units within those Fortresses. Building City Walls (City Improvement) will boost a city's defense strength against all attacks, and then adding a Coastal Fortress (City Improvement) will maximize your city's defense capabilities. As an additional defensive measure, you can also build one or more ships and place them on Sentry Duty (sleep mode) in the water near the city. Thus, if enemy ships approach your city, your city's first line of defense will be ships. (If you're placing ships on Sentry Duty to protect a city, there is no need to have Military Units on those ships.)

TABLE 6.4: AIR/GROUND MILITARY UNITS

UNIT	ICON	SCIENTIFIC ADVANCE REQUIREMENT	COST	ATTACK STRENGTH	DEFENSE STRENGTH	HIT POINTS	FIRE-POWER	MOVE-MENT
Alpine Troops		Tactics	50	5	5	2	1	1
Cruise Missile		Rocketry	60	20	0	1	3	12
Nuclear Missile[1]		Rocketry	160	99	0	1	1	16
Para-trooper[2]		Combined Arms	60	6	4	2	1	1

[1] Nuclear Missiles represent the strongest weapon/Military Unit you have available.

[2] Using the Paradrop command on the Orders pull-down menu, these units can drop down from an aircraft to launch a ground-based attack.

What's the Best Way to Use Paratrooper Units?

When a Paratrooper Unit becomes active, and is within a friendly city or an airbase, you have the ability to have it perform a Paradrop, which allows it to move extremely quickly. A Paratrooper that's ordered to perform a Paradrop can instantly move up to ten terrain squares and land on any terrain square that's not occupied by an enemy unit or city. Once they land, Paratroopers can move one terrain square at a time over land. If you have a friendly city that's located near a rival empire's city, you can build Paratroopers in that friendly city and then quickly launch an attack by Paradropping the units right outside the enemy city.

Paradropping Paratroopers is similar to airlifting a unit from one location to another; however, when you use the Airlift command (on the Orders pull-down menu), the unit must be within a friendly city containing an Airport (City Improvement)—or be standing on an Airbase—and it must be ordered to travel to another friendly city containing an Airport (or a terrain square with an Airbase). Paratroopers, however, must begin in a city or Airbase, but they can land anywhere within a ten-terrain-square radius of their origination point. Only active Paratroopers can be ordered to perform a Paradrop from the Orders pull-down menu.

NONMILITARY UNITS

Much of your job as the ruler of your civilization involves managing and building up your military. To expand your empire without military conquests, however, you must create Settler Units and other nonmilitary units. Table 6.5 lists the specifications for all of *Civilization II*'s nonmilitary units.

TABLE 6.5: NON-MILITARY UNITS

UNIT	ICON	SCIENTIFIC ADVANCE REQUIREMENT	COST	ATTACK STRENGTH	DEFENSE STRENGTH	HIT POINTS	FIRE-POWER	MOVE-MENT
Caravan		Trade	50	0	1	1	1	1
Diplomat		Writing	30	0	0	1	1	2

(Continued on next page)

(Continued from previous page)

UNIT	ICON	SCIENTIFIC ADVANCE REQUIREMENT	COST	ATTACK STRENGTH	DEFENSE STRENGTH	HIT POINTS	FIRE-POWER	MOVE-MENT
Engineer		Explosives	40	0	2	2	1	2
Explorer		Seafaring	30	0	1	1	1	1
Freight		Corporation	50	0	1	1	1	2
Settler		None	40	0	1	2	1	1
Spy		Espionage	30	0	0	1	1	3

Settler Units allow you to found new cities and build Terrain Improvements. To more quickly build Terrain Improvements (such as roads, irrigation, railroads, or mines), Engineer Units should also be used.

What Are Some Ways to Boost Trade and Wonder Production Between Cities and Among Empires?

Caravan Units become available to you in a simulation once your empire has acquired Trade (Knowledge Advance). Later in the game, when The Corporation (Knowledge Advance) is discovered by your empire's scientists, Freight Units will become available and replace the now outdated Caravan Units. Freight Units have the ability to move two terrain squares per turn (as opposed to the one square per turn that a Caravan Unit can travel).

Caravan Units and later Freight Units allow you to established trade routes between both friendly and rival cities. Establishing a trade route between two cities will boost production in both cities that are involved in the trade route; however, the city in which the Caravan or Freight Unit originated will also receive a cash and science bonus for establishing the trade route. Each city within your empire can maintain up to three trade routes simultaneously, so the amount of money, goods, and science that can be generated from trade routes might become significant. As your empire grows, maintaining large cities and a strong military will get expensive. Establishing well-planned trade routes will provide the fund you need (on an on-going basis) to keep your empire prospering. At any time during a simulation, if you see that the costs associated with maintaining your empire have exceeded the amount of revenue being produced during each turn, you must take steps to turn your finances around. Having trade routes will help keep this from happening.

After a Caravan or Freight Unit has been created within a city, it's your job to determine what goods or commodities that unit will offer to whatever city with which it eventually establishes a trade route. A special menu will appear listing the various types of goods and commodities that are available. At the bottom of this window is a Supply and Demand button that allows you to analyze the wants and needs of each city, before you determine what the Caravan or Freight Unit will carry.

Some of the goods and commodities that cities can trade are: hides, wool, beads, cloth, salt, coal, copper, dye, wine, silver, spice, gems, gold, oil, uranium, and food supplies. If a city is suffering from a famine or food shortage, using Caravan Units from other cities to send food and supplies to the city in need can and will often rescue that city. Also, even if you assign the Caravan or Freight Unit to carry one of the above-mentioned types of goods, if the unit arrives at a city that is building a Wonder of the World, you will have the option to establish a trade route with that city, or use that Caravan or Freight Unit to help build that wonder.

You can try several ways to maximize the benefits of establishing trade routes. First, send the Caravan or Freight Unit to establish a trade route with a city that is at least ten terrain squares away from its home city. Next, use the Supply and Demand button to determine the needs or wants of the the city with which you're planning to establish a trade route. (This Supply and Demand information is also always available from your Trade Advisor.) If your Caravan or Freight Unit meets a specific demand, you'll receive extra benefits from establishing the trade route. Establishing trade routes with cities from rival empires (with which you have treaties) will generate the biggest benefits for your empire, especially if the rival city is located at least ten terrain squares away, and is located on a different continent (land mass) from the Caravan or Freight Unit's home city. Finally, your empire as a whole will reap greater benefits by establishing trade routes between larger cities.

Once you have selected a destination for the Caravan or Freight Unit, you'll save time by using the GoTo command to command that unit to travel directly to the city with which you want to establish the trade route. You'll also be able to establish trade routes more quickly if the cities are connected via roads or railroads.

Diplomat and Spy Units will come in handy when it comes time to deal with rival civilizations. To develop trade routes between your own cities, or between your cities and foreign cities, you must use either Caravan or Freight Units. Trade routes can only be established between cities that are located at least ten terrain squares apart from each other. The farther apart the cities are, the more profitable the trade route will be. Every city within your empire can maintain up to three trade routes. The following list describes the nonmilitary units in detail:

- **Caravan Unit**   These Units are used to develop trade routes with other friendly cities. If one of your cities is building a Wonder of the World (which takes many turns), a Caravan Unit from another friendly city can travel to the city building a wonder and assist in its development. Once a Caravan Unit develops a trade route or helps build a wonder, it is disbanded. Caravan Units cannot attack enemy units, and they should avoid being attacked because their defense strength is low.

- **Diplomat Unit**   The capabilities of Diplomat Units has been expanded in *Civ II*. In addition to establishing Embassies in foreign cities, Diplomat Units can also prevent friendly cities from being sabotages. They can also invade a city to perform one of several tasks.

- **Engineer Unit**   Engineer Units cannot found new cities, but they can build Terrain Improvements faster than Settler Units can. Use these units to build roads, railroads, irrigation, mines, fortresses, and airbases.

- **Explorer Unit**   In the early stages of a simulation, Explorer Units can be used for exploring territory, because they have the ability to move quickly, as if they were traveling along roads (even if no roads have been built).

- **Freight Unit**   In later stages of a simulation, Freight Units can replace Caravan Units. Trade routes established by Freight Units are more profitable.

- **Settler Unit**   Settler Units play a vital role in *Civ II* because they are used to found new cities and to build all types of Terrain Improvements.

- **Spy Unit** Spy Units are like Diplomat Units, with the difference that they become available later in a simulation. They are capable of performing more tasks that will benefit your empire. If used correctly, Spy Units will allow you to conquer enemies without actually entering into battles.

USING DIPLOMATS AND SPY UNITS AS WEAPONS

The capabilities and usefulness of Diplomat and Spy Units have been greatly enhanced in *Civ II*. In fact, these two types of units can be powerful tools for conquering cities and sabotaging (or *recruiting!*) enemy units. Spy Units can perform all the tasks of a Diplomat Unit, plus they have a few extra capabilities. Use your Spy Units to investigate enemy cities before you launch an all-out attack. When a Spy or Diplomat Unit approaches an enemy city, a window similar to the one shown in Figure 6.3 will appear with a list of the following tasks that can be accomplished:

- Investigate City (Free)
- Steal Technology
- Industrial Sabotage
- Pollute Water Supply
- Plant Nuclear Device
- Incite a Revolt

Investigating a city allows you to view the City screen of that city. Stealing Technology allows your Diplomat or Spy Unit to steal one Scientific Advance that has been acquired by a rival empire (one that your empire hasn't yet acquired). Industrial Sabotage lets your unit destroy whatever the enemy city has in production, whether it's a unit, improvement, or wonder. Polluting the water supply will help weaken the city, making it easier to invade and conquer.

Choosing to plant a nuclear device is a dangerous mission for a Spy Unit and will wreak major havoc on the city (but could start an all-out war between your empire and the empire whose city you blew up), as shown in Figure 6.4. Planting a nuclear device doesn't always work. In fact, you can count on your Spy Unit getting captured

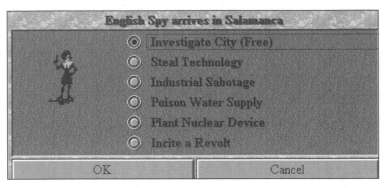

FIGURE 6.3: This window will appear when a Spy Unit attempts to enter an enemy city. It's your job to decide what type of damage, if any, you want the unit to attempt to inflict on the city.

(although the unit will often escape later). Obviously, if you're already at war, this won't matter. After the detonation of the device, you can have a team of Engineers and/or Settlers standing by to clean up the pollution.

If you command a Spy Unit to incite a revolt, it's going to cost you, as shown in Figure 6.5. You must decide if the cost of taking over the city without a battle is worth the price. Although inciting a riot will cost you money, this is an easy way to take over a city without launching any type of attack. In essence, you're paying off the inhabitants of the city, causing them to join your empire. From an economic standpoint, inciting a riot doesn't usually make sense, but it's a nice ability to have at your disposal, especially if your empire has money to spare.

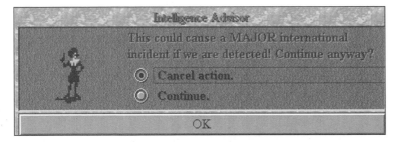

FIGURE 6.4: This Intelligence Advisor window tells you the consequences that could result when you use a Spy Unit to plant a nuclear device in an enemy city.

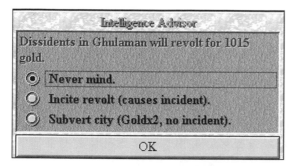

FIGURE 6.5: The Intelligence Advisor window tells you how much inciting a revolt in an enemy city will cost you.

Another useful task that a Spy Unit is capable of is bribing or sabotaging an enemy unit that it encounters. When a Spy Unit approaches an enemy unit, the window shown in Figure 6.6 will appear. Using the mouse, you can choose to bribe the unit (which will cost your empire money) or you can sabotage the unit (which will often injure it, not destroy it). If you successfully bribe a unit and pay the necessary amount of money, that unit will join your empire and begin working for you. If you sabotage the unit, have one of your Military Units on hand to move in and attack after the Spy Unit does its thing (because the Spy Unit will often just weaken the enemy unit).

As you can see, Diplomat Units are also extremely useful, although they are not as powerful as Spy Units when it comes to inflicting damage on an enemy city. Diplomats can investigate enemy cities, steal technology, perform industrial sabotage, and incite riots, as shown in Figure 6.7.

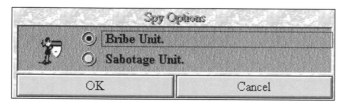

FIGURE 6.6: This Spy Options window allows you to either bribe or sabotage an enemy unit.

Often, once a Diplomat or Spy Unit has accomplished the task you assigned it, it will automatically be disbanded. Sometimes, the Diplomat or Spy Unit will remain available to embark on additional missions.

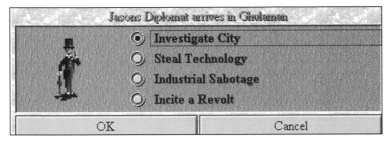

FIGURE 6.7: This window will appear when a Diplomat Unit attempts to enter an enemy city. It's your job to decide what type of damage, if any, you want the Unit to attempt to inflict on the city.

7

Planning
Knowledge Advances

O ne of your ongoing objectives in *Civ II* is to keep the scientists within your empire working to develop new Knowledge Advances. It is with this knowledge that you can create new types of units, City Improvements, and Wonders of the World. Of course, it's vital to balance the scientific development efforts with the need to keep your population happy and productive—all of which is done by accessing the Kingdom pull-down menu, selecting the Tax Rate option, and adjusting your empire's distribution of wealth.

THE *CIVILIZATION II* KNOWLEDGE ADVANCES

This section offers information about each Knowledge Advance available to you in *Civ II*, and describes what new units, City Improvements, and Wonders of the World you'll be able to create within your cities once each Knowledge Advance is acquired during a simulation. The advances are organized in this chapter by five distinct categories— military, economic, social, academic, and applied—within each epoch of civilization: the Ancient World, the Renaissance, the Industrial Revolution, and the Modern World. For easy reference, advances within each category are provided in alphabetical order.

Most Knowledge Advances have a prerequisite—that is, a Knowledge Advance that you must obtain first before you can acquire the Knowledge Advance you are seeking to acquire. For example, if your empire just obtained Advanced Flight and you want to pursue Rocketry, you must first obtain Electronics (or already have acquired

Electronics) before it will be possible to obtain Rocketry. The prerequisite associated with an advance is listed along with the information for each Knowledge Advance that follows shortly. If applicable, secondary prerequisites—such as Electronics as a secondary prerequisite for Advanced Flight in the previous example—are also indicated for each Knowledge Advance.

Additional information for each advance includes a summary of the units, City Improvements, and Wonders of the World that will now be available to you from the Production window of any City screen within your empire, once you acquire the advance. The specifications pertaining to each of the units, which were covered in detail in Chapter 6, *The Civilization II Units*, have also been included here, along with the costs associated with each type of improvement and wonder.

The extensive list of Knowledge Advances that follow can be used as a directory to assist you in developing a strategy for determining which Knowledge Advances you want your empire's scientists to pursue during the course of a simulation. By looking up the information for any specific advance, you can map out the course of advance requirements that will play a pivotal role in helping your empire to meet its ultimate goal.

UNITS THAT DO NOT REQUIRE ADVANCE PREREQUISITES

The units listed in Table 7.1 do not require you to obtain a previous Knowledge Advance. They can be built at the very start of a simulation, before any knowledge has been obtained by your empire's scientists. The Barracks improvement is the only City Improvement that can be built as soon as you found your first city, because it does not require obtaining a Knowledge Advance.

TABLE 7.1: UNITS WITH NO KNOWLEDGE ADVANCE PREREQUISITE

UNIT	COST	ATTACK STRENGTH	DEFENSE STRENGTH	HIT POINTS	FIRE-POWER	MOVEMENT PER TURN
Settlers	40	0	1	2	1	1
Warrior	10	1	1	1	1	1

Advances of the Ancient World

Just as in real-life history, the events that take place during a simulation happen during specific epochs, and the advances your civilization can acquire during each period is loosly equivalent to the major advances that have taken place over the course of history in real life. During the Ancient World epoch of the simulation, you will want to begin working on acquiring Knowledge Advances that will lay the foundation for achieving your ultimate goals. What knowledge and advances you aquire in the early stages of a simulation will have a tremendous impact on your empire's future.

MILITARY ADVANCES

Feudalism—Requirements: *Monarchy* and *Masonry*

UNIT	COST	ATTACK STRENGTH	DEFENSE STRENGTH	HIT POINTS	FIRE-POWER	MOVEMENT PER TURN
Pikemen	20	1	2	1	1	1

Wonder: **Sun Tzu's War Academy**—cost is 300

Knowledge Advances: **Chivalry**—when combined with *Horseback Riding*

Theology—when combined with *Monotheism*

Horseback Riding—Requirements: None

UNIT	COST	ATTACK STRENGTH	DEFENSE STRENGTH	HIT POINTS	FIRE-POWER	MOVEMENT PER TURN
Horsemen	20	2	1	1	1	2

Knowledge Advances: **The Wheel**

Chivalry—when combined with *Feudalism*

Polytheism—when combined with *Mysticism*

Warrior code—Requirements: None

UNIT	COST	ATTACK STRENGTH	DEFENSE STRENGTH	HIT POINTS	FIRE-POWER	MOVEMENT PER TURN
Archer	30	3	2	1	1	1

⊕ Knowledge Advance: **Iron Working**—when combined with *Bronze Working*

ECONOMIC ADVANCES

Currency—Requirement: *Bronze Working*

⊕ City Improvements: **Marketplace**—cost is 80; maintenance cost/turn is 1

⊕ Knowledge Advances: **Construction** when combined with *Masonry*

                                  Trade when combined with *Code of Laws*

Map Making—Requirement: *Alphabet*

UNIT	COST	ATTACK STRENGTH	DEFENSE STRENGTH	HIT POINTS	FIRE-POWER	MOVEMENT PER TURN
Trireme	40	1	1	1	1	3

⊕ Wonder: **Lighthouse**—cost is 200

⊕ Knowledge Advance: **Seafaring** when combined with *Pottery*

Pottery—Requirements: None

⊕ City Improvement: **Granary**—cost is 60; maintenance cost/turn is 1

⊕ Wonder: **Hanging Gardens**—cost is 200

⊕ Knowledge Advances: **Sanitation** when combined with *Engineering*

                                    Seafaring when combined with *Map Making*

Seafaring—Requirements: *Map Making* and *Pottery*

UNIT	COST	ATTACK STRENGTH	DEFENSE STRENGTH	HIT POINTS	FIRE-POWER	MOVEMENT PER TURN
Explorer	30	0	1	1	1	1

⊕ City Improvement: **Harbor**—cost is 60; maintenance cost/turn is 1

⊕ Knowledge Advance: **Navigation** when combined with *Astronomy*

Trade—Requirements: *Currency* and *Code of Laws*

UNIT	COST	ATTACK STRENGTH	DEFENSE STRENGTH	HIT POINTS	FIRE-POWER	MOVEMENT PER TURN
Caravan	50	0	1	1	1	1

⊕ Wonder: **Marco Polo's Embassy**—cost is 200

⊕ Knowledge Advances: **Banking** when combined with *Republic*

Medicine when combined with *Sanitation*

What Steps Can Be Taken to Ensure a City's Growth?

The key to keeping your cities growing is to keep their populations happy (or at least content), and supply them with the City Improvements and Terrain Improvements that allow for maximum production and growth.

As soon as possible, use a Settler or Engineer Unit to begin building irrigated terrain squares surrounding the city. Early on, build a Granary (City Improvement) within your cities. A Granary allows for food storage, and encourages faster growth early in a simulation. You'll also want to build an Aqueduct (City Improvement) so that the city can grow beyond the size of 8. Later, a Sewer System (City Improvement) will allow your cities to grow beyond the size of 12.

If you want to give the production within a city a boost, build any or all of the following City Improvements: Factory (and later a Hydro Plant in conjunction with the Factory); Manufacturing Plant; Power Plant; Solar Plant or Nuclear Plant; and an Offshore Platform.

SOCIAL ADVANCES

Ceremonial Burial—Requirements: None

⊕ City Improvement: **Temple**—cost is 40; maintenance cost/turn is 1

⊕ Knowledge Advances: **Mysticism**

Monarchy when combined with *Code of Laws*

Code of Laws—Requirement: *Alphabet*

⊕ City Improvement: **Courthouse**—cost is 80; maintenance cost/turn is 1

⊕ Knowledge Advances: **Literacy** when combined with *Writing*

Monarchy when combined with *Ceremonial Burial*

Republic when combined with *Literacy*

Trade when combined with *Currency*

Monarchy—Requirements: *Code of Laws* and *Ceremonial Burial*

⊕ Knowledge Advance: **Feudalism** when combined with *Masonry*

The Monarchy advance also allows you to change the form of government under which you're ruling your empire to a Monarchy.

Mysticism—Requirements: Ceremonial Burial

⊕ Wonder: **Oracle**—cost is 300

⊕ Knowledge Advances: **Astronomy** when combined with *Mathematics*

Philosophy when combined with *Literacy*

Polytheism—Requirements: *Mysticism* and *Horseback Riding*

UNIT	COST	ATTACK STRENGTH	DEFENSE STRENGTH	HIT POINTS	FIRE-POWER	MOVEMENT PER TURN
Elephant	40	4	1	1	1	2

⊕ Knowledge Advance: **Monotheism** when combined with *Philosophy*

Republic—Requirements: *Code of Laws* and *Literacy*

⊕ Knowledge Advance: **Banking** when combined with *Trade*

This advance also allows you to change the form of government under which you are ruling your empire to a Republic. Select the REVOLUTION command on the Kingdom pull-down menu.

ACADEMIC ADVANCES

Alphabet—Requirements: None

⊕ Knowledge Advances: **Code of Laws**

Map Making

Writing

Mathematics when combined with *Masonry*

Literacy—Requirements: *Writing* and *Code of Laws*

⊕ Wonder: **Great Library**—cost is 300

⊕ Knowledge Advances: **Republic**

Invention when combined with *Engineering*

Philosophy when combined with *Mysticism*

Physics when combined with *Navigation*

Mathematics—Requirements: *Alphabet* and *Masonry*

UNIT	COST	ATTACK STRENGTH	DEFENSE STRENGTH	HIT POINTS	FIRE-POWER	MOVEMENT PER TURN
Catapult	40	6	1	1	1	1

⊕ Knowledge Advances: **Astronomy** when combined with *Mysticism*

The University when combined with *Philosophy*

Writing—Requirements: *Alphabet*

UNIT	COST	ATTACK STRENGTH	DEFENSE STRENGTH	HIT POINTS	FIRE-POWER	MOVEMENT PER TURN
Diplomat	30	0	0	1	1	2

⊕ City Improvement: **Library**—cost is 80; maintenance cost/turn is 1

⊕ Knowledge Advance: **Literacy** when combined with *Code of Laws*

APPLIED ADVANCES

Bridge Building—Requirements: *Iron Working* and *Construction*

⊕ Knowledge Advance: **Railroad** when combined with *Steam Engine*

This advance also allows Settler and Engineer Units to build roads over River terrain squares.

Bronze Working—Requirements: None

UNIT	COST	ATTACK STRENGTH	DEFENSE STRENGTH	HIT POINTS	FIRE-POWER	MOVEMENT PER TURN
Phalanx	20	1	2	1	1	1

⊕ Wonder: **Colossus** Cost: 200

⊕ Knowledge Advances: **Currency**

Iron Working when combined with *Warrior Code*

Construction—Requirements: *Currency* and *Masonry*

⊕ City Improvements: **Aqueduct**—cost is 80; maintenance cost/turn is 2

Colosseum—cost is 100; maintenance cost/turn is 4

⊕ Knowledge Advances: **Bridge Building** when combined with *Iron Working*

Engineering when combined with *The Wheel*

Engineering—Requirements: *The Wheel* and *Construction*

⊕ Wonder: **King Richard's Crusade**—cost is 300

⊕ Knowledge Advances: **Invention** when combined with *Literacy*

Sanitation when combined with *Pottery*

Iron Working—Requirements: *Bronze Working* and *Warrior Code*

UNIT	COST	ATTACK STRENGTH	DEFENSE STRENGTH	HIT POINTS	FIRE-POWER	MOVEMENT PER TURN
Legion	40	4	2	1	1	1

⊕ Knowledge Advances: **Bridge Building** when combined with *Construction*

Gunpowder when combined with *Invention*

Magnetism when combined with *Physics*

Masonry—Requirements: None

⊕ City Improvement: **City Walls**—cost is 80; maintenance cost/turn is 0

Palace—cost is 100; maintenance cost/turn is 0

⊕ Wonders: **Great Wall**—cost is 300

Pyramids—cost is 200

⊕ Knowledge Advances: **Construction** when combined with *Currency*

Feudalism when combined with *Monarchy*

Mathematics when combined with *Alphabet*

The Wheel—Requirements: None

UNIT	COST	ATTACK STRENGTH	DEFENSE STRENGTH	HIT POINTS	FIRE-POWER	MOVEMENT PER TURN
Chariot	30	3	1	1	1	2

⊕ Knowledge Advance: **Engineering** when combined with *Construction*

Advances of the Renaissance

As time passes, your empire will enter the Renaissance era. During this time you will earn the opportunity to build more advanced Militrary Units, City Improvements, and Wonders of the World. Now that you can build stronger and more advanced Military Units, you might consider eliminating some of your outdated Military Units to help conserve the resources required to maintain them. Now, more than ever, it is imporant to determine in advance what type(s) of Military Units you'll want to build within your empire, and then develop a strategy that will allow you to aquire the appropriate Knowledge Advances required to build these units.

MILITARY ADVANCES

Chivalry—Requirements: *Feudalism* and *Horseback Riding*

UNIT	COST	ATTACK STRENGTH	DEFENSE STRENGTH	HIT POINTS	FIRE-POWER	MOVEMENT PER TURN
Knight	40	4	2	1	1	2

⊕ Knowledge Advance: **Leadership** when combined with *Gunpowder*

Gunpowder—Requirements: *Invention* and *Iron Working*

UNIT	COST	ATTACK STRENGTH	DEFENSE STRENGTH	HIT POINTS	FIRE-POWER	MOVEMENT PER TURN
Musketeer	30	3	3	2	1	1

⊕ Knowledge Advances: **Explosives** when combined with *Chemistry*

Leadership when combined with *Chivalry*

Metallurgy when combined with *The University*

Leadership—Requirements: *Chivalry* and *Gunpowder*

UNIT	COST	ATTACK STRENGTH	DEFENSE STRENGTH	HIT POINTS	FIRE-POWER	MOVEMENT PER TURN
Dragoon	50	5	2	2	1	2

⊕ Knowledge Advance: **Tactics** when combined with *Conscription*

Metallurgy—Requirements: *Gunpowder* and *The University*

UNIT	COST	ATTACK STRENGTH	DEFENSE STRENGTH	HIT POINTS	FIRE-POWER	MOVEMENT PER TURN
Cannon	80	8	1	2	1	1

⊕ City Improvement: **Coastal Fortresses**—cost is 80; maintenance cost/turn is 1

⊕ Knowledge Advances: **Conscription** when combined with *Democracy*

Electricity when combined with *Magnetism*

ECONOMIC ADVANCES

Banking—Requirements: *Trade* and *Republic*

⊕ City Improvement: **Bank**—cost is 120; maintenance cost/turn is 3

⊕ Knowledge Advances: **Economics** when combined with *The University*

Industrialization when combined with *Railroad*

Medicine—Requirements: *Sanitation* and *Trade*

- ⊕ Wonder: **Shakespeare's Theatre**—cost is 300
- ⊕ Knowledge Advances: **Chemistry** when combined with *The University*

  Genetic Engineering when combined with *Corporation*

Navigation—Requirements: *Seafaring* and *Astronomy*

UNIT	COST	ATTACK STRENGTH	DEFENSE STRENGTH	HIT POINTS	FIRE-POWER	MOVEMENT PER TURN
Caravel	40	2	1	1	1	3

- ⊕ Wonder: **Magellan's Expedition**—cost: 400
- ⊕ Knowledge Advances: **Amphibious Warfare** when combined with *Tactics*

  Physics when combined with *Literacy*

SOCIAL ADVANCES

Monotheism—Requirements: *Philosophy* and *Polytheism*

UNIT	COST	ATTACK STRENGTH	DEFENSE STRENGTH	HIT POINTS	FIRE-POWER	MOVEMENT PER TURN
Crusader	40	5	1	1	1	2

- ⊕ City Improvement: **Cathedral**—cost is 120; maintenance cost/turn is 3
- ⊕ Wonder: **Michelangelo's Chapel**—cost is 400
- ⊕ Knowledge Advances: **Theology** when combined with *Feudalism*

  Fundamentalism when combined with *Conscription*

Philosophy—Requirements: *Mysticism* and *Literacy*

⊕ Knowledge Advances: **Communism** when combined with *Industrialization*

Monotheism when combined with *Polytheism*

The University when combined with *Mathematics*

The civilization that obtains Philosophy first will receive a bonus Knowledge Advance of their choice.

Theology—Requirements: *Monotheism* and *Feudalism*

⊕ Wonder: **J. S. Bach's Cathedral**—cost is 400

This advance also makes the Oracle obsolete and adds one content citizen to every city that has a Cathedral City Improvement built within it.

ACADEMIC ADVANCES

Astronomy—Requirements: *Mysticism* and *Mathematics*

⊕ Wonders: **Copernicus' Observatory**—cost is 300

⊕ Knowledge Advances: **Navigation** when combined with *Seafaring*

Theory of Gravity when combined with *The University*

Chemistry—Requirements: *The University* and *Medicine*

⊕ Knowledge Advances: **Explosives** when combined with *Gunpowder*

Refining when combined with *Corporation*

Magnetism—Requirements: *Physics* and *Iron Working*

UNIT	COST	ATTACK STRENGTH	DEFENSE STRENGTH	HIT POINTS	FIRE-POWER	MOVEMENT PER TURN
Frigate	50	4	2	2	1	4
Galleon	40	0	2	2	1	4

⊕ Knowledge Advance: **Electricity** when combined with *Metallurgy*

This advance also makes the Lighthouse advance obsolete.

Physics—Requirements: *Navigation* and *Literacy*

⊕ Knowledge Advances: **Atomic Theory** when combined with *Theory of Gravity*

Magnetism when combined with *Iron Working*

Steam Engine when combined with *Invention*

Theory of Gravity—Requirements: *Astronomy* and *The University*

⊕ Wonder: **Isaac Newton's College**—cost is 400

⊕ Knowledge Advances: **Atomic Theory** when combined with *Physics*

Flight when combined with *Combustion*

The University—Requirements: *Mathematics* and *Philosophy*

⊕ City Improvement: **University**—cost is 160; maintenance cost/turn is 3

⊕ Knowledge Advances: **Chemistry** when combined with *Medicine*

Economics when combined with *Banking*

Metallurgy when combined with *Gunpowder*

Invention—Requirements: *Engineering* and *Literacy*

- ⊕ Wonder: **Leonardo's Workshop**—cost is 400
- ⊕ Knowledge Advances: **Democracy** when combined with *Banking*

  Gunpowder when combined with *Iron Working*

  Steam Engine when combined with *Physics*

Machine Tools—Requirements: *Steel* and *Tactics*

UNIT	COST	ATTACK STRENGTH	DEFENSE STRENGTH	HIT POINTS	FIRE-POWER	MOVEMENT PER TURN
Artillery	50	10	1	2	2	1

- ⊕ Knowledge Advances: **Advanced Flight** when combined with *Radio*

  Miniaturization when combined with *Electronics*

Advances of the Industrial Revolution

Welcome to the Industrial Revolution. From a technology and Knowledge Advance perspective, things should start happening a bit faster now. The Militrary Units you'll be able to build in this era are far more powerful. It is during this epoch that you'll want to take larger steps toward colonizing space or using your stronger military to conquer rival empires.

MILITARY ADVANCES

Conscription—Requirements: *Democracy* and *Metallurgy*

UNIT	COST	ATTACK STRENGTH	DEFENSE STRENGTH	HIT POINTS	FIRE-POWER	MOVEMENT PER TURN
Riflemen	40	5	4	2	1	1

- ⊕ Knowledge Advances: **Fundamentalism** when combined with *Theology*

  Tactics when combined with *Leadership*

Tactics—Requirements: *Conscription* and *Leadership*

UNIT	COST	ATTACK STRENGTH	DEFENSE STRENGTH	HIT POINTS	FIRE-POWER	MOVEMENT PER TURN
Alpine Troop	50	5	5	2	1	1
Cavalry.	60	8	3	2	1	2

Knowledge Advances: **Amphibious Warfare** when combined with *Navigation*

Guerrilla Warfare when combined with *Communism*

Steel when combined with *Tools*

Mobile Warfare when combined with *Automobile*

ECONOMIC ADVANCES

Corporation—Requirements: *Industrialization* and *Economics*

UNIT	COST	ATTACK STRENGTH	DEFENSE STRENGTH	HIT POINTS	FIRE-POWER	MOVEMENT PER TURN
Freight	50	0	1	1	1	2

City Improvement: **Capitalization**—cost is 600; maintenance cost/turn is 0

Knowledge Advances: **Electronics** when combined with *Electricity*

Genetic Engineering when combined with *Medicine*

Mass Production when combined with *Automobile*

Refining when combined with *Chemistry*

Economics—Requirements: *The University* and *Banking*

⊕ City Improvement: **Stock Exchange**—cost is 160; maintenance cost/turn is 4

⊕ Wonder: **Adam Smith's Trading Co.**—cost is 400

⊕ Knowledge Advance: **Corporation** when combined with *Industrialization*

Industrialization—Requirements: *Railroad* and *Banking*

UNIT	COST	ATTACK STRENGTH	DEFENSE STRENGTH	HIT POINTS	FIRE-POWER	MOVEMENT PER TURN
Transport	50	0	3	3	1	5

⊕ City Improvement: **Factory**—cost is 200; maintenance cost/turn is 4

⊕ Wonders: **Women's Suffrage**—cost is 600

⊕ Knowledge Advances: **Communism** when combined with *Philosophy*

Corporation when combined with *Economics*

Steel when combined with *Electricity*

This advance also makes the King Richard's Crusade wonder obsolete.

Railroad—Requirements: *Steam Engine* and *Bridge Building*

⊕ Wonder: **Darwin's Voyage**—cost is 400

⊕ Knowledge Advance: **Industrialization** when combined with *Banking*

This advance also allows Settler and Engineer Units to begin building Railroad terrain improvements, and it makes the Hanging Gardens wonder obsolete.

Sanitation—Requirements: *Engineering* and *Pottery*

⊕ City Improvement: **Sewer System**—cost is 120; maintenance cost/turn is 2

⊕ Knowledge Advances: **Medicine** when combined with *Trade*

Refrigeration when combined with *Electricity*

SOCIAL ADVANCES

Communism—Requirements: *Philosophy* and *Industrialization*

⊕ City Improvement: **Police Station**—cost is 60; maintenance cost/turn is 2

⊕ Wonder: **United Nations**—cost is 600

⊕ Knowledge Advances: **Espionage** when combined with *Democracy*

Guerrilla Warfare when combined with *Tactics*

This advance also allows you to switch to Communism as the form of government under which you rule your empire, and it makes Marco Polo's Embassy obsolete.

Democracy—Requirements: *Banking* and *Invention*

⊕ Wonder: **Statue of Liberty**—cost is 400

⊕ Knowledge Advances: **Conscription** when combined with *Metallurgy*

Espionage when combined with *Communism*

Recycling when combined with *Mass Production*

This advance also allows you to switch to Democracy as the form of government under which you rule your empire.

Fundamentalism—Requirements: *Theology* and *Conscription*

UNIT	COST	ATTACK STRENGTH	DEFENSE STRENGTH	HIT POINTS	FIRE-POWER	MOVEMENT PER TURN
Fanatics	20	4	4	2	1	1

This advance also allows you to switch to Fundamentalism as the form of government under which you rule your empire.

ACADEMIC ADVANCES

Atomic Theory—Requirements: *Theory of Gravity* and *Physics*

⊕ Knowledge Advance: **Nuclear Fission** when combined with *Mass Production*

Steam Engine—Requirements: *Physics* and *Invention*

UNIT	COST	ATTACK STRENGTH	DEFENSE STRENGTH	HIT POINTS	FIRE-POWER	MOVEMENT PER TURN
Ironclad	60	4	4	3	1	4

⊕ Wonder: **Eiffel Tower**—cost is 300

⊕ Knowledge Advance: **Railroad** when combined with *Bridge Building*

APPLIED ADVANCES

Combustion—Requirements: *Refining* and *Explosives*

UNIT	COST	ATTACK STRENGTH	DEFENSE STRENGTH	HIT POINTS	FIRE-POWER	MOVEMENT PER TURN
Submarine	60	10	2	3	2	3

⊕ Knowledge Advances: **Automobile** when combined with *Steel*

Flight when combined with *Theory of Gravity*

Explosives—Requirements: *Gunpowder* and *Chemistry*

UNIT	COST	ATTACK STRENGTH	DEFENSE STRENGTH	HIT POINTS	FIRE-POWER	MOVEMENT PER TURN
Engineer	40	0	2	2	1	2

⊕ Knowledge Advance: **Combustion** when combined with *Refining*

Flight—Requirements: *Combustion* and *Theory of Gravity*

UNIT	COST	ATTACK STRENGTH	DEFENSE STRENGTH	HIT POINTS	FIRE-POWER	MOVEMENT PER TURN
Fighter	60	4	2	2	2	10

⊕ Knowledge Advance: **Radio** when combined with *Electronics*

This advance also makes the Colossus wonder obsolete.

Refining—Requirements: *Chemistry* and *Corporation*

⊕ City Improvement: **Power Plant**—cost is 160; maintenance cost/turn is 4

⊕ Knowledge Advances: **Combustion** when combined with *Explosives*

Plastics when combined with *Space Flight*

Steel—Requirements: *Electricity* and *Industrialization*

UNIT	COST	ATTACK STRENGTH	DEFENSE STRENGTH	HIT POINTS	FIRE-POWER	MOVEMENT PER TURN
Cruiser	80	6	6	3	2	5

⊕ Knowledge Advances: **Automobile** when combined with *Combustion*

Machine Tools when combined with *Tactics*

Advances of the Modern World

It's during this era that you'll want to put the finishing touches on your ever-growing empire. Now is the time you can begin your quest into space, or take advantage of air-based units and nuclear weapons to conquer rivals. The City Improvements that will now become available to you will help each of your cities grow.

MILITARY ADVANCES

Amphibious Warfare—Requirements: *Navigation* and *Tactics*

UNIT	COST	ATTACK STRENGTH	DEFENSE STRENGTH	HIT POINTS	FIRE-POWER	MOVEMENT PER TURN
Marine	60	8	5	2	1	1

City Improvement: **Port Facility City Improvement**—cost is 80; maintenance cost/turn is 3

Combined Arms—Requirements: *Mobile Warfare* and *Advanced Flight*

UNIT	COST	ATTACK STRENGTH	DEFENSE STRENGTH	HIT POINTS	FIRE-POWER	MOVEMENT PER TURN
Helicopter	100	10	3	2	2	6
Paratrooper	60	6	4	2	1	1

Espionage—Requirements: *Communism* and *Democracy*

UNIT	COST	ATTACK STRENGTH	DEFENSE STRENGTH	HIT POINTS	FIRE-POWER	MOVEMENT PER TURN
Spy	30	0	0	1	1	3

Guerrilla Warfare—Requirements: *Communism* and *Tactics*

UNIT	COST	ATTACK STRENGTH	DEFENSE STRENGTH	HIT POINTS	FIRE-POWER	MOVEMENT PER TURN
Partisan	50	4	4	2	1	1

Knowledge Advance: **Labor Unions** when combined with *Mass Production*

Mobile Warfare—Requirements: *Automobile* and *Tactics*

UNIT	COST	ATTACK STRENGTH	DEFENSE STRENGTH	HIT POINTS	FIRE-POWER	MOVEMENT PER TURN
Armor	80	10	5	3	1	3

⊕ Knowledge Advances: **Combined Arms** when combined with *Advanced Flight*

Robotics when combined with *Computers*

This advance also makes Sun Tzu's War Academy obsolete.

Robotics—Requirements: *Computers* and *Mobile Warfare*

UNIT	COST	ATTACK STRENGTH	DEFENSE STRENGTH	HIT POINTS	FIRE- POWER	MOVEMENT PER TURN
Howitzer	70	12	2	3	2	2

⊕ City Improvement: **Manufacturing Plant**—cost is 320; maintenance cost/turn is 6

⊕ Knowledge Advance: **Stealth** when combined with *Superconductor*

Rocketry—Requirements: *Advanced Flight* and *Electronics*

UNIT	COST	ATTACK STRENGTH	DEFENSE STRENGTH	HIT POINTS	FIRE- POWER	MOVEMENT PER TURN
Cruise Missile	60	20	0	1	3	12
Nuclear Missile	160	99	0	1	1	16
AEGIS Cruiser	100	8	8	3	2	5

⊕ City Improvement: **SAM Missile Battery**—cost is 100; maintenance cost/turn is 2

⊕ Knowledge Advance: **Space Flight** when combined with *Computers*

Stealth—Requirements: *Superconductor* and *Robotics*

UNIT	COST	ATTACK STRENGTH	DEFENSE STRENGTH	HIT POINTS	FIRE- POWER	MOVEMENT PER TURN
Stealth Bomber	160	14	3	2	2	12
Stealth Fighter	80	8	3	2	2	14

ECONOMIC ADVANCES

Refrigeration—Requirements: *Electricity* and *Sanitation*

⊕ City Improvement: **Supermarket**—cost is 80; maintenance cost/turn is 3

Settler and Engineer Units can begin transforming terrain into farm land and can double-irrigate terrain squares for improved food production.

SOCIAL ADVANCES

Environmentalism—Requirements: *Recycling* and *Space Flight*

⊕ City Improvement: **Solar Plant**—cost is 320; maintenance cost/turn is 4

Labor Unions—Requirements: *Mass Production* and *Guerrilla Warfare*

UNIT	COST	ATTACK STRENGTH	DEFENSE STRENGTH	HIT POINTS	FIRE-POWER	MOVEMENT PER TURN
Mechanized Infantry	50	6	6	3	1	3

Recycling—Requirements: *Mass Production* and *Democracy*

⊕ City Improvement: **Recycling Center**—cost is 200; maintenance cost/turn is 2

⊕ Knowledge Advances: **Environmentalism** when combined with *Space Flight*

Future Technology when combined with *Fusion Power*

ACADEMIC ADVANCES

Fusion Power—Requirements: *Nuclear Power* and *Superconductor*

⊕ Knowledge Advance: **Future Technologies** when combined with *Recycling*

This advance also eliminates the chance of a Nuclear Plant meltdown.

Future technology—Requirements: *Fusion Power* and *Recycling*

⊕ City Improvement: **Future Technologies**—Adds 10 points each to your *Civilization II* game score

Genetic Engineering—Requirements: *Medicine* and *Corporation*

⊕ Wonder: **Cure for Cancer**—cost is 600

Nuclear Fission—Requirements: *Atomic Theory* and *Mass Production*

⊕ Wonder: **Manhattan Project**—cost is 600

⊕ Knowledge Advance: **Nuclear Power** when combined with *Electronics*

Nuclear Power—Requirements: *Nuclear Fission* and *Electronics*

⊕ City Improvement: **Nuclear Plant**—cost is160; maintenance cost/turn is 2

⊕ Knowledge Advances: **Fusion Power** when combined with *Superconductor*

The Laser when combined with *Mass Production*

Space Flight—Requirements: *Computers* and *Rocketry*

⊕ City Improvement: **Spaceship Structural**—cost is 80; maintenance cost/turn is 0

⊕ Wonder: **Apollo Program**—cost is 600

⊕ Knowledge Advances: **Environmentalism** when combined with *Recycling*

Plastics when combined with *Refining*

Superconductor—Requirements: *Plastics* and *The Laser*

⊕ City Improvement: **Spaceship Module**—cost is 320; maintenance cost/turn is 0

⊕ Knowledge Advances: **Fusion Power**

Stealth when combined with *Robotics*

The Laser—Requirements: *Mass Production* and *Nuclear Power*

⊕ City Improvement: **SDI Defense**—cost is 200; maintenance cost/turn: 4

⊕ Knowledge Advance: **Superconductor** when combined with *Plastics*

To Enter the Great Space Race, How Do You Create the Best Spaceships in the Later Portion of a Simulation?

Begin by acquiring or developing the Apollo Program (Wonder of the World). This allows your cities to begin building Spaceship Structural Components (SS Structural), which is the first step of your trek into space.

The ability to build a spaceship and eventually travel into space requires that your empire first acquire the majority of the Knowledge Advances that are available in the game, which is a major challenge unto itself. Because of the time limitations of a simulation (all simulations end in the year A.D. 2020), chances are you'll only have one opportunity to build and launch a spaceship during each simulation—so careful planning is critical for success. Once a spaceship is built and launched, another spaceship cannot be built unless the original spaceship gets destroyed.

The only way your empire can colonize space is by first building a spaceship that's capable of carrying colonists to Alpha Centauri. For a spaceship to survive the journey, it must be equipped with several different types of components and modules. The better equipped a spaceship is before it gets launched, the better chance it has of reaching its destination safely and quickly.

Once the race into space begins, and the first Spaceship Structural Component (City Improvement) is created, the special Spaceship screen will be displayed. Now, at any time, you can view this screen by selecting the Spaceship command on the World pull-down menu. From this screen, you can see a graphical representation of the spaceship your empire is building, and you can see a display that lists the following:

- The number of Structural Components built
- The number of Propulsion Components built
- The number of Fuel Components built
- The number of Habitation Modules built
- The number of Life Support Modules built
- The number of Solar Panels built
- The current population of the spaceship (in multiples of 10,000)
- The Support % of the spaceship
- The Energy % of the spaceship
- The Mass of the spaceship (in tons)
- The Fuel % of the spaceship
- The Flight Time for the spaceship's journey (in years)
- The Probability of Success % for the mission

A population of a spaceship can be increased in multiples of 10,000. You will receive bonus points for every 10,000 people who reach Alpha Centauri. Obviously, the more people in the spaceship, the larger the ship must be—and the more energy, fuel, and resources it will require. As a result, it will take longer to build the additional Spaceship Components and Modules needed for the spaceship to survive its journey. As you build your spaceship, the simulation will be in its final stages, so pay careful attention to the Flight Time and Probability of Success that's listed on the Spaceship screen, along with the current year of the simulation. If the year is A.D. 2000, and the Flight Time for the ship to reach Alpha Centauri is 21 years (with a 100 percent probability for success), the spaceship won't reach its destination before the simulation comes to an end, so you must first add the necessary components and modules to your spaceship to speed up the journey.

At this point in the simulation, you should access the City screen for each of your cities, and allocate all production toward the development of Spaceship Components, Spaceship Modules, and Spaceship Structural Improvements. Plan ahead, so that by the time you can build these City Improvements, your empire's military is strong enough to protect your empire. When you enter the space race, you'll also greatly improve your chances of success if you have established a Cease-Fire or Peace Treaty with all the other rival empires. It's virtually impossible to fight wars and build a spaceship at the same time. All your empire's resources should go toward building the spaceship, as soon as this capability becomes available. (This, of course, is assuming your *goal* in the simulation is to colonize space. If you want to *conquer the world*, forget about building a spaceship altogether, and work on building strong Military Units and launching attacks.)

Spaceships are made up of three types of City Improvements—Spaceship Structural Improvements, Spaceship Components, and Spaceship Modules. Structural Improvements help build the ship itself and are what hold all the other Spaceship Modules and Components together. If the Components and Modules you build are not connected to the ship itself, using Structural Improvements, they will offer no benefit to the ship. Normally, a city can only produce one of each type of City Improvement, though cities can produce multiple SS Structural, SS Module, or SS Component Improvements.

Once a Component is built by a city, you must choose which type of Component it should be—Propulsion or Fuel. Propulsion represents the engines of the ship, while Fuel will power the engines. One Fuel Component is needed for each Propulsion Unit you build. There are also several types of Spaceship Modules. Habitation Modules are the areas of the ship where your population will live during the journey through space. Each module can hold 10,000 people. For each Habitation Module built, you must also build at least one Life Support Module, which provides the food and other requirements the population will need to survive the journey. Finally, Solar Panel Modules are needed to provide energy to the Habitation Units. One Solar Panel will support two Habitation Modules.

Spaceship Modules require the Superconductor Knowledge Advance, which will most likely be developed after your empire has acquired the ability to build Spaceship Structural and Spaceship Component City Improvements. When the space race begins, you should boost your Science Tax Rate, so that your scientists will develop the Superconductor knowledge as quickly as possible. Remember, at this point in a simulation, you're in a race against time to get your spaceship built and launched.

When enough Spaceship Structural Improvements, Components, and Modules have been built, and the Spaceship screen reports that the probability of success is good, a special Launch icon will appear on the Spaceship screen that'll allow you to launch your spaceship. Before you launch your ship, check the Flight Time to ensure that the ship will reach its destination before a simulation ends. Also, if you have some extra time, you can also add Habitation Modules (plus the support Modules and Components needed) to increase the population of your spaceship, boosting your point score.

Once your spaceship is ready to go, click on the Launch icon. You'll see a computer animation and your spaceship will now be on its way (and out of your control!). You will return to the Main Game screen. At this point in a simulation, you have two choices. First, you can reassign all your cities to begin building Military Units, so that while your spaceship is traveling, you can attempt to conquer rival empires to boost your point score Or, second, you can focus on building your empire internally, by assigning cities to build City Improvements and any remaining Wonders of the World (which will also boost your point score). When the spaceship reaches Alpha Centauri, the simulation will automatically come to an end, and you'll be victorious!

The very early stages of a simulation are the best time to determine what your ultimate goal for the simulation will be. If you choose to pursue colonizing space, then you'll want to enter into Peace Treaties with rival empires as quickly as possible, so that you can keep the size of your military to a minimum, and instead focus on internal growth and the pursuit of knowledge. It is possible to complete a simulation without ever fighting a rival empire, or participating in any battles (except for fighting Barbarians). To maintain peace throughout a simulation, it's an excellent idea to periodically trade Knowledge Advances with other empires when such trades are proposed to you by the other leaders. Not only will this help maintain peace, but trading Knowledge Advances will often benefit your empire as well.

APPLIED ADVANCES

Advanced Flight—Requirements: *Machine Tools* and *Radio*

UNIT	COST	ATTACK STRENGTH	DEFENSE STRENGTH	HIT POINTS	FIRE-POWER	MOVEMENT PER TURN
Bomber	120	12	1	2	2	8
Carrier	160	1	9	4	2	5

Knowledge Advances: **Combined Arms** when linked with *Mobile Warfare*

Rocketry when combined with *Electronics*

Automobile—Requirements: *Combustion* and *Steel*

UNIT	COST	ATTACK STRENGTH	DEFENSE STRENGTH	HIT POINTS	FIRE-POWER	MOVEMENT PER TURN
Battleship	160	12	12	4	2	4

City Improvement: **Superhighways**—cost is 200; maintenance cost/turn is 5

Knowledge Advances: **Mass Production** when combined with *Corporation*

Mobile Warfare when combined with *Steel*

Computers—Requirements: *Miniaturization* and *Mass Production*

City Improvement: **Research Lab**—cost is 160; maintenance cost/turn is 3

Wonder: **SETI Program**—cost is 600

Knowledge Advances: **Robotics** when combined with *Mobile Warfare*

Space Flight when combined with *Rocketry*

Electricity—Requirements: *Metallurgy* and *Magnetism*

UNIT	COST	ATTACK STRENGTH	DEFENSE STRENGTH	HIT POINTS	FIRE-POWER	MOVEMENT PER TURN
Destroyer	60	4	4	3	1	6

Knowledge Advances: **Electronics** when combined with *Corporation*

Refrigeration when combined with *Sanitation*

Steel when combined with *Industrialization*

This advance also makes the Great Library wonder obsolete.

Electronics—Requirements: *Electricity* and *Corporation*

⊕ City Improvement: **Hydro Plant**—cost is 240; maintenance cost/turn is 4

⊕ Wonder: **Hoover Dam**—cost is 600

⊕ Knowledge Advances: **Miniaturization** when combined with *Machine Tools*

Nuclear Power when combined with *Nuclear Fission*

Radio when combined with *Flight*

Rocketry when combined with *Advanced Flight*

Mass Production—Requirements: *Automobile* and *Corporation*

⊕ City Improvement: **Mass Transit**—cost is 160; maintenance cost/turn is 4

⊕ Knowledge Advances: **Computers** when combined with *Miniaturization*

Labor Union when combined with *Guerrilla Warfare*

Nuclear Fission when combined with *Nuclear Power*

Recycling when combined with *Atomic Theory*

The Laser when combined with *Democracy*

Miniaturization—Requirements: *Machine Tools* and *Electronics*

⊕ City Improvement: **Offshore Platform**—cost is 160; maintenance cost/turn is 3

⊕ Knowledge Advance: **Computers** when combined with *Mass Production*

Plastics—Requirements: *Refining* and *Space Flight*

- ⊕ City Improvement: **Spaceship Component**—cost is 160; maintenance cost/turn is 0

- ⊕ Knowledge Advance: **Superconductor** when combined with *The Laser*

Radio—Requirements: *Flight* and *Electronics*

- ⊕ City Improvement: **Airport**—cost is 160; maintenance cost/turn is 3

- ⊕ Knowledge Advance: **Advanced Flight** when combined with *Machine Tools*

Settlers and Engineer Units can build air bases once the Radio Knowledge Advance is acquired.

For more detailed information about City Improvements and Wonders of the World, see Chapter 8, *The Benefits of City Improvements and Wonders of the World*.

8

The Benefits of City Improvements and Wonders of the World

Simply building cities isn't enough to keep your empire growing. One of your biggest ongoing challenges during this game is to keep each of your cities expanding, while at the same time keeping your military strong. Throughout a simulation, you must decide how you will allocate each city's production capabilities. You can build Military Units, Settler Units, Engineer Units, Caravan Units, Diplomat Units, Spy Units, Explorer Units, City Improvements, or Wonders of the World. Because each city can only build one thing at a time, strategy plays an important role as you decide what needs to be built and when.

WEIGHING THE BENEFITS OF CITY IMPROVEMENTS

City Improvements offer benefits to the specific cities in which they are built. At different times during a simulation, the needs of a city will change. When determining what to build, you must study the needs of that city and your empire as a whole. For example, even though most Wonders of the World are built within a single city, acquiring a wonder has an impact on all cities within your empire.

This chapter lists and describes the benefits of each City Improvement and Wonder of the World that can be built during a simulation. Keep in mind, your ability to build these improvements and wonders is totally dependent on the Knowledge Advances your empire's scientists have acquired, plus the production capabilities of each specific city. To determine how the production capabilities of each city will be allocated, you must access a city's City screen, and select the unit, improvement, or wonder you wish to build from the Production window. An example City screen is shown in Figure 8.1. Improvements can be selected manually, or you can take advantage of the *Civ II* Auto Production feature, which will automatically choose which improvements (or units) to build in your cities for you.

In *Civ II*, the benefits that each City Improvement offers to the city in which it's built, along with the maintenance cost per turn to maintain each improvement, have changed from previous versions of the game. Additionally, several new types of improvements are now available to you (once the proper Knowledge

> **SEE**
> For more information on the units, improvements, and wonders that acquired Knowledge Advances allow you to obtain, see Chapter 7, *Planning Knowledge Advances*.

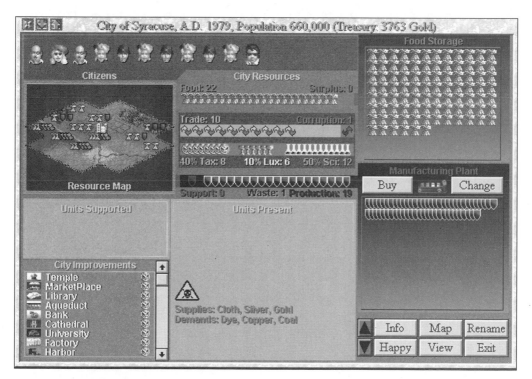

FIGURE 8.1: Choose which improvement, wonder, or unit you want to produce from the Production window in the lower-right corner of a city's City screen.

Advances have been acquired), giving your cities capabilities that were not possible in previous versions of the *Civilization* game. For easy reference, descriptions of each City Improvement are provided in alphabetical order.

What Should You Do When Your Empire's Finances Are Running Very Low?

There are six primary steps you can take to begin boosting revenue in your empire:

1. Create Taxmen (Specialists)—Creating these Specialists cuts down production waste within a city and boosts revenue, though creating Specialists *also* cuts the workforce of that city. Eventually, you'll probably want to create Taxmen in your cities, but you should wait until the cities are well-established.

2. Sell Off City Improvements—This is a quick fix. By selling off City Improvements, the money you earn from the sale(s) will be added to your treasury, giving you additional funds in the short term. This doesn't fix the problem(s) that originally caused your empire to go broke in the first place, however. When you see your finances getting close to zero, you'll want to manually select which City Improvement(s) you want to sell, and from which city you want to sell it/them. Otherwise, the computer will automatically make the decision for you, on your behalf.

3. Adjust the Tax Rate—From the Kingdom pull-down menu, select the Tax Rate option, and increase the Tax Rate (thus cutting the Luxuries and Science rates). If you boost the Tax Rate too high, your population will get angry, so be sure to keep a balance.

4. Trim the Number of Military Units—Cut down on the ones you have outside their home cities. Consider disbanding out-of-date Units (or sending them into battle), and relocate Units that are far away from home by assigning them to a new home city that's closer to their present location.

5. Use Caravans and Freight Units—These will let you establish trade routes that generate the maximum revenue. Create Trade Routes with cities that are far apart, and study what each city needs the most, and then set up the trade route to provide for those needs.

6. Build City Improvements—Create such improvements as Banks, Marketplaces, Stock Exchanges, and Capitalization, designed to boost revenue generation. Other City Improvements will cut corruption, which will also save you money in the long run.

THE *CIVILIZATION II* CITY IMPROVEMENTS

Airport

⊕ Cost: 160

⊕ Maintenance cost/turn: 3

⊕ Knowledge Advance Requirement: Radio

Cities with this improvement will be able to produce Veteran air-based Units. (The attack and defense strength of Veteran Units is increased by 50 percent.) Also, aircraft will be completely repaired after a battle by spending one turn within a friendly city. Finally, Airports allow air-based units to airlift ground-based units to other locations.

What Is the Best Way to Use Airports and Airbases in *Civ II*?

Note that there is a major difference between Airports and Airbases. Airports are City Improvements that are built within cities, and that allow air-based units to refuel. Airports are also used for airlifting ground-based units from one city to another (those that contain an Airport). When a unit is airlifted, it can move instantly from one city to another city, as long as both cities contain Airports. Use the Airlift command on the Orders pull-down menu to accomplish this. Airlifting from airport to airport is an extremely fast way to move units around on the Main Map. The drawback is that you can only airlift one unit from an airport per turn. Airports are also used to quickly repair damaged air-based units.

Airbases are terrain improvements that can be built by Engineer or Settlers Units on any terrain square. Every air-based unit can only travel across a predetermined number of terrain squares per turn, and then they must stop at a friendly city or Airbase to refuel. The benefit to Airbases is that they can be built to act like stepping stones, allowing air-based units to travel greater distances by landing at Airbases to refuel. When air-based units must cross oceans, strategically placing Carrier Units in the ocean can serve the same purpose as Airbases, as shown in Figure 8.2. Notice in the figure that the air-based unit is traveling from the friendly city in the lower-left corner of the screen, will make refueling stops on two Carriers, and will eventually reach the Airbase located in the upper-right corner of the screen. From there, it can attack nearby enemy cities. Based on the types of air-based units you're using, you will want to place the Carrier Units and Airbases at greater distances apart to maximize how quickly the air-based unit will be able to reach its destination. Be sure to check the distances (the number of terrain squares) each type of air-based unit can move per turn, to help you determine how far apart these support units and Terrain Improvements should be placed. Using a combination of Airbases, friendly cities with Airports, and Carrier Units, air-based units can travel between continents and over great distances, yet still have enough fuel to launch attacks on enemy cities.

FIGURE 8.2: By strategically placing friendly cities containing Airport improvements, Airbases, and Carrier Units in a path that leads to a distant continent containing enemy cities, you can launch air-based units and have them travel greater distances, over several turns, without running out of fuel and crashing.

Aqueduct

- ⊕ Cost: 80
- ⊕ Maintenance cost/turn: 2
- ⊕ Knowledge Advance Requirement: Construction

The Aqueduct improvement allows a city to expand beyond the size of eight terrain squares.

Bank

- ⊕ Cost: 120
- ⊕ Maintenance cost/turn: 3
- ⊕ Knowledge Advance Requirement: Banking

The Bank improvement increases tax and luxury production by an additional 50 percent. The benefits of a Bank can be combined with those from a Market Place improvement, if both of these improvements are built within the same city.

Barracks

- ⊕ Cost: 40
- ⊕ Maintenance cost/turn: 1
- ⊕ Knowledge Advance Requirement: None

The Barracks improvement allows a city to create Veteran ground-based Military Units. Veteran Units have 50 percent stronger attack and defensive strengths. Ground-based units can also have injuries healed (damage indicated by their energy meters repaired) after battle by spending one turn within a friendly city.

Capitalization

- Cost: 600
- Maintenance cost/turn: 0
- Knowledge Advance Requirement: Corporation

With this improvement, all Shield production is converted into tax revenue.

Cathedral

- Cost: 120
- Maintenance cost/turn: 3
- Knowledge Advance Requirement: Monotheism

The Cathedral improvement transforms three unhappy people within a city into content citizens. After Communism (Knowledge Advance) is acquired, the benefits of a Cathedral are diminished; two citizens within a city go from being unhappy to content. To improve the power of the Cathedral, concentrate on acquiring Theology (Knowledge Advance), which makes one additional citizen go from being unhappy to content in all cities containing a Cathedral. Keeping a city's population happy (or at least content) goes a long way toward preventing a city from entering a state of civil disorder.

What Can You Do When a City Encounters Civil Disorder? How Can You Keep Your Population Happy (or at Least Content)?

You'll find that a city enters into a state of civil disorder when the number of unhappy people within that city exceeds the number of happy people. You'll want to boost morale as quickly as possible when this happens because growth and production within a city that's experiencing civil disorder comes to a complete halt.

To change the attitude of the city's population, you can do several things:

1. **Increase the Luxuries rate**—From the Kingdom pull-down menu, choose the Tax Rate command, and then increase Luxuries. As a result, you'll have to reduce the Tax rate,

Scientific rates, or both. If you're ruling as a Monarchy or Republic, 20 percent Luxuries will usually make the people within your cities happier.

2. **Order Military Units to return home**—If there are several Military Units from a city that have traveled outside of the city, order up to three of these units to return home. Three Military Units within a city force a state of martial law, and each unit that returns home will make one citizen content (as opposed to unhappy). This works when you're ruling under a Despotism, Monarchy, or Communist form of government.

3. **Buy a Temple, Cathedral, or Colosseum City Improvement for the city as quickly as possible**—The more of these improvements that you build, the more citizens you'll make happy (or at least content) on an ongoing basis. Because the city's production is halted, you must buy an improvement or create Entertainers to reverse the civil disorder quickly, and then implement a long-term strategy of gradually building the rest of these morale-boosting improvements. Under a Democratic form of government, building a Courthouse in each city will also keep one extra citizen happy. Also, because sending Military Units away from the city (to fight battles or explore) creates unhappy citizens, building a Police Station City Improvement decreases the number of unhappy citizens created as a result of traveling Military Units.

4. **Acquire wonders**—Certain Wonders of the World also benefit either the city in which they are built, or the entire empire, by making citizens happy. If you're having a serious civil disorder problem, consider focusing your production efforts to develop the Cure for Cancer or acquire the Hanging Gardens Wonders of the World.

5. **Create Entertainers (Specialists)**—From the city's City Screen, create Entertainers (Specialists) to provide a quick fix that works in the short term. Be aware that this action can be detrimental to a city in the long term, because creating Specialists actually *cuts* the work force. Once you have built a Temple, Cathedral, Colosseum, or any combination of these, transform the Entertainers back into normal citizens to increase the city's production.

6. **Consider changing the empire's form of government**—If many of your cities are entering into a state of civil disorder, this might be a good time to change the form of government under which you're ruling your empire. Choose a Fundamentalist form of government. This quick fix will make the population happy, yet it has serious drawbacks in terms of overall production and scientific advancement. You won't want to rule under this form of government for long, so while your population is happy under this form of government, take steps to keep them happy once you initiate another revolution to again change the empire's form of government.

City Walls

- ⊕ Cost: 80
- ⊕ Maintenance cost/turn: 0
- ⊕ Knowledge Advance Requirement: Masonry

Military Units positioned within a city with City Walls have their defense capabilities tripled against all attacks, with the exception of those from enemy Howitzers. Building City Walls within a city and then stationing one or more Military Units within that city will help to dramatically boost a city's defenses against surprise enemy and Barbarian attacks. When City Walls are built around a city, this improvement will be shown graphically on the Main Map as a wall around the city.

Coastal Fortress

- ⊕ Cost: 80
- ⊕ Maintenance cost/turn: 1
- ⊕ Knowledge Advance Requirement: Metallurgy

Cities located adjacent to water will benefit from this improvement because all Military Units stationed within that city will have their defense strength doubled against attacks from enemy ships. Since it is necessary to build cities adjacent to water (rivers and oceans) for your empire to launch its own ships, building Coastal Fortresses within those cities, and then stationing one or more Military Units within those cities, will go a long way toward protecting them from attacks. Cities that are not located near water have no need for Coastal Fortresses, but *will* benefit from City Walls.

Colosseum

- ⊕ Cost: 100
- ⊕ Maintenance cost/turn: 4
- ⊕ Knowledge Advance Requirement: Construction

Three unhappy citizens within the city where a Colosseum is built will be transformed into content citizens. Once Electronics (Knowledge Advance) is acquired, a fourth citizen will be transformed from unhappy to content.

Courthouse

- ⊕ Cost: 80
- ⊕ Maintenance cost/turn: 1
- ⊕ Knowledge Advance Requirement: Code of Laws

Corruption within a city containing a courthouse will be reduced by 50 percent. That city will also be stronger against bribery attempts made by enemy diplomats or spies. When ruling an empire under a Democracy, one content citizen will also be made happy. Until corruption becomes an issue within your empire, Courthouse Improvements are not really needed, thus your production efforts should be directed elsewhere.

Factory

- ⊕ Cost: 200
- ⊕ Maintenance cost/turn: 4
- ⊕ Knowledge Advance Requirement: Industrialization

Shield production within the city containing this improvement will be boosted by 50 percent. The drawback is that Factories cause pollution, which will have to be controlled.

Granary

- ⊕ Cost: 60
- ⊕ Maintenance cost/turn: 1
- ⊕ Knowledge Advance Requirement: Pottery

When a city grows in size, only half its food storage will be depleted. Early in a simulation, a Granary should be one of the first improvements built within your cities.

Harbor

- Cost: 60

- Maintenance cost/turn: 1

- Knowledge Advance Requirement: Seafaring

All cities built adjacent to an ocean will generate one extra food unit per turn.

Hydro Plant

- Cost: 240

- Maintenance cost/turn: 4

- Knowledge Advance Requirement: Electronics

A Factory (City Improvement) within a city where a Hydro Plant is built will have a 50 percent boost in output. Meanwhile, pollution generated by that Factory will be cut by 50 percent. Hydro Plants are also a safer form of energy than Nuclear Plants.

Library

- Cost: 80

- Maintenance cost/turn: 1

- Knowledge Advance Requirement: Writing

The Library improvement boosts science output of a city by 50 percent. A Library improvement's benefits for scientific output can be combined with other improvements for greater overall scientific output to a city.

Manufacturing Plant

⊕ Cost: 320

⊕ Maintenance cost/turn: 6

⊕ Knowledge Advance Requirement: Robotics

Shield production within a city will get a 50 percent boost. Manufacturing Plants can be combined with the benefits of a Factory for maximum Shield output.

Marketplace

⊕ Cost: 80

⊕ Maintenance cost/turn: 1

⊕ Knowledge Advance Requirement: Currency

Tax and luxury output will increase by 50 percent within a city.

What's the Best Way to Control Pollution in Your Cities?

Several types of City Improvements, such as Factories and Manufacturing Plants, create pollution. Launching Nuclear Missiles and operating Nuclear Power Plants also cause pollution. When pollution becomes an issue, the best way to deal with it is to eliminate it quickly. This can be done by building the following City Improvements: Recycling Centers, Hydro Plants, Solar Plants, and Mass Transit.

A more direct approach is to create a team of Engineer (or Settler) Units that can travel quickly by air (by getting airlifted) or boat to polluted locations and then work to eliminate pollution, one terrain square at a time. Pollution will appear graphically on the Main Map, so you'll know exactly where to send your Engineer or Settler Units. Once these units are at the polluted location, use the Orders pull-down menu and select the Clean Up Pollution command to assign them to the task of clearing up the pollution.

Before a simulation reaches an end, you can improve your point score by ordering Engineer Units (or Settlers) to clean up all polluted terrain squares. Any polluted square that exists when the simulation ends will result in your losing game points.

Mass Transit

⊕ Cost: 160

⊕ Maintenance cost/turn: 4

⊕ Knowledge Advance Requirement: Mass Production

This improvement eliminates all pollution that a city's population is creating.

Nuclear Plant

⊕ Cost: 160

⊕ Maintenance cost/turn: 2

⊕ Knowledge Advance Requirement: Nuclear Power

A Factory's output within a city will be boosted by 50 percent with this improvement, plus pollution will be cut by 50 percent. Nuclear Plants, however, run the risk of experiencing a nuclear meltdown (which can be disastrous to a population and a city). The danger of a meltdown is eliminated once Fusion Power (Knowledge Advance) is discovered.

Offshore Platform

⊕ Cost: 160

⊕ Maintenance cost/turn: 3

⊕ Knowledge Advance Requirement: Miniaturization

In cities built near oceans, shield production will increase by one, once this improvement is built.

Palace

⊕ Cost: 100

⊕ Maintenance cost/turn: 0

⊕ Knowledge Advance Requirement: Masonry

The city in your empire that contains a Palace is your capital city. At the start of a simulation, the first city you build automatically becomes your capital city. Should that city get destroyed or conquered, or if you wish to move your capital city elsewhere, you can build a Palace within a different city, and that city becomes your capital city. An empire may only build one Palace at a time, so before building a new Palace, your old one must be destroyed or sold.

What's the Throne Room, and Does Building It Impact a Simulation?

Among the most obvious improvements to the *Civ II* game are the new "bells and whistles." By taking advantage of the multimedia capabilities of your PC, this game now offers animation that appears when triggered by particular events, such as when you discover a new Wonder of the World, hold a High Council Meeting, or have the opportunity to build an addition to your Throne Room.

Previous versions of *Civilization* allowed you, the ruler, to occasionally build additions to your Palace, *if* your leadership skills were worthy of a reward. In this edition of the game, you can build and improve your Throne Room at certain times within the game.

Are these animation sequences a necessary part of the game? No. They've been added for the sole purpose of providing eye-candy to the game-play experience. Do they make the game more exciting? Well, that's up to you to decide. You can choose to turn off the game animation (thus speeding up the game) by accessing the Select Graphic Options window from the Game pull-down menu.

To save hard disk space on your computer when installing the game, you can choose not to copy these extra graphic files. Later, if you want to view them during a simulation, however, it will be necessary to have the *Civ II* Program CD inserted in the computer's CD-ROM drive during game play.

Police Station

- Cost: 60
- Maintenance cost/turn: 2
- Knowledge Advance Requirement: Communism

When Military Units are far away from their home city, unhappy citizens within those cities are created. Building a Police Station will make one fewer unhappy citizen as a result of having moved too many Military Units far from the home city.

Port Facility

- Cost: 80
- Maintenance cost/turn: 3
- Knowledge Advance Requirement: Amphibious Warfare

This improvement allows cities to produce sea-based Veteran Units. Also, after a battle, any ship that returns to a city containing a Port Facility will be completely repaired after one turn.

Power Plant

- Cost: 160
- Maintenance cost/turn: 4
- Knowledge Advance Requirement: Refining

The Power Plant improvement will boost Factory output within the city by 50 percent.

Recycling Center

- ⊕ Cost: 200

- ⊕ Maintenance cost/turn: 2

- ⊕ Knowledge Advance Requirement: Recycling

The Recycling Center improvement cuts pollution generated by Shield production by 66 percent within a city.

Research Lab

- ⊕ Cost: 160

- ⊕ Maintenance cost/turn: 3

- ⊕ Knowledge Advance Requirement: Computers

The Research Lab improvement boosts a city's scientific output by an additional 50 percent. Build this improvement in conjunction with a Library and a University within cities to boost scientific production a total of 150 percent.

SAM Missile Battery

- ⊕ Cost: 100

- ⊕ Maintenance cost/turn: 2

- ⊕ Knowledge Advance Requirement: Rocketry

The defense strength of all units within a city will double against attacks from all air-based enemies, except from a Nuclear Missile attack.

SDI Defense

- Cost: 200

- Maintenance cost/turn: 4

- Knowledge Advance Requirement: The Laser

All units and Terrain Improvements located within three terrain squares from a city containing the SDI Defense improvement will be protected against nuclear attack.

Sewer System

- Cost: 120

- Maintenance cost/turn: 2

- Knowledge Advance Requirement: Sanitation

The Sewer System improvement allows a city to expand beyond the size of 12 terrain squares. You must first build an Aqueduct to expand a city past the size of 8 squares.

Solar Plant

- Cost: 320

- Maintenance cost/turn: 4

- Knowledge Advance Requirement: Environmentalism

Factory output within a city is boosted by 50 percent when this improvement is built. Pollution generated as a result of Shield Production is also eliminated. This improvement also reduces the chances of global warming.

Spaceship Component

- Cost: 160

- Maintenance cost/turn: 0

- Knowledge Advance Requirement: Plastics

Spaceship Components add Thrust or Fuel to the spaceship your empire is building, once you enter into the race to colonize space. Each Spaceship Thrust Component you build adds 25 percent more thrust to the spaceship you're building. The Spaceship Fuel Component provides the ship you are building with enough fuel for one Thrust Component. You can build multiple Spaceship Component, Spaceship Module, and Spaceship Structural City Improvements within each city. As each Spaceship Component is complete, you must decide if it will be a Thrust Component or a Fuel Component. To speed up the creation of these space-related City Improvements, order Caravan Units from other cities to visit the city building Spaceship Components and assist in the building process.

Spaceship Module

- Cost: 320

- Maintenance cost/turn: 0

- Knowledge Advance Requirement: Superconductor

There are three types of Spaceship Modules—Population modules, Life Support modules, and Solar Panels. You must determine the number of each module you will create. Each Population module holds 10,000 space colonists. A Life Support module contains enough food, air, and support for one Population module. Solar Panels provide enough power to support two other types of modules.

Spaceship Structural

⊕ Cost: 80

⊕ Maintenance cost/turn: 0

⊕ Knowledge Advance Requirement: Space Flight

This improvement provides the structure needed to hold the other spaceship modules together. The number of Space Structural improvements you build will impact the size and capabilities of the spaceship you ultimately build.

Stock Exchange

⊕ Cost: 160

⊕ Maintenance cost/turn: 4

⊕ Knowledge Advance Requirement: Economics

The tax and luxuries rates created for a city will increase by 50 percent. When combined with the Marketplace and Bank improvements, you can boost the tax and luxuries production rates by a total of 150 percent for a city.

Superhighway

⊕ Cost: 200

⊕ Maintenance cost/turn: 5

⊕ Knowledge Advance Requirement: Automobile

All terrain squares within a city's immediate radius that contain road or railroad Terrain Improvements will produce 50 percent more output. Additionally, revenue generated by trade routes between the city with Superhighways and others will increase.

Supermarket

- Cost: 80
- Maintenance cost/turn: 3
- Knowledge Advance Requirement: Refrigeration

Cities with double-irrigated terrain squares (Farmland) surrounding it will produce 50 percent more food in those terrain squares.

Temple

- Cost: 40
- Maintenance cost/turn: 1
- Knowledge Advance Requirement: Ceremonial Burial

One unhappy citizen within a city where a Temple is built will become content. After Mysticism (Knowledge Advance) is acquired, two citizens within the city will go from being unhappy to content.

University

- Cost: 160
- Maintenance cost/turn: 3
- Knowledge Advance Requirement: The University

The University improvement will boost the science output of the city by 50 percent. This improvement should be combined with the Library and Research Lab improvements for maximum benefit.

THE *CIVILIZATION II* WONDERS OF THE WORLD

When you assign a city to build a Wonder of the World, you are initiating a long-term plan that, when complete, will benefit your entire empire, not just the city in which the wonder is built. This is what sets Wonders of the World apart from City Improvements. City Improvements benefit a single city within your empire, while in most cases, wonders benefit the entire empire. Each wonder that you build will offer a different benefit. Some wonders actually enhance the benefits of City Improvements, and should be used in conjunction with them.

Just as with City Improvements, the Wonders that you can build within your empire are totally dependent on the Knowledge Advances that your scientists develop or acquire. During a simulation, each wonder can only be developed once, by one empire. The empire that builds the wonder is the one that will benefit from it. Of course, if a rival city that contains a wonder is conquered, the benefits of that wonder will be transferred to the conquering city.

One excellent strategy is to build a few cites within your empire in safe, well-protected locations, that will be used for the sole purpose of building Wonders of the World. If you choose to do this, be sure that the cities you assign to be wonder builders are protected by the military units from nearby cities.

The following alphabetical list of the game's Wonders of the World provides their costs, their Knowledge Advance requirement, and a brief description of their benefits. Like City Improvements, assigning a city to build a wonder is done from the Production window in a city's City screen. Keep in mind that you cannot use *Civ II*'s Auto Production feature to build wonders. You must assign a city to build each wonder manually.

Adam Smith's Trading Company

⊕ Cost: 400

⊕ Knowledge Advance Requirement: Economics

All City Improvements that normally cost one coin per turn to maintain will become free of maintenance costs for the remainder of the simulation when this wonder is built.

Apollo Program

- ⊕ Cost: 600

- ⊕ Knowledge Advance Requirement: Space Flight

Once this wonder is discovered by any empire, it allows all empires to begin building Spaceship Improvements—and the space race has begun! Start building your empire's spaceships immediately, once this wonder is discovered.

Colossus

- ⊕ Cost: 200

- ⊕ Knowledge Advance Requirement: Bronze Working

This wonder only benefits the city in which it is built. All trade routes with that city will produce one extra unit per turn. The benefit of the Colossus wonder will become obsolete when Flight (Knowledge Advance) is acquired. Until Flight is discovered, be sure to build this wonder in a city that has the greatest number of trade route opportunities.

Copernicus' Observatory

- ⊕ Cost: 300

- ⊕ Knowledge Advance Requirement: Astronomy

Science output in the city in which this wonder is built will increase by 50 percent. Build this wonder in a city containing the following City Improvements—Library, University, and Research Lab—to create some serious science output.

Cure for Cancer

⊕ Cost: 600

⊕ Knowledge Advance Requirement: Genetic Engineering

This Cure for Cancer wonder will make one citizen happy in every friendly city. In the long run, this will help keep your cities from falling into civil disorder.

Darwin's Voyage

⊕ Cost: 400

⊕ Knowledge Advance Requirement: Railroad

When this wonder is created, your empire will automatically receive two Scientific Knowledge Advances.

Eiffel Tower

⊕ Cost: 300

⊕ Knowledge Advance Requirement: Steam Engine

This wonder has two main purposes. First, it will make your entire population 25 percent happier with your performance as their ruler. Second, the Eiffel Tower will also make rival empires more quickly forget your reputation—an advantage, if you tend to break treaties often.

Great Library

⊕ Cost: 300

⊕ Knowledge Advance Requirement: Literacy

The empire that discovers this wonder will automatically receive all Knowledge Advances that have already been discovered by at least two other civilizations. Unfortunately, this wonder's power becomes obsolete once Electricity (Knowledge Advance) has been acquired.

Great Wall

⊕ Cost: 300

⊕ Knowledge Advance Requirement: Masonry

Once this wonder is built, all the cities within your empire will immediately benefit from having City Walls, even if the City Walls improvement hasn't been built in each city. Likewise, this wonder will double the attack strength of units that attack Barbarians. Finally, when you make contact with a rival civilization when you possess this wonder, the rival will be forced to offer you either a cease-fire agreement or a peace treaty. The benefits of the Great Wall wonder expire once Metallurgy (Knowledge Advance) is acquired.

Hanging Gardens

⊕ Cost: 200

⊕ Knowledge Advance Requirement: Pottery

Within the city in which this wonder is built, three citizens will be made happy on an ongoing basis. In all other friendly cities within your empire, one citizen will be made happy. The impact of this wonder becomes obsolete once Railroad (Knowledge Advance) is acquired.

Hoover Dam

⊕ Cost: 600

⊕ Knowledge Advance Requirement: Electronics

Once this wonder is built, every city will benefit from the effects of having a Hydro Plant within it.

Isaac Newton's College

⊕ Cost: 400

⊕ Knowledge Advance Requirement: Theory of Gravity

The science output doubles in the city where this wonder is built. Be sure to build this wonder in a city that has the Library, Research Lab, and University City Improvements, which also boost science output to maximize the benefit of this wonder.

J. S. Bach's Cathedral

⊕ Cost: 400

⊕ Knowledge Advance Requirement: Theology

Every friendly city located on the same continent on which this wonder is built will benefit by having two unhappy people made content.

King Richard's Crusade

⊕ Cost: 300

⊕ Knowledge Advance Requirement: Engineering

Production in every terrain square in the immediate vicinity of the city in which this wonder is built will produce one extra Shield per turn. This will continue until Industrialization (Knowledge Advance) is acquired.

Leonardo's Workshop

⊕ Cost: 400

⊕ Knowledge Advance Requirement: Invention

This wonder will automatically update all your empire's units as new Knowledge Advances are acquired because Military Units become obsolete. The impact of this wonder becomes obsolete once the Automobile (Knowledge Advance) is acquired. Until then, this wonder is vital for keeping your military force up-to-date inexpensively with the latest types of units available.

Lighthouse

⊕ Cost: 200

⊕ Knowledge Advance Requirement: Map Making

Triremes (ships with three ranks of oars) can sail in the open ocean without the risk of sinking, once this wonder is built. All other sea-based units will be able to move one extra terrain square (ocean) per turn. Once this wonder is built, all sea-based units that are produced by any city in your empire will be created as Veteran Units. The benefit of this wonder expires once Magnetism (Knowledge Advance) is acquired.

Magellan's Expedition

⊕ Cost: 400

⊕ Knowledge Advance Requirement: Navigation

All sea-based units will be able to move two extra terrain squares (ocean) per turn when this wonder is acquired.

Manhattan Project

⊕ Cost: 600

⊕ Knowledge Advance Requirement: Nuclear Fission

Once this wonder is built, all civilizations will have the ability to build nuclear weapons, the most powerful weapons available to you in this game.

Marco Polo's Embassy

- ⊕ Cost: 200

- ⊕ Knowledge Advance Requirement: Trade

An embassy is automatically established within every rival city, when this wonder is built. Your Foreign Minister will now be able to provide you with enhanced intelligence reports and recommendations. The benefit of this wonder continues until the discovery of Communism (Knowledge Advance) occurs.

Michelangelo's Chapel

- ⊕ Cost: 400

- ⊕ Knowledge Advance Requirement: Monotheism

When you build this wonder, every city in your empire will benefit from having a Cathedral City Improvement within it, even if this improvement isn't actually built within each city.

Oracle

- ⊕ Cost: 300

- ⊕ Knowledge Advance Requirement: Mysticism

The benefits of all Temples within your empire will double, until Theology (Knowledge Advance) is discovered, when you are able to build this wonder.

Pyramids

- ⊕ Cost: 200

- ⊕ Knowledge Advance Requirement: Masonry

When you build this wonder, you will experience the benefit of having a Granary (City Improvement) within each of your empire's cities.

SETI Program

⊕ Cost: 600

⊕ Knowledge Advance Requirement: Computers

When you acquire this wonder, your empire's science will double, because every city will benefit from having the equivalent of a Research Lab within it. Those cities that already contain the Research Lab improvement will experience even greater rewards.

Shakespeare's Theatre

⊕ Cost: 300

⊕ Knowledge Advance Requirement: Medicine

When this wonder is built, all unhappy citizens in the city that contains this wonder will become content and remain that way.

Statue of Liberty

⊕ Cost: 400

⊕ Knowledge Advance Requirement: Democracy

Normally, when you change between types of governments by causing a revolution, your empire goes into a state of temporary Anarchy. With this wonder, as long as you have already acquired the necessary Knowledge Advances to switch to a new form of government, your empire will not go into a state of Anarchy during the transition period.

Sun Tzu's War Academy

⊕ Cost: 300

⊕ Knowledge Advance Requirement: Feudalism

With the building of this wonder, all ground-based units created from this point on in the simulation will be Veteran Units, and any unit that already exists will automatically achieve Veteran status once it wins a battle. This wonder's benefits become obsolete once Mobile Warfare (Knowledge Advance) is acquired.

United Nations

⊕ Cost: 600

⊕ Knowledge Advance Requirement: Communism

When you build this wonder, your empire will establish an embassy in every rival city. Plus, when you encounter an enemy, it will be forced to offer you a cease-fire agreement or peace treaty every time. If you're ruling under a Democracy, you will be able to override your Senate and declare war on rival empires about 50 percent of the time.

Women's Suffrage

⊕ Cost: 600

⊕ Knowledge Advance Requirement: Industrialization

With this wonder in your empire, you will benefit from having the equivalent of a Police Station within every one of your cities. This wonder also causes unhappy citizens—which are a result of Military Units being far away from their home city—to become content. If you're going to be fighting battles when ruling your empire under a Republic or Democratic form of government, this is a useful Wonder of the World to acquire because it keeps your maintenace costs down and moral (population's happiness) up, as you send your military out to fight.

9

Civilization II
Governments and
Types of Terrain

This chapter is designed to help you become more familiar with the benefits and drawbacks associated with each form of government under which you can rule your empire, as well as the types of terrain that are available in *Civ II*.

Civilization II offers you new types of government and terrain, along with the ability to build new types of Terrain Improvements, so even if you're familiar with other versions of the *Civilization* game, you'll want to review this information to update your strategy.

CHOOSING A GOVERNMENT YOUR PEOPLE CAN TRUST

The people of your civilization rely on their government for everything. As the leader of the government, you're in the hot seat. Within *Civ II*, there are now seven types of government; however, most of them are available only after you have obtained certain Knowledge Advances. For example, Democracy only becomes available in later stages of a simulation, after you have acquired several advances, including Trade, Republic, Engineering, Literacy, Banking, and finally Invention. The best time to switch to Democracy is when most of the rival empires have been defeated and you are living in peaceful, stable times.

Other forms of government are available only under certain circumstances—for example, Anarchy takes place in a time of civil disorder after an invasion or during a revolution when you're trying to switch from one form of government to another.

CHANGING GOVERNMENTS

Each form of government offers its own advantages and disadvantages in terms of your civilization's growth and well-being. At the start of the simulation, Despotism (defined in the next section of this chapter) is in place. By ordering a Revolution (this can be done by selecting the REVOLUTION command on the Kingdom pull-down menu), you have the ability to change the existing form of government at any time, as long as you have the required advances necessary to sustain the form of government you select.

TYPES OF GOVERNMENT

The seven types of government that are or will be available within a *Civ II* simulation are:

- Anarchy
- Despotism
- Monarchy
- Fundamentalism
- Communism
- Republic
- Democracy

Now, in case you were asleep in class when you were taught about different forms of government, here are brief descriptions that should prove helpful.

Anarchy

In reality, anarchy isn't a type of government, but rather a lack of one. In *Civ II*, anarchy occurs when civil disorder erupts. While no central government is in existence, no taxes are collected, no scientific research is conducted, and no progress is made on City Improvements. The other drawback during periods of anarchy is that corruption is extremely high. In other words, do your best to avoid periods of anarchy. If you're going to be switching government types multiple times during a simulation (which is common), be sure to acquire the Statue of Liberty wonder to prevent a state of anarchy from taking place during the period when you are switching types of government.

Despotism

Under this form of government, you have absolute control over the people in your empire. While this gives you greater control over your empire, the production capabilities within cities will be limited. Furthermore, each unit produced above the city size will cost one Shield per turn, and Settler Units eat one unit of food per turn. In terms of keeping the citizens in each city happy, three Military Units within a city represent martial law, resulting in up to three citizens being kept content. When ruling under despotism, the further cities are away from your capital city, the higher corruption and waste will be. Finally, the Tax, Science, and Luxuries rates that you set cannot go higher than 60 percent, and the production capabilities of terrain squares are reduced. In the early stages of a simulation, operating under this form of government is actually somewhat beneficial, but to grow into a productive empire, you'll soon have to change to another type of government.

Monarchy

A monarchy is a government led by a monarch (a person who reigns by *divine right* over a kingdom or empire.) This form of government gives less control to the ruler than despotism, but makes the population happier and more productive, allowing for greater long-term growth. In reality, the benefits and drawbacks to a monarchy are similar to those of despotism, although the drawbacks are less severe. When ruling under a Monarchy, one easy way to keep the citizens within your cities happy (or at least content) is to place up to three Military Units within each city. This enforces a state of martial law and makes one unhappy citizen content. This form of government also allows up to three units per city to travel outside the city limits without incurring financial costs. The Tax, Science, and Luxuries rates that you can set cannot go above 70 percent.

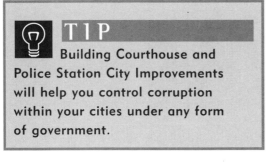

TIP

Building Courthouse and Police Station City Improvements will help you control corruption within your cities under any form of government.

Fundamentalism

This is a new form of government that's available in *Civ II*. This form of government is based on a set of beliefs that usually derive from religion, and both the population and the rulers are totally dedicated to their beliefs. They are willing to do just about anything to uphold them. Fanatics are a new type of Military Unit that can only be created under this form of government, which doesn't penalize you financially until more than ten units per city are active. Under this form of government, no citizens are ever unhappy, which means that your individual cities won't ever enter into a state of civil disorder and that corruption is kept extremely low. The Tax, Science, and Luxuries rates cannot be set above 80 percent under a Fundamentalist government. Also, the City Improvements and Wonders of the World that are dedicated to making citizens content or happy will now generate money because the population is happy by default. The drawback to this form of government is that all science production is cut in half, so your empire's progress toward developing new advances will be limited. Finally, if an enemy spy or diplomat (terrorist) is captured, the penalty for them will be lighter than the death penalty, which is standard under other forms of government.

Communism

All goods and production are commonly owned under this form of government; however, you (the leader) still retain all decision-making powers. There is no corruption under a Communist government, and all Spy Units produced are immediately given Veteran status. The Tax, Science, and Luxuries rates cannot be set above 80 percent. When you place three military units within a city, under this form of government, two unhappy citizens are made content.

Republic

This form of government represents a political system where elected representatives exercise power over the people. When your civilization opens trade routes with other countries, you'll want to rule your empire as a Republic, because your empire will receive Trade bonuses. One drawback with this type of government is that your Senate can and will often override your decisions to break treaties or invade a foreign country. Also, if a foreign government approaches you to make peace, your Senate will always accept. Under less-structured forms of governments, it's your job as the ruler to make peace or declare war, and you have nobody to answer to. The Tax, Science, and Luxuries rates cannot be set above 80 percent. Under this form of government, you can not declare martial law (by placing 3 Military Units within the city. To help keep your population happy (or at least content), boost the Luxuries Tax Rate to at least 20 percent and build City Improvements that help boost happiness (Cathedrals, Colosseums, Police Stations, Marketplaces, Banks, etc.).

Democracy

The rulers of a Democracy are put in a position of power based on majority vote. This is the most advanced form of government within *Civ II*, and it gives you the most opportunity to make your population happy while at the same time giving your empire the most growth potential. The Tax, Science, and Luxuries rates can be set to any level (up to 100 percent), the benefits of trade routes are enhanced, and your units and cities cannot be bribed by enemy Diplomat or Spy Units. Just like when ruling under a Republic, you can't declare martial law, so you have to use other strategies for keeping the populations in your cities happy. If you find that keeping citizens happy requires more than one or two Entertainers (Specialists) per city, then you might want to switch to another form of government, because this is an indication that your empire isn't ready for a Democracy. Just as the Presid-ent must do in real-life democracies, you will have to answer to your Senate, which can and sometimes will override your decisions to enter into war or invade rivals. In almost every circumstance, the Senate will insist on peaceful negotiations.

> **TIP**
>
> In *Civ II*, the happier your people are, the harder they will work, the faster they will reproduce, and the less you will have to do to keep them happy. If you're forced to take actions to keep the citizens within your cities happy, start by creating Entertainers (Specialists), increase the Luxuries rate (select the Tax Rate command on the Kingdom pull-down menu), or build City Improvements like Temples, Cathedrals, or Colosseums.

UNDERSTANDING THE LAY OF THE LAND

One key to succeeding in *Civ II* is understanding the terrain and taking full advantage of it. Just as on Earth, the planet you inhabit while playing this simulation contains many types of both land (continents and islands with different types of terrain) and water (rivers, lakes, and oceans). At the start of a game, your knowledge of the terrain will be quite limited, which is why you must explore.

EXPLORING AND EXPLOITING TERRAIN SQUARES

In *Civ II*, the entire planet is divided into squares (or units on a grid). To see this more clearly on the Main Map, activate the Show Map Grid command (Ctrl + G) on the View pull-down menu. Each square represents an area of land that contains a specific type of terrain—such as Grasslands, Plains, or Swamps—that you can take advantage of as you establish your cities and expand your civilization. Land can be used to provide natural resources, such as food, or additional wealth in the form of gems or minerals—or it can be used to defend your cities from enemies. As you will soon discover, some terrain is more useful and valuable for your purposes than other terrain.

Types of Terrain

There are many more types of terrain in *Civ II* than were available in other versions of the game. Table 9.1 provides a list of the types of terrain available in *Civ II* and tells what they provide.

TABLE 9.1: TERRAIN TYPES

TERRAIN	MOVE COST	UNIT DEFENSE BONUS	FOOD	SHIELDS	TRADE EFFECTS	IRRIGATION IRRIGATE
Desert	1	100%	0	1	0	+1 Food
Forest	2	150%	1	2	0	Plains
Glacier	2	100%	0	0	0	N/A
Grassland	1	100%	2	0	0	+1 Food
Hills	2	200%	1	0	0	+1 Food
Jungles	2	150%	1	0	0	Grassland
Mountains	3	300%	0	1	0	N/A
Oasis	N/A	N/A	3	1	N/A	N/A
Ocean	1	100%	1	0	2	N/A
Plains	1	100%	1	1	0	+1 Food
River	N/A	50%	N/A	N/A	2	N/A
Swamp	2	150%	1	0	0	Grassland
Tundra	1	100%	1	0	0	+1 Food

† Provides source of water for irrigation of other terrain

TURNS TO EFFECTS	MINING TO MINE	TURNS TRANSPORMATION EFFECTS	ENGINEERING EFFECTS	ROAD
5	+1 Shield	5	Plains	Move cost is ⅓ point +1 Trade
5	N/A	N/A	Grassland	Move cost is ½ point.
N/A	+1 Shield	15	Tundra	Move cost is ½ point
5	Forest	10	Hills	Move cost is ½ point +1 Trade
10	+3 Shield	10	Plains	Move cost is ½ point
15	Forest	15	Plains	Move cost is ⅓ point
N/A	+1 Shield	10	Hills	Move cost is ½ point
N/A	N/A	N/A	N/A	
N/A	N/A	N/A	N/A	N/A
5	Forest	15	Grassland	Move cost is ½ point +1 Trade
†	N/A	N/A	N/A	N/A
15	Forest	15	Plains	Move cost is ½ point
10	N/A	N/A	Desert	Move cost is ½ point

Natural Resource Benefits

Within each type of terrain, *Civ II* offers special resources. Table 9.2 lists the resources you may find scattered throughout the planet during a simulation.

TABLE 9.2:	*CIVILIZATION II* RESOURCE LOCATIONS	
RESOURCE	**TERRAIN WHERE FOUND**	**STRATEGIC BENEFIT**
Buffalo	Plains	Increases the amount of shields produced from 1 to 3.
Coal	Hill	Increases the amount of shields produced from 0 to 2.
Fish	Ocean	Increases the amount of shields produced from 1 to 3.
Fruit	Jungle	Increases the amount of food produced from 1 to 4 and the amount of trade from 0 to 1.
Furs	Tundra	Increases the amount of food produced from 1 to 2 and the amount of trade from 0 to 3.
Gems	Jungle	Increases the amount of trade produced from 0 to 4.
Gold	Mountain	Increases the amount of trade produced from 0 to 6.
Grassland Shield	Grassland	Increases the amount of shields produced from 0 to 1.
Iron	Mountain	Increases the amount of shields produced from 1 to 4.
Ivory	Glacier	Increases the amount of food produced from 0 to 1, the amount of shields produced from 0 to 1, and the amount of trade from 0 to 4.
Musk Ox	Tundra	Increases the amount of food produced from 1 to 3 and shields produced from 0 to 1.
Oil	Desert and Glacier	Increases the amount of shields produced from 0 to 4.
Peat	Swamp	Increases the amount of shields produced from 0 to 4.
Pheasant	Forest	Increases the amount of food produced from 1 to 3.
Silk	Forest	Increases the amount of trade produced from 0 to 3.
Spice	Swamp	Increases the amount of food produced from 1 to 3, and boosts trade from 0 to 4.
Whales	Ocean	Increases the amount of food produced from 1 to 2, the amount of shields produced from 0 to 2, and the amount of trade produced from 2 to 3.
Wheat	Plains	Increases the amount of food produced from 1 to 3.
Wine	Hills	Increases the amount of trade produced from 0 to 4. Cities built on this type of terrain square also have increased knowledge production.

TERRAIN IMPROVEMENTS

Settlers and Engineer Units are the two types of units that have the ability to alter terrain. They can convert one type of terrain to another, or they can add Terrain Improvements to an existing terrain square. Terrain Improvements are built outside cities, and have nothing to do with a city's production, though the Terrain Improvements you build around or near a city will often benefit that city dramatically.

While Engineer Units don't have the ability to found new cities (like Settlers Units do), they work much more quickly when it comes to building Terrain Improvements. To build a Terrain Improvement, place the Active Settler or Explorer Unit on the terrain square you want to build on, and then select the proper command from the Orders pull-down menu.

Following are Terrain Improvements that can be built during a *Civ II* simulation by either Settlers or Engineer Units, along with their strategic descriptions.

Airbases

An Airbase acts a refueling station for air-based Military Units, such as Fighters, Bombers, Stealth Fighters, and Stealth Bombers. Build an Airbase on any terrain square that's not located near a friendly city. Air-based units must refuel by stopping at a friendly city or by landing at an Airbase, otherwise they will crash. Strategically placing Airbases on the planet will greatly enhance the distance your air-based units will be able to travel over the course of each turn. (Carrier Units are ships that air-based units can land on in the middle of the ocean to refuel.)

Fortresses

Settler or Engineer Units can build Fortresses around cities to dramatically enhance their defensive capabilities. They can also be used to build blockades and keep enemy units from getting past a specific area of land. When a Military Unit is positioned within a Fortress (built on a terrain square), that unit's defense capabilities double. Thus, to develop the ultimate line of defense, build Military Units with the strongest defense capabilities, help them achieve Veteran status, and then Fortify them within a Fortress. On the Main Map, a Fortress looks like a square made up of stone walls.

How Do You Deal with Food Shortages in Individual Cities?

Building cities during a simulation is how you will make your empire grow. Once cities are established, however, they must be able to grow and prosper—and that will sometimes require your assistance. To ensure that a city will be able to prosper, before it's actually established, it's critical that you choose a good location on the map to establish the city. Remember, the population of a city will be forced to cultivate the land surrounding the city to generate good and resources needed to survive, so not only make sure that the actual terrain square is suitable for the city that will be placed on it, but also make sure that the surrounding terrain can be cultivated. Later, Settler or Engineer Units can always transform the terrain near a city into a better type of terrain, plus these two types of units can build Irrigation and eventually create farmland, though these improvements take time to build.

Cities that are built near water will have the ability to create irrigation, which is vital. (Thus, cities placed inland must be built near a river or lake to have a source of water. Cities with no supply of water will have difficulty surviving.) Also, when founding a city, look for terrain squares that contain special resources, such as fish, fruit, pheasant, wheat, and other types of food resources. If possible, make sure that these additional resources fall within a city's radius (the terrain squares surrounding a city).

As you determine where cities will be built, make sure you don't build cities too close together, or the radius of the cities will overlap. If this happens, the two cities will have to share the resources of the terrain, and chances are that terrain won't be able to support the needs of both cities. Lack of resources can and will lead to problems.

From a city's City screen, you can view the resource map, located in the upper-right portion of the screen. This map, along with the recourse charts located to the right of the map, allow you to graphically see how the people in a city are spread out around the terrain squares surrounding the city. Using the mouse, you can move the citizens around, and order them to cultivate other nearby terrain squares to produce food and needed resources. As you move icons around on the map, you'll notice that the graphics in the resource chart also change. A city's radius (and the amount of terrain shown on the resource map) will expand as a city's population grows. The maximum number of terrain squares that can become part of a city's radius is 21.

Irrigation

This Terrain Improvement allows a city to produce more food and ultimately to grow bigger andmore rapidly. Build irrigation on grasslands, plains, deserts, and hills. This type of Terrain Improvement must be built adjacent to a water supply, such as a lake, river, ocean, or another irrigated square. After the discovery of Refrigeration (Knowledge Advance), Settlers or Engineer Units can double-irrigate a terrain square to create Farmland, which allows for the production of even more food. On the Main Map, irrigation looks like small grids made up of thin blue lines (to simulate water).

Mining

Building Mines on desert or mountain terrain squares increases a nearby city's shield production by one (per turn). When a Mine is built on a hill terrain square, shield production increases by three (per turn). On the Main Map, Mines look like black domes.

Pillaging

Any type of ground-based Military Unit has the ability to Pillage a terrain square, which destroys any Terrain Improvements built on that square. As your military approaches an enemy city to launch an attack, you can pillage the nearby irrigated terrain squares, which will stun the production of that city, even if you don't manage to conquer it. This command must be used multiple times if multiple Terrain Improvements exist on a single terrain square.

Railroads

Once your empire discovers the Railroad (Knowledge Advance), any or all of the Roads your empire has built to connect cities can be transformed into Railroads. Units moving along a railroad track use no movement points, which means they can travel the full length of the railroad track in a single turn. Railroads also increase shield and trade production by 50 percent for the cities they connect. On the Main Map, Railroads look like darker (more defined) Roads.

Roads

Settler or Engineer Units can build roads on any type of terrain, except oceans, to allow for easier and faster travel for all units. If you want to build a road to cross a river,

Bridge Building (Knowledge Advance) must first be acquired. Any unit that travels along a road will be able to travel three times farther than their normal movement limit per turn. Roads also increase trade. On the Main Map, Roads look like solid brown (tan) lines that connect two or more cities.

Transform Terrain

This command, also found on the Orders pull-down menu, allows Settler or Engineer Units to change terrain that surrounds a city, if the surrounding terrain doesn't offer enough resources to sustain a city. Thus, if a city is having a serious food shortage, one of the possible ways to remedy the situation is to have multiple Settler or Engineer Units move in and transform the terrain into a type that's more useful, such as grasslands.

10

CivNet and Multiplayer
Simulations

The original *Civilization* offered strategy that was intense. Still, it was a one-player game—providing a challenge that pitted you against the computer. Sid Meier's *CivNet* for the PC is a Windows-based adaptation of *Civilization* that adds multiplayer gaming capabilities along with several other exciting new features. Now you can play *Civilization* against other people over a network, via a PC-to-PC direct cable connection, over the Internet, or through a specialized on-line gaming service.

CivNet's game play is extremely similar to that of the original game. Your overall objective is to take a small nomadic tribe of people and do whatever is necessary to expand it into a thriving, space-traveling society or a world-dominating military force. *CivNet* isn't a flashy, action-packed game, nor is it a military shoot 'em-up game. (You will, however, be forced to protect your people and perhaps enter into small battles or even all-out wars.) From the moment the game begins, you will be asked to make decisions that will have ramifications later. Everything in *Civilization* is somehow connected—just as it is in real life—and has a cause-and-effect relationship.

When experiencing a *CivNet* simulation, you must build and control your empire as it comes into contact with other *Civilization*s as well as with small tribes of Barbarians. What sets *CivNet* apart from its *Civilization* predecessors is that instead of the enemy *Civilization*s you encounter being controlled by the computer, human players and computer-controlled players will be attempting to build up rival empires. There can ultimately be only one world leader in this game, so you'll have to beef up your military and conquer the competition, while at the same time continuing to discover new technological advancements and boost productivity. A simulation ends when one player has conquered the entire planet, or is the first to colonize space.

This chapter describes many of the important menus and commands found in *CivNet*, outlines the new features in the game, plus offers some game-play strategies that are specific to *CivNet*, particularly in multiplayer simulations. Because actual *CivNet* play is very similar to playing simulations in the *Civilization* series, consult previous chapters for additional strategies and tips specific to the game itself.

MAJOR *CIVNET* FEATURES

CivNet allows you to compete against up to seven other rival empires, each controlled by another human player or the computer. As you compete against other human players on-line, the new chat feature allows you to communicate in real-time by typing messages. While the overall game play and strategy used when playing this game are virtually identical to those used when playing *Civilization*, there are some pregame features that allow you to better customize your game-play experience. The King Builder feature, shown in Figure 10.1, allows leaders to create an on-screen visual representation of themselves. Before a simulation begins, you can choose the gender, nationality, clothing, and weapons of the king or queen character that you'll be controlling.

Another major new pregame option is the ability to totally design the terrain on which your simulation will take place. Using *CivNet*'s MapEditor, you can choose the size of the land masses, as well as specify the types of terrain that make up the land masses. You can also use CivMaps to create your own world from scratch. Finally, if you happen to be bilingual, you can experience *CivNet* in English, French, or German. For help mastering this game, MicroProse has developed a highly detailed interactive guide that's included with the *CivNet* package.

SYSTEM REQUIREMENTS FOR *CIVNET*

CivNet is designed for use on an IBM PC 486, Pentium, or 100 percent compatible computer (operating at 33MHz or faster). The game operates in the Windows 3.1 (or later) environment. *CivNet* requires 8MB of RAM, plus hard disk space of between 18MB and 32MB. Your computer must be capable of displaying SVGA graphics and be equipped with a CD-ROM drive and Microsoft-compatible mouse. To take advantage of the multiplayer capabilities, *CivNet* supports Novell, PC Bios, and Artisoft LAN networks, together with a 9600 baud (or faster) modem. To use the Head-To-Head multiplayer gaming mode, a null modem cable is also required.

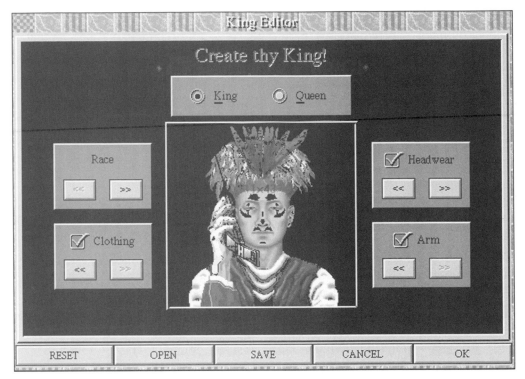

FIGURE 10.1: The King Editor window lets you create an on-screen representation of your-self as leader of your empire.

Installing *CivNet* onto Your PC

CivNet is distributed on CD-ROM, so begin by turning on your computer, loading Windows, and then placing the *CivNet* disc into your PC's CD-ROM drive. Once Windows is running, double-click on the File Manager icon to activate the File Manager program.

Choose the Run command on the File menu, and in the command box, type: **d:\install**, and then click on the OK button. (If your CD-ROM drive is assigned to a drive letter other than D, use the appropriate letter when typing the install command.) The installation process will now begin.

When the Sid Meier's *CivNet* Installation window shown in Figure 10.2 appears, you can choose one of the following install option buttons—Full Install, Custom Install, or Exit Install—and determine in what directory of your hard disk you will store the *CivNet* files. The default options are Full Installation (requiring approximately 29MB of hard disk space) and the directory c:\mps\civnet. Click on the Full Install button, and files will begin copying from the CD-ROM to your hard disk.

During the installation process, while the computer is copying files, be sure to complete the software registration card that comes with the *CivNet* package. After you register the software, MicroProse will know how to reach you to keep you posted on major upgrades to the software that are made available. If you have access to one of the major on-line services, be sure to visit the MicroProse forum and see if there have been any upgrades to the software. At the time this book was written, Version 1.1 of the software was available for download.

Toward the end of the installation process, a second window will appear on the screen, allowing you to determine the name of the icon group that will be displayed in the Windows Program Manager. The default option selection is *CivNet*. Click on the

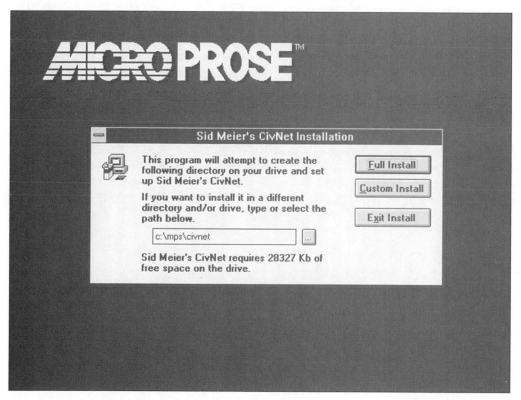

FIGURE 10.2: The *CivNet* Installation dialog box allows you to select the type of installation you want.

Create button to continue. Within a minute, a message saying, "Setup Successful!" should appear on the screen. Click on the OK button.

You will now automatically be returned to the Windows Program Manager. A program group called *CivNet* has been created and appears on-screen. Within the group are five program icons: CivNet, CivMaps, CivGuide, Internet Setup Win 3.1, and Internet Setup Win 95. Descriptions for these program icons are listed in Table 10.1.

TABLE 10.1: THE *CIVNET* PROGRAM GROUP ICONS		
PROGRAM NAME	**ICON**	**DESCRIPTION**
CivNet	CivNet	Starts the *CivNet* game and lets you begin a simulation.
CivMaps	CivMaps	Before you begin a simulation, starts the CivMaps program so that you can create from scratch the world your simulation will take place on, which can have a major impact on your overall simulation.
CivGuide	CivGuide	This is an interactive guide or tutorial for CivNet. This is separate from the Help feature that's built into the game.
Internet Setup Win 3.1	Internet setup Win 3.1	Starts a separate set of utilities needed to experience *CivNet* in multiplayer mode via the Internet, if you're operating under Windows 3.1.
Internet Setup Win 95	Internet setup Win 95	Starts a separate set of utilities to experience *CivNet* in multiplayer mode via the Internet, if you're operating under Windows 95.

RUNNING *CIVNET*

By double-clicking the mouse on the *CivNet* program icon, you can begin playing the game. Within a few seconds, the game's opening title sequence will appear inside a window. The game's Menu Bar is at the top of the window, though none of the options will be accessible at this time. Press any key to skip the opening sequence and begin the actual game.

The first *CivNet* window that you see will appear with several options, as shown in Figure 10.3. Use the mouse to select the option of your choice, and then click on the OK button located in the lower-right corner of this window. Each option does the following:

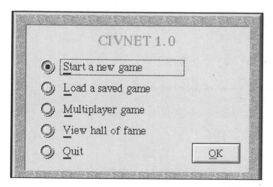 **Start a new game**   Select this option to begin a new simulation. This is the default option.

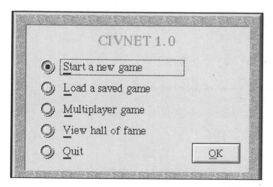 **Load a saved game**   Select this option to resume a previously saved simulation.

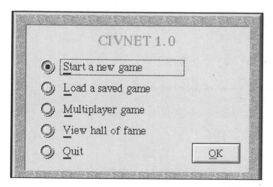 **Multiplayer game**   Select this option to begin playing a multiplayer game. Additional menu options will appear allowing you to select the type of multiplayer game you want to experience.

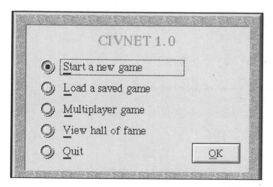 **View hall of fame**   Select this option to see final scores from completed simulations.

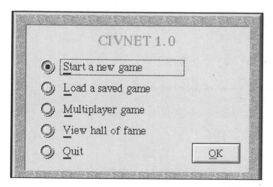 **Quit**   Select this option to return to the Windows Program Manager.

SELECTING PREGAME OPTIONS

When you choose the *Start a new game* option, several additional pregame menu windows will appear. These options allow you to customize your game-play experience.

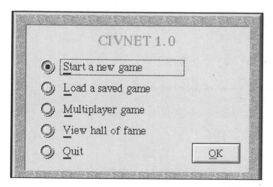

FIGURE 10.3: The *CivNet* 1.0 window presents you with several pregame options.

As shown in Figure 10.4, you will be asked to select the Difficulty Level for the upcoming simulation. You can choose from the following Difficulty Level options:

- Chieftain (easiest)
- Warlord
- Prince
- King
- Emperor (toughest)

The Difficulty Level you select will affect how easy it is to keep your population content, the number of Barbarian units you can expect to encounter during an attack, the speed at which your civilization will acquire technological advancements, and the year when the simulation will end. If you're a new *Civilization* or *CivNet* player, you'll want to begin by experiencing a simulation on the Chieftain level. This easy level provides

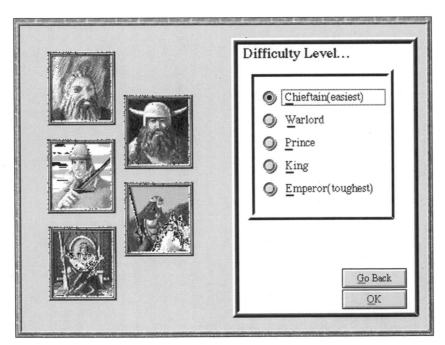

FIGURE 10.4: Choose the Difficulty Level of the game from this menu.

you with extra advice throughout the game and gives you the maximum number of years in which to accomplish your ultimate goal—whether to colonize space or conquer the world. Once you have selected the Difficulty Level, click on the OK icon to continue.

Next you must choose the Level of Competition. You will be controlling one civilization that will exist on the planet. Now, you must choose how many additional civilizations will coexist with you at the start of the game. When playing alone, the fewer rival civilizations you choose, the easier it will be to achieve world domination because your goal is to conquer these rivals. Thus, if this is your first time playing *CivNet*, you might want to keep things simple and select three rival civilizations. Click on your selection, and then click on the OK button to continue on with pregame selections.

The Setup the World options shown in Figure 10.5 allow you to experience your upcoming simulation on a computer-generated Earth (the default option). An alternative is to choose the Generate New World option and adjust the Land Mass, Temperature, Climate, and Age settings of the planet you'll be playing on. If you choose the Generate New World option, the four graphic icons on the left side of this window can be adjusted. To change any of the four options, click on one of the graphic icons. If you click on the icon for Land Mass, for example, you can choose a Small, Normal, or Large sized land mass. If you selected a large number of competing civilizations at the previous menu, and now choose a small land mass, things could get crowded—which means you can expect to encounter the enemy very early in the simulation. The ability to customize the land mass is a new feature added to *CivNet*. Adjusting the Land Mass, Temperature, Climate, and Age options will impact your civilization and affect how quickly and easily it can grow.

If you used the CivMaps program to design your own land mass before running the *CivNet* program, you can load this file into the game by selecting the Load Customized Map option in the Setup the World window. Once you select

NOTE Do not confuse the Generate New World option in the Setup the World window with the CivMaps program, which allows you to design your own terrain from scratch.

the Play on Earth, Generate New World, or Load Customized Map option, click on the OK button to proceed.

The next pregame menu option is also a new feature added to *CivNet*. Here you choose one of two Select A Play Method options: Turn Based Movement or Simultaneous Movement. Turn Based Movement is what you're already familiar with if

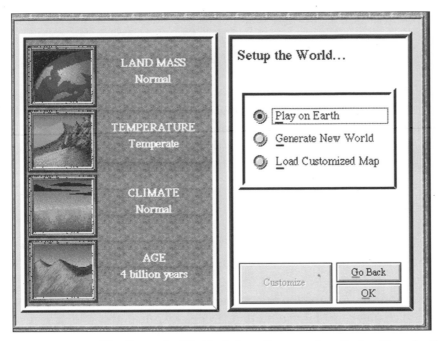

FIGURE 10.5: The Setup the World window allows you to adjust settings for the world in which your simulation will take place.

you've already played any of the *Civilization* series games. All the decisions you make when playing *Civilization* and *CivNet* are done during a player's turn. A turn represents the passing of time (which is measured in years). Choosing the Turn Based Movement option means that players make all their decisions during their turn, and once they are done, the next player (or the computerized opponents) will then be able to perform whatever moves they wish to make during that turn. Playing a turn-based game gives each player time to consider each action they make. To speed up the game and add an extra element of challenge, you can choose to experience a Simultaneous Movement game, where all the players make decisions and execute their strategies at the same time. This speeds up the game, but also makes battles between civilizations far more intense.

When the next pregame window appears, as shown in Figure 10.6, each player will have the opportunity to select the nationality of their tribe. You can choose a tribe based on reality, or select the Custom option and type in any name for your tribe. Once again, use the mouse to select one of the options and then click on the OK button to continue. If you're playing a one-player game, you can choose the names of the computer-controlled tribes as well, or allow the computer to make random selections.

If you chose to customize your tribe, you'll also have the option to determine what you, the leader of your tribe, will look like. The King Editor window shown in Figure 10.7 allows you to create your own custom king or queen by choosing the sex, race, clothing, headwear, and arm of the character that represents you—the leader of your tribe. Go ahead, be creative and have some fun creating a persona for yourself (see Figures 10.8 and 10.9). How you look will have no impact on your performance or capabilities during the game, though if you're playing a multiplayer game, the persona you create is how your opponents will see you throughout the game. This window only appears if you chose to create a Custom tribe.

The final pregame menu has one simple question—your name. All you have to do is enter your name. If you selected one of the predefined nationalities previously, the default for this menu will be a famous leader from that country. For example, if you chose Rome, the default name appearing in the Your Name pregame window will be Caesar. At this point, you can accept the default option, or enter your own name. Continue by clicking the OK button.

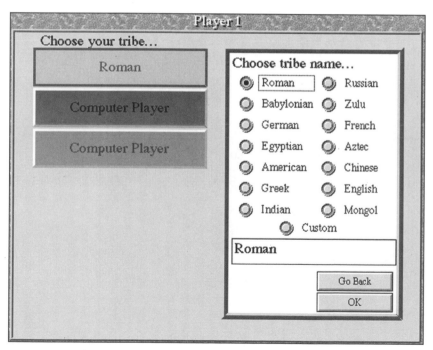

FIGURE 10.6: Select a real-life tribe name, or make up your own using the Custom option.

FIGURE 10.7: If you elect to create a custom tribe, the King Editor window will appear so that you can customize your own on-screen appearance as the leader of your tribe.

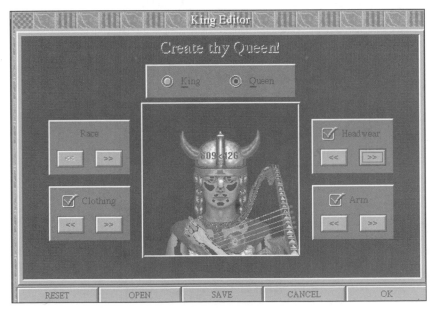

FIGURE 10.8: Be creative when you devise your on-screen persona as the King or Queen of your tribe.

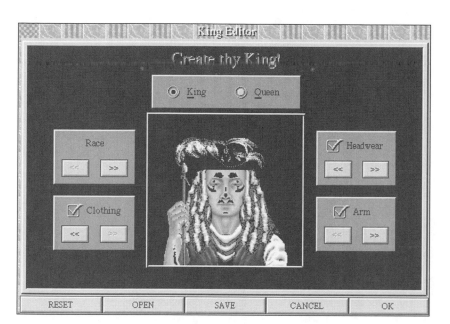

FIGURE 10.9: Don't be afraid to experiment with different "looks" as you customize your appearance.

All of the major pregame decisions have now been made. The computer will create a world based on the selections you've just made. An introductory screen will then appear as shown in Figure 10.10, giving you a brief background about your civilization and a list of the knowledge it already possesses. Click on the OK button when you're ready to begin your simulation.

THE *CIVNET* MAIN GAME SCREEN

When the *CivNet* Main Game screen appears, as you see in Figure 10.11, the *CivNet* simulation has officially begun. This screen is very much like the Main Same screen in the original *Civilization* game. Everything you do from this point on will have an impact on the remainder of the game.

The Main Game screen is basically your control center for the entire game. At the top of the screen is the Menu Bar, which offers nine pull-down menu options that will be described in detail shortly. Just below the Menu Bar, on the upper-left side of the

Jason, you have risen to become leader of the The Jasonians. May your reign be long and prosperous. The The Jasonians have knowledge of Irrigation, Mining, and Roads.

OK

FIGURE 10.10: This screen provides you with general information about your civilization at the start of a simulation.

screen is a small World Map. Right now, that map is almost totally black, because it represents the territory that you've explored (and in which you haven't done anything yet). Under the World Map is the Status window, which will also be described shortly. In the lower-left corner of the screen is the End Turn button. This should be used when you've taken all the actions you wish to take during a single turn, and you're ready for the simulation to proceed.

The biggest window on the screen is the main area where all the on-screen action takes place. Right now, what you'll see is a primarily black square with a flashing Settler Unit in the center. (Just as in other *Civilization* games, your population is made up of many different types of units.) Later, as the simulation progresses, you will see more of the map area in the Normal view mode, as shown in Figure 10.12.

Between this large window and the Menu Bar are three small buttons. From left to right, the first two are labeled with a minus sign (–) and a plus sign (+). The button furthest to the right appears as a small, unlabeled colored square. If you click on the minus sign (–) the large window will zoom outward, allowing you to see a large area of the overall world map, as shown in Figure 10.13; however, everything in this

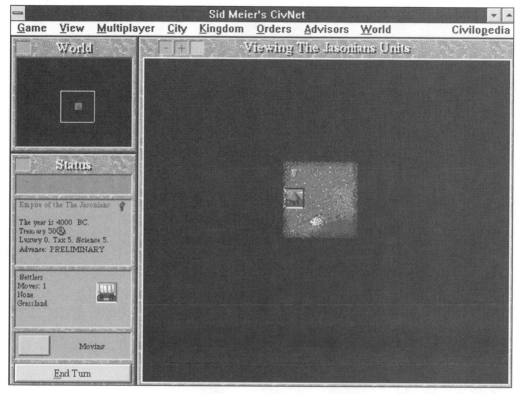

FIGURE 10.11: *CivNet's* Main Game screen appears after all pregame options have been selected.

window will appear smaller. The plus sign (+), on the other hand, lets you zoom in and get a close-up view of a specific area of the world, as shown in Figure 10.14. As for the small, colored button, every civilization is given a color to make identifying its units easier. You can customize your view of the large window by selecting to simultaneously view all units, or just your own units, or no units, or only the units of any one civilization. Click on this button to scroll through the possible options. As a general rule, you'll want to continue viewing all units.

THE STATUS WINDOW

The Main Game screen's Status window, as shown in Figure 10.15, is quite similar to the one found in other versions of *Civilization*. This window is divided into four main sections and provides you with a vast amount of information during the simulation.

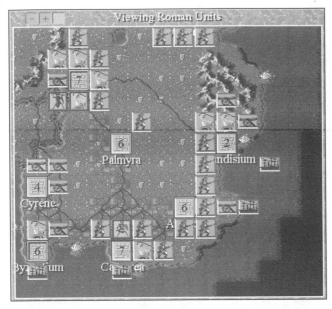

FIGURE 10.12: A world map shown in Normal view.

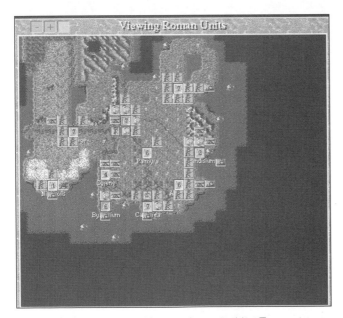

FIGURE 10.13: A world map shown in Min Zoom view to see a larger area.

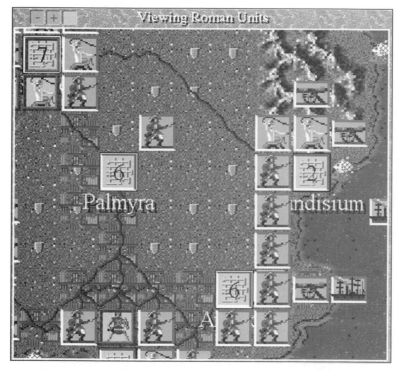

FIGURE 10.14: A world map shown in Max Zoom view to see more detail.

Just below its title is a light-blue rectangle that will soon be your Palace Display and Peace Bar. When you first begin a simulation, there is nothing inside this area because you have not yet begun building your castle, and you have experienced no turns in the simulation. Once you begin building your castle, a small graphic picture of that castle will appear in this area. Just above the castle graphic will be a thin yellow line that represents how long you've been at peace with rival civilizations. To conquer the world, you will have to fight battles and wage all-out wars against rival civilizations; however, you are also rewarded for maintaining peaceful relations. The longer this yellow line becomes, the longer you have been at peace. This Peace Bar is not affected by military conflicts with Barbarians.

Below the blue rectangle in the Status window is a line of text that tells the name of the active tribe's nationality. Moving downward, you'll see the population of the tribe displayed, followed by the current year and the amount of money the tribe has in its treasury. The next line down displays your civilization's Trade rates. These rates can be adjusted by selecting the appropriate commands on the Kingdom pull-down menu. These three numbers show how your Trade revenue is derived (from Luxuries,

FIGURE 10.15: The Status window provides you with a wealth of information during a simulation.

Taxes, and Science). Each of these numbers should be multiplied by ten to determine the percentage of Trade that is allocated to each. The default settings are: Luxury 0, Tax 5, and Science 5.

Moving downward in the Status window, you'll find the Research Progress indicator. This line indicates the status of the Knowledge Advance research being done by your civilization. When your civilization begins developing a new technological Advance, the rating will be "Preliminary." This rating will change until the Knowledge Advance is about to be completed, at which time the rating will be displayed as "Validating." How long it actually takes to achieve each Knowledge Advance depends entirely on the percentage of Trade you allocate to Science. The higher the percentage that's allocated to Science, the faster your civilization will obtain new knowledge. The trade-off is that the amount of revenue your civilization generates will go down. The speed at which Scientific Research (the quest for new advances) is being done is also signified by the brightness of the tiny light bulb located in the upper-right corner of the Status window, just below the blue rectangle.

In the middle or later portions of a simulation, Global Warming will become something you must contend with. The danger from Global Warming will be displayed just below the Advance Progress line in the Status window. Global Warming is measured as Slight, Growing, Menacing, and Imminent. Global Warming is a direct result of the number of pollution-generating terrain squares on the World Map.

The next section of the Status window pertains to the active unit. The unit type is displayed along with the number of squares that the unit can travel during a single turn. Other information in this area includes the active unit's home city and the type of terrain the active unit is currently on. If the terrain the active unit is on contains improvements, such as irrigation facilities, mines, or a road, this will also be indicated here. Likewise, if other units occupy the same terrain square, pictures of those units will be displayed. A picture of the active unit will be displayed on the right side of this portion of the Status window.

The final section of the Status window keeps you informed on what's happening at any given time. The colored square tells you which player is currently moving, by changing to reflect that player's color. This colored square is most important when playing a multiplayer game, because it helps you to determine which player is taking a turn.

THE *CIVNET* MENU BAR

Above the Main Game screen is the Menu Bar that is displayed throughout the game. Many of the commands available to you from these pull-down menus can also be selected using the keyboard. This section summarizes the commands available on each of the pull-down menus.

To activate any of these pull-down menus, you can point to its name and click the left mouse button to display the menu, or you can use the keyboard's Alt key in conjunction with the underlined letter in each menu's name. For example, to access the Game pull-down menu, press Alt + G.

The Game Pull-Down Menu

The following commands can be selected on the Game pull-down menu:

- ⊕ **Save Game (Ctrl + S)**   At any time during a simulation, you can save your game, so that you can continue later. Some simulations can take upward of ten or more hours to run their course, thus this Save feature can be quite handy. When you save your game, the Select A File window will appear. *CivNet* will automatically provide a filename for your saved game, which abbreviates your tribe's name and the year. You can accept the filename provided and click on the OK button, or enter any filename you choose. If *CivNet*

> **NOTE**
> The various commands available from these pull-down menus differ slightly from those found in other versions of *Civilization* and *Civilization II*.

> **NOTE**
> When the game crashes, hangs or freezes, it basically stops running. When this happens, you may be forced to reboot your computer and reload the game. Once the game has reloaded, you can reload your simulation using the Load command found under the Game pull-down menu. To reload a simulation you must have either Saved your game (using the Save Game command) before the problem with the game occured, or you must have the Save After Every Turn command activated.

appears to crash, hang, or freeze, you can always go back to your previously saved game.

⊕ **Retire**   You can end a simulation before conquering the world or colonizing space by selecting this command. This feature tabulates your score before ending the game.

⊕ **Pause Game**   If you need to take a quick break during a simulation, this command comes in handy, especially when playing a multiplayer game.

⊕ **Options**   This command displays a separate Game Options window, as shown in Figure 10.16. Use the mouse to activate or deactivate the various options that customize your game-play experience.

⊕ **Change Language**   If you feel like adding an international flare to your game, you can choose for all the text in the game to be displayed in English, French, or German.

⊕ **Set Password**   When resuming a multiplayer game, this password feature allows you to protect your empire from being tampered with by

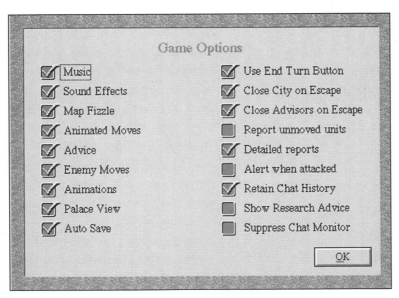

FIGURE 10.16: The Game Options window contains numerous options for customizing the simulation environment.

other players. Before saving your game, set the password. Now, your empire can't be reloaded without first entering the proper password.

- ⊕ **Quit (Ctrl + Q)**   You can end a simulation and return to Windows File Manager quickly by using this command. If you're in the middle of a simulation, however, be sure to save your game data *first*.

The View Pull-Down Menu

The following commands can be selected on the View pull-down menu:

- ⊕ **Zoom In (+)**   Use this command to get a closer look at the large Map window by zooming inward. You'll see a smaller area of terrain, though all the units on the screen will be larger.

- ⊕ **Zoom Out (–)**   Use this command to obtain a view of more terrain in the large Map window. The units will appear smaller, but you'll be able to see a larger area.

- ⊕ **Zoom Level Max**   Instantly switch to an ultra-close-up view of the action taking place in the large Map window.

- ⊕ **Zoom Level Normal**   If you've zoomed in or zoomed out, you can switch back to the default view instantly.

- ⊕ **Zoom Level Min**   Instantly switch to a bird's-eye view of the large Map window. This view will show you the most terrain possible from this window, yet the units and cities will appear tiny.

- ⊕ **Jump To Unit (Ctrl + U)**   This feature automatically centers your viewing perspective of the large Map window on the active unit.

- ⊕ **Jump To City (Ctrl + I)**   This feature centers the viewing perspective of the large Map window on the city whose City screen was last activated.

- ⊕ **Default Desktop**   Each of the windows that make up the Main Game screen can be moved or resized by the player. This command restores all the windows to their original size and location.

New Map (F1)   This command opens a separate window that allows you to focus on a specific area where action is taking place. This feature comes in handy when you're fighting multiple battles at once in different locations on the World Map. By opening up multiple windows, you can view multiple events happening atthe same time.

 Status (F2)   This command opens or reopens the large Map window.

 World (F3)   This command opens or reopens the small World Map window.

 City Display (F4)   Instantly reaccess the City screen that was most recently activated. You can close the City screen window by clicking in the upper-left corner of the window.

 Reports (F5)   Use this command to display the Reports window.

The Multiplayer Pull-Down Menu

The options on this pull-down menu are used only when experiencing a multiplayer game. All these commands are new to *CivNet*, and none are available in the original *Civilization* game.

 Anonymous Broadcast (Ctrl + A)   If you're playing a game against multiple human players, you can send an instant anonymous message to all other players using this command.

 Chat Monitor (Ctrl + C)   This window appears when players communicate in real-time by typing messages to each other. All messages will appear within this Chat Monitor window, which can be closed or repositioned anytime.

 Meet With A King (Ctrl + M)   If you want to converse with a specific player, use this command to type a private message to that person. You can only send messages to leaders of rival civilizations you have already encountered during a simulation. (If you're playing the game on the Chieftain level, you can communicate freely with all other leaders.)

⊕ **Quit HotSeat Game**   If you're experiencing a multiplayer game and you want to drop out, use this command and the computer will take over the management of your civilization. The simulation will continue.

⊕ **Who's On**   Use this command to display a list of who's currently participating in your simulation.

The City Pull-Down Menu

The following commands can be selected on the City pull-down menu:

⊕ **List City**   Select this command to see a quick list of the cities within your empire. You can then use the mouse to click on any city name to quickly access that city's City screen.

⊕ **Aerial View of City (Ctrl + V)**   When a city in your empire builds a new improvement or wonder, a graphic view of the city automatically appears, similar to the one shown in Figure 10.17. You can view this display for any city in your empire using this command.

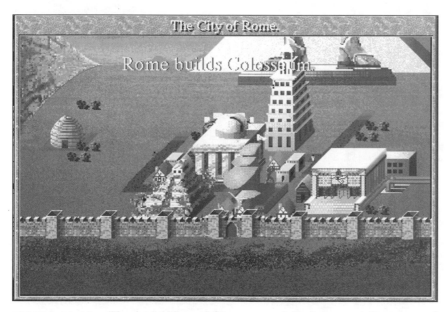

FIGURE 10.17: The Aerial View of City command displays a graphic image of a city, which also appears each time an improvement or wonder is created within a city.

Rename City (Ctrl + N) Each time you found a city within your empire, you'll have the opportunity to name that city (or accept the default name provided). This command you rename any city in your empire to suit your own tastes.

The Kingdom Pull-Down Menu

The following commands can be selected on the Kingdom pull-down menu:

  Tax Rate (Ctrl + T) Adjusting the Tax Rate impacts the proportion of funds and light bulb icons that each city generates during a turn. By generating more revenue, you will cut the amount of scientific knowledge each city generates during a turn. As you can see in Figure 10.18, you

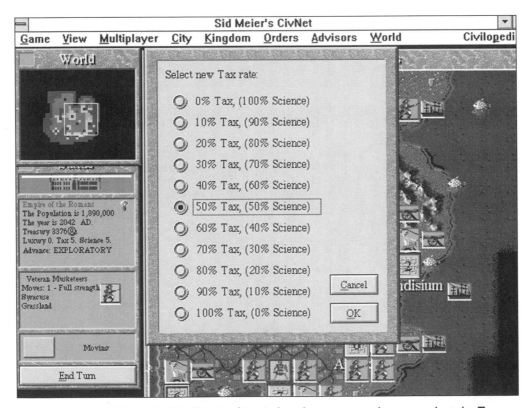

FIGURE 10.18: Adjust the Tax Rate in this window that appears when you select the Tax Rate command.

can adjust the Tax Rate anywhere from 0 percent tax (100 percent Science) to 100 percent tax (0 percent Science), in 10 percent increments. If you choose the 0% Tax (100% Science) option, for example, during a turn, your cities will generate zero revenue, and 100 percent of the empire's resources will be dedicated to improving scientific knowledge.

⊕ **Luxuries Rate (Ctrl + L)**   Adjusting the Luxuries Rate changes the proportion of resources that goes toward generating light bulbs (scientific knowledge) and diamonds (which contributes directly to your population's happiness).

⊕ **Revolution (Ctrl + R)**   Use this command to bring a new form of government into power for your empire. In *CivNet*, there are several different government types, just as in *Civilization*. Each government type offers different benefits and drawbacks to your empire. The government types available to you depend on the knowledge you have already acquired during the simulation. A description of each government type in *CivNet* follows later in this chapter.

The Orders Pull-Down Menu

As you maintain and continue to expand your empire, the commands under this pull-down menu will be used constantly, because they are control the active units under your command. Depending on the type of unit that is active, not all these options will be available.

⊕ **No Orders (N)**   An active unit will do nothing during a turn.

⊕ **Found New City (B)**   Command Settler Units to create a new city.

⊕ **Build Road (R)**   Command Settler Units to construct a road between two locations.

⊕ **Build Irrigation (I)**   Command Settler Units to provide irrigation. You can only build irrigation in a terrain square that's adjacent to water or another irrigated terrain square.

⊕ **Build Mines (M)**   Command Settler Units to dig a mine. Mines can only be built on hill, desert, or mountain terrain squares.

⊕ **Clean Up Pollution (K)** In the later stages of a simulation, when you begin erecting factories and other pollution-generating City Improvements, you will have to keep the pollution under control by commanding Settler Units to clean up polluted terrain squares. You'll know a terrain square is polluted because the letter "P" will appear on that square.

⊕ **Build Fortress (F)** This command causes a non-Settler Unit to fortify itself where it happens to be at the time. If this command is used when a Settler Unit is active, the Settler Unit will build a defensive wall in the terrain square that it occupies.

⊕ **Wait (W)** If you want to issue commands to other active units, and then return (during the same turn) to issue a command to the original active unit, use the Wait command.

⊕ **Sentry (S)** Placing a unit on Sentry duty commands it to be on guard. The unit will turn gray, positioning itself on the terrain square where it is currently located and where it will remain, on Sentry duty, until an enemy unit approaches, or until you manually take the unit off Sentry duty.

⊕ **GoTo (G)** Instead of constantly commanding an active unit to move toward a specific location, you can use the GoTo command once and command the active unit to move, over a period of multiple turns, to anywhere on the land mass that you indicate. The GoTo command is a time-saving tool when you're moving many units during each turn.

⊕ **Pillage (P)** If your active unit is near enemy territory, you can command it to pillage the terrain square it's on. This will cause your active unit to destroy enemy mines, irrigation, or other improvements that are on that terrain square.

⊕ **Home City (H)** Each unit is created by a specific city, which then becomes its home city. If a unit has traveled a great distance, you can reassign it to a closer city. To reassign a unit to a new city, that unit must be within the new city.

⊕ **Unload (U)**   When units are placed on ships, they are temporarily deactivated while they are passengers. When the ship approaches land, you can reactive the units on the ship using this command.

⊕ **Disband Unit (Shift + D)**   This command allows you to disband (delete) an active unit. This means that the unit will no longer be part of your empire—it will disappear—and cannot be brought back.

⊕ **Create Smart Settlers**   This is a new feature added to *CivNet*. It lets you command Settler Units to automatically build mines, roads, railroads, or irrigation on terrain squares where the computer deems these enhancements are needed, as shown in Figure 10.19. Once you choose the basic function of a Smart Settler, you won't have to keep issuing commands during each turn. Another use of Smart Settlers is to build a Highway between two cities that you define.

The Advisors Pull-Down Menu

In *CivNet*, you are the supreme ruler of your empire. To help you make intelligent decisions, you have access to a variety of advisors who are always at your disposal. Taking

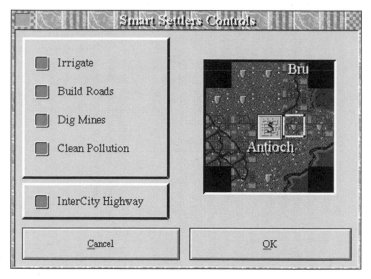

FIGURE 10.19: You can choose what you want your Smart Settlers to do.

advantage of your various advisors will help you manage your empire and plan long-term strategies; however, you are under *no obligation* to take advantage of the information these advisors provide.

- **City Status (Ctrl + 1)**   This command causes a window to appear that displays useful information about each city within your empire.

- **Military Advisor (Ctrl + 2)**   This command causes a window to appear that displays important information about the military assets of your empire. Two separate screens display information for each city, as shown in Figures 10.20 and 10.21.

- **Intelligence Advisor (Ctrl + 3)**   This command causes a window to appear that summarizes the intelligence information acquired by your embassies.

- **Attitude Advisor (Ctrl + 4)**   Are you keeping the citizens within your

MILITARY STATUS			
Empire of the Romans			
Emperor Caesar. 2042 AD			
MILITARY ASSETS			
Unit Type	Units	Units	In Production
Militia	(1 / 1 / 1)	1 active	
Legion	(3 / 1 / 1)	1 active	
Musketeers	(2 / 3 / 1)	31 active	1 in production
Cavalry	(2 / 1 / 2)	1 active	
Cannon	(8 / 1 / 1)	9 active	6 in production
Chariot	(4 / 1 / 2)	8 active	
Ironclad	(4 / 4 / 4)	7 active	
CASUALTIES			

FIGURE 10.20: This first Military Status screen shows each city's military assets in your empire.

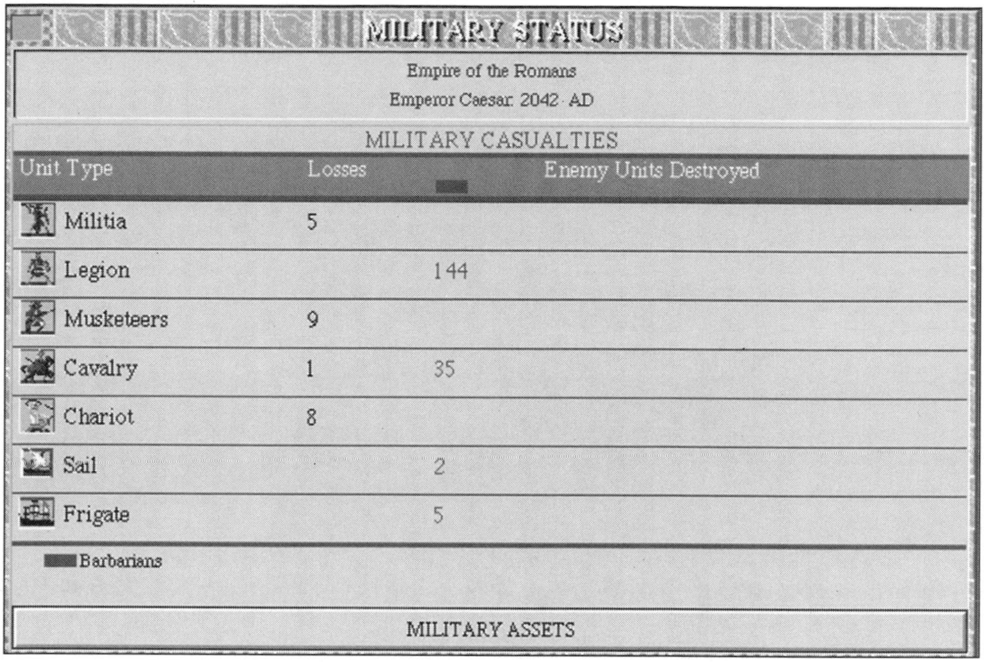

MILITARY STATUS		
Empire of the Romans		
Emperor Caesar 2042 AD		
MILITARY CASUALTIES		
Unit Type	Losses	Enemy Units Destroyed
Militia	5	
Legion		144
Musketeers	9	
Cavalry	1	35
Chariot	8	
Sail		2
Frigate		5
Barbarians		
MILITARY ASSETS		

FIGURE 10.21: The second Military Status screen shows each city's military casualties.

empire happy and content, or are they ready to revolt? Get a quick overview of your entire population using this command.

Trade Advisor (Ctrl + 5)   Once trade has been established between cities in your empire, use this command to view a summary of what benefits each city is achieving from the trade that's taking place during each turn.

Science Advisor (Ctrl + 6)   This command provides a list of the technologies and knowledge that your empire has acquired thus far in the simulation. You will also see your progress toward developing the next advance.

Research Advisor   Are you confused about which Knowledge Advances your empire needs to develop? Your research advisor will help you keep track of which one you need and suggest how to go about obtaining it. There is no keyboard shortcut. To access the Research Advisor, you must select this command from the pull-down menu using the mouse.

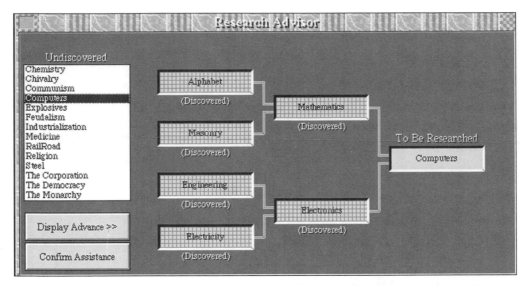

FIGURE 10.22: Use these flowcharts provided by your Research Advisor to help you determine what Knowledge Advance to pursue next. A flowchart can be created for any Knowledge Advance.

The World Pull-Down Menu

The following commands can be selected on the World pull-down menu:

- **Wonders of the World (Ctrl + 7)** This command allows you to see a list of the Wonders of the World that have already been built.

- **Top Five Cities (Ctrl + 8)** This command provides a list of the top five cities, and shows you how many of those cities are part of your empire. This is just one way to determine the strength of your competition.

- **Civilization Score (Ctrl + 9)** In addition to having the ultimate goal of conquering the world or colonizing space, throughout each simulation you can earn points to build up your overall score. This command lets you see how well you're progressing.

- **World Map (Ctrl + 0)** This command displays a slightly larger version of the World Map that's found in the upper-left corner of the Main Game screen.

- **Demographics (Ctrl + D)**   This command allows you to find out about the citizens living within your empire.

- **Spaceships (Ctrl + P)**   In the later stages of a simulation this command allows you to track the progress of your race into space, which begins after the Apollo Program Window of the World has been created.

The Civilopedia Pull-Down Menu

CivNet's Civilopedia is an on-line help feature that provides helpful information for all aspects of the *CivNet* game. The Civilopedia pull-down menu's commands categorize the information as follows:

- **Complete**   This command summons a list of all the topics available to you in the Civilopedia. Use the mouse to highlight the option you're interested in learning about, and that information will be displayed on the screen.

- **Civilization Advances**   This command leads you to find out about each Knowledge Advance that is available in *CivNet*.

- **City Improvements**   This command gives information on each City Improvement available in *CivNet*.

- **Military Units**   This command provides extensive information about each type of Military Unit available in *CivNet*.

- **Terrain Types**   Use this command to learn more about each type of terrain.

- **Miscellaneous**   This command allows you to obtain information about other aspects of the *CivNet* game.

- **Game Help**   This command provides information to help you when you might be stuck with game-related topics.

- **About Civilization**   This command provides an animated sequence that will shed some insight into what this game is all about. Find out about the formation of the world on which your simulation is based.

THE CITY SCREEN

The second most important game screen in *CivNet* is the City screen. Each city that you create within your empire has its own City screen. From this screen, you can manage a city. Just like the Main Game screen, the City screen has several components, as you can see in Figure 10.23. You'll find that the City screen in *CivNet* is similar in several ways to the City screen in the original *Civilization* game. However, *CivNet* has one major new feature that can be used for allocating a city's production resources. If you want to exit this screen, simply click on the small square in the upper-left corner of the City screen window.

At the top of the City screen, the city's name appears along with its population. A graphic display also shows the type of citizens living within that city. Each graphically depicted person on this display represents one point of city strength. This display also

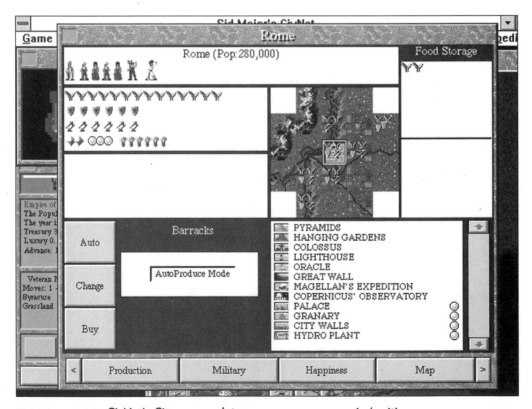

FIGURE 10.23: *CivNet's* City screens let you manage your empire's cities.

depicts the type of work force the city has. The majority of a city's population works toward producing food, raw materials, and trade materials. You'll be able to tell the mood of your population (happy, content, or angry) by examining this display. Using the mouse, you can also create Specialists—Taxmen, Scientists, and Entertainers. These features are all very similar to those found in the *Civilization* and *Civilization II* games.

THE CITY RESOURCES WINDOW

As you can see in Figure 10.23, just below the graphic display of the population on the left side of the City screen is the City Resources window. This graphic display depicts the amount of food, raw materials, and trade generated by a city. The wheat symbols on the top line of this display indicate the amount of food being created. Unless two units of food are being produced for each member of the population, food shortages will occur.

The second line in the City Resources window shows the amount of raw materials being developed. These raw materials, displayed graphically as shield icons, are used to support the city's Military Units. If a separate group of shield icons appears to the right of this line, they represent surpluses or shortages in raw materials.

The third line in the City Resources window indicates the amount of trade revenue generated by the city. Roads, rivers, mines, caravans, and railroads contribute to trade revenue for the city. If there is a separate group of icons to the right of this line, it shows whether the city is losing revenue due to corruption.

Trade revenue for a city is divided into three categories—Luxuries (diamond icons), Tax Revenues (gold coin icons), and Science (light bulb icons). These categories are displayed on the fourth line of the City Resources window. You can adjust the percentage of resources allocated to each category by changing the Tax Rate and Luxuries Rate from the Kingdom pull-down menu. To generate more revenue within a city, you can also create Taxmen. One way to improve Science Advancements is to create Scientists.

THE GENERAL INFORMATION WINDOW

This window will keep you posted on how pollution is affecting your population (once you reach The Industrial Age). The biggest causes of pollution are Factories and Manufacturing Plants built within your cities; however, a city that is generating a large volume of raw materials, or cities with large populations, can also create pollution that will have to be kept under control. Within this window, dark smoke stacks will appear, indicating pollution. Each smoke stack icon represents a 1 percent chance that pollution will be generated during a turn. Thus, if many smoke stack icons are displayed, and nothing is done to clean up the pollution, an empire-wide pollution problem can quickly get out of control. Once pollution is generated, terrain squares on the City screen's City Map will turn dark.

To clean up pollution and keep it under control, there are several steps you should take. First, create Smart Settlers (and allocate them to clean up the area). Then build Nuclear Power Plants or Hydro Power Plants, and build Mass Transit or a Recycling Center in the cities affected by pollution. On a larger scale, developing the Hoover Dam Wonder of The World helps to prevent pollution throughout your entire empire.

The General Information window is also used to display information about active trade routes that have been established by that city's Caravan units. Once a trade route is established, on-going revenue is generated. For a trade route to be created, one city must create a Caravan Unit and send that unit to another city located at least ten terrain squares away.

THE PRODUCTION WINDOW

Shown by itself in Figure 10.24, the Production window is located below the General Information window on the City screen. This component allows you to determine what that city will build. Throughout a simulation, the resources of a city can be allocated to build any type of unit (Military, Settler, or Diplomat), City Improvements, or Wonders of the World. Each city can only build one thing at a time, so based on your specific game-play strategies and the immediate needs of each city, you must make important decisions as to what each city in your empire will be used for.

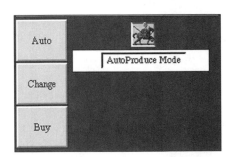

FIGURE 10.24: The Production window lets you establish what a particular city will produce.

Similar to a feature in the *Civilization II* game, a new feature in *CivNet* is the Auto Production capability. Instead of having to keep deciding what your cities need to produce next, by activating the Auto Production feature, the computer makes the decision on your behalf—once, that is, you have decided if you want to pursue military, peaceful, or custom expansion. Military expansion causes the computer to allocate the city's resources toward building military units, while the peaceful expansion option allocates the city's resources toward building City Improvements. To create Wonders of the World, you cannot use the Auto Production feature. If you choose the Custom option after activating Auto Production mode, a sub-menu will appear asking you to select the types of units or improvements you want that city to build, and in what order.

At the top of the Production window, the name of the unit, City Improvement, or Wonder of the World being created will appear. A city's ability to build something is directly related to the surplus of resources that is created by a city. The more surplus that's created during each turn, the faster a unit, City Improvement, or Wonder of the World will be built. At any time (whether you're in Auto Production mode or not), you can click on the Change button and alter what a city is building.

When you click on the Change button, the menu of available units, City Improvements, and Wonders of the World shown in Figure 10.25 will be displayed, along with the number of turns it will take that city to build each item. Highlight and select what you want the city to produce from the menu that's displayed. Keep in mind that a city with a lot of extra surplus will be able to build a wonder or a unit much faster than a city with little or no surplus production. Therefore, it's a good strategy to use your larger, more productive, and most-protected cities to build Wonders of the World.

Buying a Unit, Improvement, or Wonder

Instead of waiting around for a city to build a unit, improvement, or wonder, if you have enough money in your empire's treasury, you can instantly buy whatever it is that the city is set to build. Note that the cost of buying a unit is more expensive than building it (that is, two gold coins for every one unit of raw materials that would be required if you waited to build the unit). However, the benefit is that whatever you buy will be available to you on your next turn. The buy feature comes in handy when you must have a new Military Unit to protect that city in a hurry.

THE CITY MAP

Near the center of the City screen appears the City Map, which offers you a view of that city and its surrounding terrain. This map is divided into 20 squares, with the city itself appearing in the center. The graphic icons that appear on the map will help you determine how much food, raw materials, and trade the city is capable of producing. Each person in the city's population is used to develop one of the city's 19 surrounding

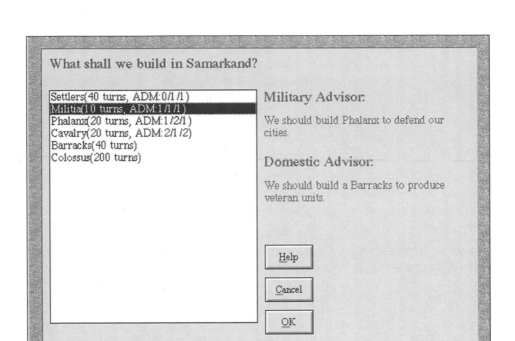

FIGURE 10.25: You can change the unit, improvement, or wonder that a city is building at any time.

terrain squares. As a city gets larger, the computer assigns one person to each terrain square on the City Map, though you can move those people around on the map to maximize their output. When you decide to transform members of a city's population into a specialist (whether Entertainer, Scientist, or Taxman), you must first decide from which terrain square you want to remove the person you want to transform.

THE FOOD STORAGE BOX

To the right side of the City screen is the Food Storage box. Refer to it periodically to determine how much food surplus a city has available. Wheat icons are used to measure the amount of surplus food. As soon as the entire Storage Box is completely filled with wheat icons, that city's size grows by one (back on the Main Game screen, the number in the city square will increase). When this happens, the storage box will empty and must be refilled with additional surplus food.

Building a Granary in a city helps you stretch that city's food supply and feed a larger population. When you build a Granary (City Improvement), a black line will appear halfway down the Food Storage box. If a food shortage is occurring within a city, during each turn several wheat icons will disappear from the Food Storage box.

THE CITY IMPROVEMENT ROSTER

Each time you build (or purchase) a City Improvement or Wonder of the World, it will be added to the list in the City Improvement roster located in the lower-right corner of the City screen (see Figure 10.26). To raise funds, City Improvements that have been built within a city can be sold by clicking on the gold coin icon next to the name of the City Improvement you wish to sell. A small window, containing the selling price for that improvement along with a sale confirmation prompt, will appear. Wonders of the World cannot be sold, so no gold coins will appear next to them in this list. Only one improvement may be sold per turn. If your empire's funds are running dangerously low, and you don't manually sell off improvements to raise cash (or take other revenue-generating steps), the computer will automatically sell off improvements on your behalf. The drawback to letting this happen is that you have no control over what improvements will be sold, or which city will be affected.

THE REPORT BUTTONS

At the bottom of the City screen are four buttons—Production, Military, Happiness, and Map. The Production button is the default and displays the Production and City Improvement roster windows. Clicking the Military button will cause the Production and City Improvement roster windows to be replaced by a window that graphically depicts the number and type of Military Units supported by that city.

The Happiness button provides information about a selected city's population and its degree of happiness. The information is indicated by rows of "people" icons. The top row depicts the number of happy citizens, without taking external factors into account. The next row takes into account the number of happy people based on the Luxuries offered to them and the Entertainers in that city. The third row helps you determine the effect that Temples, Cathedrals,

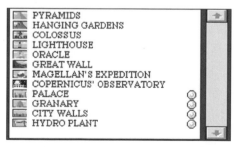

FIGURE 10.26: Sometimes you have to sell an improvement to raise money quickly. You can select an improvement you want to sell from this City Improvement roster.

and Coliseums have on making the city's population happier. Building these City Improvements is an easy way to make people happy, without your having to create Specialists and give up production capabilities within the city.

The fourth line in this display gives you insight into how the population feels about the Military Units it's supporting. The impact the military has on the population depends on the type of government under which your empire is being ruled. If you're ruling your empire as a Republic or Democracy, each military unit that's outside of the city causes one or two people to become unhappy. The bottom row in this display shows how many people are being made happy, based on the Wonders of the World that your empire has built. The Population roster displayed just under the city's name at the top of the City screen takes all the above into account, and summarizes the overall happiness of the city's population.

THE *CIVNET* UNITS

The majority of the units available to you in *CivNet* are similar to the ones available in *Civilization*, though some of the units' strength values differ in this version of the game. Table 10.2 lists the attack strength, defense strength, and number of terrain squares of movement per turn for each ground unit. Tables 10.3 and 10.4 show similar information for air and naval units, respectively. Table 10.5 provides information for *CivNet*'s nonmilitary units.

These tables will help you determine the best units to produce for specific tasks. For example, if you're looking to launch a long-range attack, you will want Military Units with strong attack strengths and the ability to move farther during each turn. If you are looking to protect a city, you'll want units with strong defense strengths, and you might want to fortify those units. With the exception of Militia and Settler Units, your empire must first discover the requisite scientific knowledge before it will be able to build advanced units.

TABLE 10.2: *CIVNET'S* GROUND-BASED MILITARY UNITS

UNIT	ICON	SCIENTIFIC ADVANCE REQUIREMENT	COST	ATTACK STRENGTH	DEFENSE STRENGTH	MOVE-MENT
Armor		Automobile	80	10	5	3
Artillery		Robotics	60	12	2	2
Cannon		Metallurgy	40	8	1	1
Catapult		Mathematics	40	6	1	1
Cavalry		Horseback Riding	20	2	1	1
Chariot		The Wheel	40	4	1	2
Knights		Chivalry	40	4	2	2
Legion		Iron Working	20	3	1	1
Mechanized Infantry		Labor Union	50	6	6	3
Militia		None	10	1	1	
Musketeer		Gunpowder	30	2	3	1

(Continued on next page)

(Continued from previous page)

UNIT	ICON	SCIENTIFIC ADVANCE REQUIREMENT	COST	ATTACK STRENGTH	DEFENSE STRENGTH	MOVE-MENT
Phalanx		Bronze Working	20	1	2	1
Riflemen		Conscription	30	3	5	1

TABLE 10.3: *CIVNET'S* AIR-BASED MILITARY UNITS

UNIT	ICON	SCIENTIFIC ADVANCE REQUIREMENT	COST	ATTACK STRENGTH	DEFENSE STRENGTH	MOVE-MENT
Bomber[1]		Advanced Flight	120	12	1	8(16)
Fighter		Flight	60	4	2	10
Nuclear Missile		Rocketry	160	99	0	16

[1]Bombers can move eight terrain squares per turn for up to two turns before returning to a friendly city or Carrier.

TABLE 10.4: *CIVNET'S* NAVAL-BASED MILITARY UNITS

UNIT	ICON	SCIENTIFIC ADVANCE REQUIREMENT	COST	ATTACK STRENGTH	DEFENSE STRENGTH	MOVE-MENT
Battleship		Steel	160	18	12	4
Carrier		Advanced Flight	160	1	12	5

UNIT	ICON	SCIENTIFIC ADVANCE REQUIREMENT	COST	ATTACK STRENGTH	DEFENSE STRENGTH	MOVE-MENT
Cruiser		Combustion	80	6	6	6
Frigate		Magnetism	40	2	2	2
Ironclad		Steam Engine	60	4	4	4
Sail		Navigation	40	1	1	3
Submarine		Mass Production	50	8	2	3
Transport		Industrialization	50	0	3	4
Trireme		Map Making	40	1	0	3

TABLE 10.5: *CIVNET*'S NON-MILITARY UNITS

UNIT	ICON	SCIENTIFIC ADVANCE REQUIREMENT	COST	ATTACK STRENGTH	DEFENSE STRENGTH	MOVE-MENT
Caravan		Trade	50	0	1	1
Diplomat		Writing	30	0	0	2
Settlers		None	40	0	1	1

CARAVAN UNITS HAVE MULTIPLE USES

Caravan Units are used to transport trade goods or food to other friendly cities. They can also be sent from their home cities to help another city build a Wonder of the World by contributing 50 shield units toward production. By sending multiple Caravan Units to a city building a wonder, that wonder can be built much faster.

When a Caravan Unit reaches a city that is ten or more terrain squares away from its home city, the menu shown in Figure 10.27 will appear, which allows you to order that Caravan Unit to keep moving, establish a trade route, or help build a wonder. If the Caravan Unit is assigned to establish a trade route or help build a Wonder of the World, that unit will serve its purpose and then be disbanded.

By establishing a trade route, you can easily generate additional revenue for your empire. Each city has the ability to benefit from up to three different trade routes. When establishing a trade route, keep in mind that you can generate more revenue if you establish trade with a rival civilization's city. Also, the farther the other city is away from the Caravan Unit's home city, the more revenue potential the trade route will have. Trade routes that span continents generate greater revenue.

CIVNET'S CITY IMPROVEMENTS

Cities become larger and more productive based on the City Improvements you build within each city. Unlike Wonders of the World, each of the improvements listed in Table 10.6 can be built within every city in your empire. Just as in *Civilization* and *Civilization* II, each improvement offers the city its built in some type of benefit. The problem with some improvements is that there is a cost per turn to maintain them. As your civilization acquires new Knowledge Advances, the list of improvements you are able to build will expand.

FIGURE 10.27: You can instruct a Caravan Unit to keep moving, establish a trade route, or help build a wonder when that unit reaches a city that's at least ten terrain squares away from its home city.

TABLE 10.6: *CIVNET'S* CITY IMPROVEMENTS

IMPROVEMENT	ICON	ADVANCE REQUIREMENT	COST	MAINT. COST (PER TURN)	BENEFIT
Aqueduct		Construction	120	2	A city can grow beyond a population of 10; it cuts fire and disease risk.
Bank		Banking	120	3	Boosts amount of taxes and luxuries in a city by 50 percent. (A city must have a Marketplace.)
Barracks		None	40	0	The attack/defense strength of Military Units increases 50 percent. Pirate raids are also prevented. After Gunpowder and Combustion are discovered, new Barracks must be built within each city
Cathedral		Religion	160	3	Makes four unhappy people in the city content. Build the Michelangelo's Chapel Wonder to boost a Cathedral's powers by 50 percent.
City Walls		Masonry	120	2	Triples the defensive strength of Military Units within a city. (Does not apply to attacks by enemy Artillery or Bombers.) Also protects the city from population reduction if a defending unit gets killed.
Coliseum		Construction	100	4	Three unhappy people in the city become content.
Courthouse		Code of Laws	80	1	Reduces trade corruption by 50 percent.

(Continued on next page)

(Continued from previous page)

IMPROVEMENT	ICON	ADVANCE REQUIREMENT	COST	MAINT. COST (PER TURN)	BENEFIT
Factory		Industrialization	200	4	Boosts raw material production by 50 percent.
Granary		Pottery	60	1	A city with a Granary uses only 50 percent of its stored food to create a larger population and boost its strength. This allows a city to expand more quickly.
Hydro Plant		Electronics	240	4	Increases a city's raw material production by 50 percent and reduces the chance of the population being created. This improvement must be built in a city near water.
Library		Writing	80	1	Increases science development in the city by 50 percent. Build in conjunction with Isaac Newton's College wonder.
Manufacturing Plant		Robotics	320	6	Doubles a city's raw material production.
Marketplace		Currency	80	1	Increases a city's tax revenue by 50 percent.
Mass Transit		Mass Production	160	4	The size of a city's population will have no impact on pollution.
Nuclear Plant		Nuclear Power	160	2	Increases raw material production by 50 percent, and decreases the possibility of pollution. Beware: a city with a Nuclear Plant that goes into civil disorder can experience a meltdown.

IMPROVEMENT	ICON	ADVANCE REQUIREMENT	COST	MAINT. COST (PER TURN)	BENEFIT
Palace		Masonry	Free	0	The Palace represents the heart of your empire. If it gets destroyed, you must build another, but it'll now cost you to build it (200 gold coins) and then maintain it (5 gold coins/turn)
Power Plant		Refining	160	4	Increases raw material generation by 50 percent, but can also cause pollution.
Recycling Center		Recycling	200	2	Cuts the chances of population by 66 percent.
SDI Defense		Superconductor	200	4	Protects a city against nuclear attack.
Temple		Ceremonial Burial	40	1	Makes one unhappy person in the city happy. Once your city discovers Mysticism, two people become happy. Combine with Oracle wonder to double the Temple's power.
University		The University	160	3	Increases Science generation by 50 percent in the city, but a Library must already be present. Combine with Isaac Newton's College for maximum benefits.

CIVNET'S WONDERS OF THE WORLD

Wonders of the World are considered to be major achievements. Each wonder offers specific benefits for your entire empire, not just the city they're built in. Once a wonder has been built within a city, it is vital to protect that city from enemy invasion. There are 21 Wonders of the World in all, divided into three categories depending on the era in which they're available.

TABLE 10.7: *CIVNET*'S ANCIENT WONDERS OF THE WORLD

IMPROVEMENT	ICON	ADVANCE REQUIRED	COST	BENEFIT
Colossus		Bronze Working	200	Trade for all production squares that produce trade.
The Great Library		Literacy	300	Automatically earn advances once they have been discovered by at least two opponents.
The Great Wall		Masonry	300	Opponents end all negotiations wanting peace.
Hanging Gardens		Pottery	300	Makes one person happy in every city's population.
Lighthouse		Map Making	200	All sea vessels can move one terrain square farther during each turn.
Oracle		Mysticism	300	Doubles the power of Temples.
Pyramids		Masonry	300	Change government type without first entering into a period of anarchy.

TABLE 10.8: *CIVNET'S* MIDDLE-AGES WONDERS OF THE WORLD

IMPROVEMENT	ICON	ADVANCE REQUIRED	COST	BENEFIT
Copernicus' Observatory		Astronomy	300	Doubles production of Science within the city where it's built.
Darwin's Voyage		Railroad	300	Finishes off current research, plus instantly gives you one extra Advance.
Isaac Newton's College		Theory of Gravity	400	All cities with a library or university will have greater Science production. (For maximum results, build this wonder in the same city as Copernicus' Observatory.)
J.S. Bach's Cathedral		Religion	400	Two people from every city on the continent where this wonder is built will become happy.
Magellan's Expedition		Navigation	400	Ships can move one extra terrain square per turn.
Michaelangelo's Chapel		Religion	300	All cathedrals in your cities become 50 percent more powerful
Shakespeare's Theatre		Medicine	400	All unhappy people in the city where this wonder is built become content.

TABLE 10.9: *CIVNET'S* MODERN WONDERS OF THE WORLD

IMPROVEMENT	ICON	ADVANCE REQUIRED	COST	BENEFIT
Apollo Program		Space Flight	600	Now you can begin building spaceships. As an added bonus, you'll be able to see all cities in the world, even if they're in unexplored territory.

(Continued on next page)

(Continued from previous page)

IMPROVEMENT	ICON	ADVANCE REQUIRED	COST	BENEFIT
Cure for Cancer		Genetic Engineering	600	One person in every friendly city becomes happy.
Hoover Dam		Electronics	600	All cities on the continent where this wonder is built will receive the benefit of the Hydro Plant.
Manhattan Project		Nuclear Fission	600	Any civilization with the knowledge of Rocketry can now build Nuclear Missile Units (mass destruction is now possible).
SETI Program		Computers	600	Science production is increased by 50 percent in all cities within your empire.
United Nations		Industrialization	600	Under the Republic or Democracy government types, one fewer person becomes unhappy with the release of a Military Unit.
Women's Suffrage		Communism	600	Opponents always end their negotiations with an offer of peace. This will keep you out of a war while you develop your space program and launch spaceships.

TYPES OF GOVERNMENT IN *CIVNET*

As you progress through a simulation, there are six different types of government under which you can rule your empire: Anarchy, Despotism, Monarchy, Communism, Republic, or Democracy. To switch types of government, initiate a Revolution. At the start of every simulation, Despotism is the form of government that all the civilizations are ruled under. When you're ready to progress to a new form of government and you initiate a Revolution, your empire will temporarily fall into a state of Anarchy for several turns as the transition is made—unless you have acquired the Pyramids Wonder of the World, which prevents Anarchy. Shortly after a Revolution, the menu shown in Figure 10.28 will appear, asking you to choose a new form of government. You can only choose a form of government for which you have acquired enough knowledge to operate. The exception to this is if you have already acquired the Pyramids Wonder of the World, in which can you can change to any form of government.

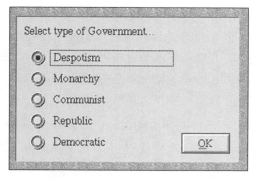

FIGURE 10.28: After a revolution, this menu appears so that you can select a new form of government.

- **Anarchy** happens only during a transitional phase when you go from one form of government to another. During this phase, it'll cost you one unit of food resources for every Settler Unit that your empire has activated. Likewise, if the number of units in any of your cities exceeds that city's population, there will be maintenance charges for those excess units.

- **Despotism** gives you absolute control over the people in your empire. A terrain square that generates three or more units of food, raw materials, or trade will have its production reduced by one unit per turn under this form of government; however, Diplomat and Caravan Units don't require any type of support. If the number of units in any of your city's exceeds that city's population, there will be maintenance charges for those excess units.

- A **Monarchy** is a government ruled by a monarch, such as a king. Under a Monarchy there is no reduction in resources that can be generated from the terrain squares. The benefit is that irrigation will cause improved production in grassland and river terrain squares, and mines also will increase production. There is a maintenance cost for units and Settler Units.

⊕ **Communism** means goods and production are commonly owned, but the leader still has the power to make decisions. The benefits of Communism are similar to those in a Monarchy, with the additional benefit that trade corruption won't increase if your trade routes are at great distances from your capital city (the city containing your Palace).

⊕ The **Republic** represents a system where elected representatives rule. For each unit of trade being produced on a terrain square under this government, one additional unit will be produced. The drawbacks are that each Military Unit that's not inside its home city will make one person unhappy, and your senate will force you to accept peace offers from rival civilizations to avoid war. You also won't be able to declare war against civilizations where a peace treaty is already in effect.

⊕ A **Democracy** is similar to the Republic form of government, but no trade revenue is ever lost because of corruption. In addition to limiting your ability to declare war, under this form of government, if one or more cities enters into a state of civil disorder and remains in that state for two more turns, a revolution will automatically happen.

DIPLOMACY IN *CIVNET*

In *CivNet*, the capabilities of Diplomat Units have been improved over other versions of *Civilization*. Once you discover Writing, your empire will have the ability to create Diplomat Units (the same way as you would create Settler or Military Units). Don't confuse Diplomat Units with Specialists. Diplomat Units have multiple functions that involve how you deal with rival civilizations. When you send a Diplomat Unit into a rival city, the menu shown in Figure 10.29 will appear. It provides the following actions you can choose to assign to the Diplomat Unit:

⊕ **No action**   The unit does nothing.

⊕ **Establish embassy**   By establishing an embassy, you can obtain useful information about the enemy civilization when you consult your Intelligence Advisor. When you establish an embassy, the Diplomat Unit will be disbanded.

⊕ **Investigate city** This option allows you to view the City screen for the enemy city. Upon investigating the city, the Diplomat Unit will be disbanded.

⊕ **Steal technology** This feature lets you steal one of the enemy empire's Knowledge Advances that your empire has not already acquired. It is only possible to steal one advance per city, and if the city has no advances that your empire doesn't already have, then you won't be able to proceed with this option. On stealing an advance, the Diplomat Unit is disbanded.

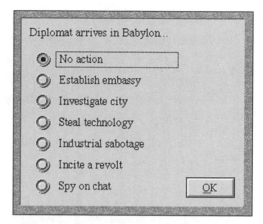

FIGURE 10.29: Diplomat Units can be assigned any of these useful jobs in *CivNet*.

⊕ **Industrial sabotage** Either your Diplomat Unit will destroy the City Improvement that's in production by the enemy city, or, if no improvement is in production, the Diplomat Unit will destroy one of the enemy city's existing improvements. On performing industrial sabotage, the Diplomatic Unit is disbanded.

⊕ **Incite a revolt** For a fee (which will be deducted from your treasury), you can have your Diplomat Unit bribe the citizens of an enemy city and get them to incite a revolt. If this happens, that city will become part of your civilization, and you will acquire all that city's Military Units. If the revolt happens, the Diplomat Unit will be disbanded.

⊕ **Spy on chat** (multiplayer games only) If your Diplomat Unit enters into a human opponent's city, and you're participating in a multiplayer game with at least three human players, this feature allows you to eavesdrop on the private chat conversations being held by the enemy leader (whose city you invaded) and anyone else they communicate with via chat mode. Once this feature is activated, the Diplomat Unit will be disbanded.

⊕ **Bribe an Enemy Unit** At any time during a simulation, if a Diplomat Unit encounters an enemy Military Unit, this option will appear below the *Spy on chat* option. In this situation, if you're willing to pay a bribe, you can get that enemy Military Unit to join your empire. The potential drawback is that if you don't pay the bribe, the enemy unit might destroy your Diplomat Unit. If the bribe is accepted, however, the Diplomat Unit will survive and continue to be active.

CIVNET MULTIPLAYER GAMING

CivNet can be used for multiplayer simulations, and there are numerous ways you can compete against other gamers: over a LAN (Local Area Network), or by connecting two computers via a null-modem cable, or through the Internet, or on a single PC (where players take turns on the same keyboard, managing their civilization), or through a computer bulletin board system (BBS) that supports the Game Connection Protocol (GCS), or by connecting to the Total Entertainment Network (a commercial venture).

Once you begin the *CivNet* program, at the pregame menu select the Multiplayer Game option if you want to experience *CivNet* as a multiplayer game. The Multiplayer Setup menu shown in Figure 10.30 will appear. Multiplayer games can be played by between two and seven human gamers, depending on the game mode you select. Keep in mind, the more players that take part in a simulation, the slower the pace of the game will be.

Upon making your multiplayer game-play mode selection, additional submenus will follow that allow you to configure your computer and the *CivNet* software to play the type of multiplayer game you select. The Multiplayer Setup menu gives you the following choices:

⊕ **Network game** This type of game is played over a Local Area Network (LAN), where multiple PCs are linked together via a server. Using this option, up to seven human players can compete simultaneously, and each player will rule their own civilization. Civilizations not being controlled by a human player can be computer controlled. One nice feature of a network game is that human players can join a simulation while it's in progress by taking over a civilization that's being computer controlled. Likewise, if a player drops out of a simulation, the computer will take over that player's civilization, so the simulation can continue unhindered.

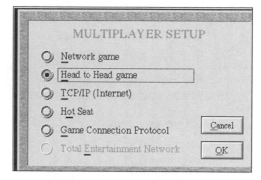

FIGURE 10.30: Before you begin a multiplayer game, you must set up the Multiplayer game-play mode.

- **Head-To-Head game** Using this game-play mode, two computers, each with a copy of *CivNet* loaded on its hard drive, can be connected via a modem or a null-modem cable. Thus, the computers can be located inches apart, across town, across the country, or even in other countries (but you'll have to pay the long-distance phone bill to connect the computers via modem). In head-to-head mode, only two human players can compete, though you can still have up to seven civilizations competing in the simulation (the remaining five civilizations will be computer controlled). Unless you're connecting two computers via a null-modem cable, you'll want to use the highest-speed modems possible to keep the pace of the game play moving. A rate of 9600 baud is the slowest modem you should consider using when playing *CivNet* via modem in this mode.

- **TCP/IP (Internet)** Two program icons in the *CivNet* Program Group relate to Internet game play. Before experiencing a simulation over the Internet, you must first run either Internet Setup Win 3.1 or Internet Setup Win 95. You must also have access to the Internet via a service provider. Within the *CivNet* packaging is a special offer from an Internet service provider that allows you to go on-line quickly.

- **Hot Seat** Multiple players can compete in *CivNet* using a single computer. This is done by playing what MicroProse calls a "hot seat" game. In this game-play mode, up to seven human players take turns managing their civilization, one at a time. If multiple players are competing and one player chooses to leave the game before it ends, that player can select the Quit Hot Seat Game command from the Multiplayer pull-down menu. The simulation will continue, but the computer will take over the civilization that belonged to the player who dropped out. Hot seat games do not support the simultaneous movement play option.

- **Game Connection Protocol** Bulletin Board Systems (BBSs) are small on-line services, most of which are operated by computer hobbyists. Some of these systems are dedicated to multiplayer computer gaming and support a special protocol that allows computer users to connect to a central system and compete via modem with other players. The process of connecting to a BBS is different from connecting to the Internet or a LAN, yet once the game play begins, everything in *CivNet* is identical to a Network Game.

- **Total Entertainment Network** (T.E.N.) This is an on-line service, similar to America Online, the Microsoft Network, CompuServe, and Prodigy; T.E.N. specializes only in multiplayer on-line gaming, however. At the time this book was written (and the *CivNet* software was released by MicroProse), T.E.N. was still in development. When the service actually goes on-line, MicroProse will make an upgrade to the *CivNet* software available, free of charge, that allows gamers to subscribe to this service and play *CivNet*. To find out whether T.E.N. is now on-line, contact MicroProse Software's technical support department via telephone, fax, or e-mail.

MULTIPLAYER NEGOTIATIONS

When you encounter an enemy civilization that's controlled by a human player, a special human-to-human negotiation window appears, allowing you to communicate with the opponent. This window lets you chat in real-time, develop treaties, make offerings, or declare war. You can also change the mood of your graphic persona that the opponent is seeing on the game screen. Possible mood options include: Bored, Happy, Angry, or Furious. From this Multiplayer Negotiations screen, by clicking on the Chat button, you can send broadcast messages, which means that all human players can read them. It's also possible to broadcast a message that's anonymous, so that everyone can read it, but nobody will know who sent it. Predefined text messages can be sent, eliminating the need to type most messages. For someone who doesn't type quickly, this is a major time-saver.

If you want to negotiate a treaty or alliance with the enemy, click on the Treaty icon. A menu of possible treaties and alliances will appear. Use the mouse to select the treaty option that you want to propose. By clicking on the Offerings button, you can trade advances, demand money, or pay money from your treasury to the opponent.

USING *CIVMAPS* TO CREATE YOUR OWN WORLDS

CivNet allows you to do something that's never before been possible in previous versions of *Civilization* you can create from scratch the world in which your simulation takes place. *CivMaps* is a separate program that comes with *CivNet*. When you installed *CivNet*, *CivMaps* was added to the *CivNet* Program Group within the Windows Program Manager.

If you're going to create your own world, it must be done *before* you begin running the *CivNet* program. From the *CivNet* Program Group in the Windows Program Manager, double-click on the CivMaps icon. The *Civilization* MapEditor screen will appear, as shown in Figure 10.31.

USING THE *CIVILIZATION* MAPEDITOR

The *Civilization* MapEditor has four main areas. At the top of the screen is a Menu Bar containing three pull-down menu options: File, View, and Brushes. Just below these pull-down menus is a small World Map, which at the moment is totally blank. This small window provides an overview of the entire planet that you're about to design. In the lower-left corner of the screen is the Tools window, containing 12 different terrain type icons. The largest window of the MapEditor is the map itself. This is an area map that shows portions of the World Map in detail, very much like the map found on the Main Game screen.

Creating your own world is easy. All it takes is a bit of creativity, but there are a few things you'll want to keep in mind when designing the terrain on which you'll soon be experiencing your simulation. First, the amount of land and the size of each

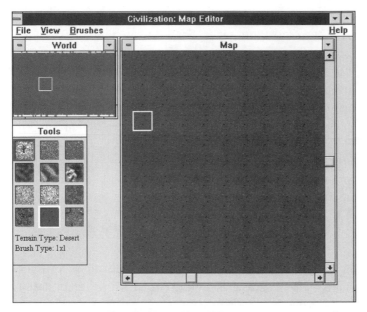

FIGURE 10.31: The CivMaps Map Editor screen appears when you double-click the CivMaps icon in the *CivNet* Program Group.

continent you create will have a major impact on the overall simulation. The less land you create, the more crowded the land mass will be with rival civilizations, which will result in your civilization encountering the enemy very early in the game. It's also important to consider the type of terrain you use to create your world. Make sure that rivers, lakes, or oceans will be accessible to the cities you build. You'll also want to add terrain types, such as hills, on which mines can be built.

You can create continents in any shape and any size by using the mouse to select the terrain type you want to use (from the Tools window), and then painting terrain squares within the large map window. If you hold down the left mouse button, you can add multiple terrain squares of that type at once, or you can place one terrain square on the map at a time by clicking the mouse button. Once the terrain squares are placed on the map, the computer will add a bit of artistic flare, rounding off the terrain and creating more realistic continents. The types of terrain in *CivNet* include: arctic, desert, forest, grassland, hill, jungle, mountain, ocean, plain, river, swamp, and tundra.

From the MapEditor's Brushes pull-down menu, you can select commands that allow you to determine how many terrain squares you paint on the Map screen at once, as follows:

- ⊕ **1×1** for placing one terrain square at a time
- ⊕ **3×3** for placing slightly larger blocks of terrain quickly
- ⊕ **5×5** for placing blocks of terrain, five squares wide by five squares high, at once to cover large areas
- ⊕ **Diamond** for placing terrain squares in a diamond shape instead of a square
- ⊕ **City Radius** for placing terrain squares in the shape of a city radius as shown in the City screen)
- ⊕ **Blob** for generating islands in random shapes and sizes

If your creative flare isn't flowing yet, you can begin creating your world with a little help from the computer, by selecting the Generate Random World command from the File pull-down menu. You can then add to or edit the world that is created.

Saving Your Maps

Once you have created your world by placing your preferred types of terrain squares where you want them, use the File pull-down menu to save your map to the hard disk. You will be asked for a filename, to which the computer will add an .mp extension. Once your world has been saved, exit the *Civilization* Map Editor and begin the *CivNet* program.

CIVNET'S CHEAT CODES, PLAY TIPS, AND STRATEGIES

To use *CivNet*'s cheat codes, you must enter a special cheat code. After entering the special cheat code, a new pull-down menu, Extras, will appear on the Menu Bar.

WARNING

Beware: all opponents will instantly know you are cheating, and will have the same cheat options available to them.

To create a special Extras pull-down menu, at the end of a turn, press the Ctrl key, release it, and then type the following letters: **A**, **O**, **D**, **B**, **A**, **M**, and **F**. The Extras pull-down menu will appear on the right end of the Menu Bar and will contain the following new cheat commands:

- **ScaleIt**   This command allows you to adjust the rate of production of food, shields, light bulbs, gold coins, and luxuries via a scaling cheat-panel window that will appear. This cheat can affect all human-controlled cities, or all cities in the game.

- **ArmyInfo**   This command provides information about the leaders of each empire.

- **MoneyAndPower**   This feature gives your empire additional funds, plus it allows you to instantly create and place any type of unit anywhere on the map. First, select the command and you will see that your treasury increases. Now, using the mouse, point to any location on the map and click the right mouse button. This will cause a Create A Unit menu to appear. Click on any of the unit types, and then click on the OK button. The unit you selected will instantly appear on the terrain square you pointed to. You can create any type of unit with this feature, regardless of what advances your empire has acquired.

- **AllSeeingEye**   This command reveals the entire World Map on the Main Game screen. You can now see the entire world and all cities.

- **GetRichQuick**   This command instantly increases your treasury by 1,000. (You can keep activating this option to generate as much money as you'd like!)

- **Get Smart Quick**   This command allows you to instantly discover whatever advance your empire was working on.

- **MissileCrisis**   A Nuclear Missile unit will instantly be created in each of your cities.

⊕ **SettlersHo!** Every one of your cities will instantly create one Settler Unit. This option can be activated multiple times in a row.

⊕ **NukeStorms** According to the information window that appears when you select this command, "The world just got a little more unstable! Watch for falling nukes! (Cheat Enabled)."

⊕ **AutoOn** This command puts the game in Auto mode.

⊕ **Armaggedon** This command allows you to instigate a world-wide nuclear war. This will virtually annihilate the entire world, your empire included. Save your game before using this command!

STRATEGIES FOR DEALING WITH DISASTERS

Rival civilizations aren't your only obstacle in *CivNet*. During a simulation, you'll be forced to contend with Land Barbarians, Barbarian leaders, corruption, famine, fire, flood, global warming, nuclear meltdown, pirate raids, plague, schism, sea raiders, and even volcanic eruptions. Each of these situations can have a negative impact on a unit, city, or your entire empire—especially if you don't react quickly.

FIGHTING RAIDERS

Sea Raiders are computer-controlled enemies that approach from the sea, but when they reach land (your land), they move in and attempt to take over your cities. Simply because these raiders want to move in, don't assume they also want to pillage your cities. They just want to take them over. If one or more of your cities is captured by Sea Raiders, you can use your Military Units to launch an attack to recapture your city.

Land Barbarians are bright-red computer-controlled enemies that often prove to be a major headache because they appear randomly and keep reappearing as they launch new attacks on your units and cities. If you allow Land Barbarians to capture one of your cities, that city (and all advances and wonders within it) will be destroyed. All Barbarian parties have a leader. If you attack a Barbarian leader who is standing alone on a terrain square, you'll receive a 100-coin ransom bonus that will be added to your treasury.

Pirates constitute another threat. Any city built near an ocean runs the risk of being attacked by a band of evil pirates. To reduce the damage caused by a Pirate attack, build Barracks within the cities that are at the greatest risk of this type of attack.

ELIMINATE CORRUPTION, RIOTS, AND SCANDALS

To prevent corruption, riots, and scandals from taking place within your cities, be sure to build Cathedral, Courthouse, Marketplace, and Temple City Improvements. Keeping tax rates as low as possible also goes a long way toward keeping your population happy. Unfortunately, earthquakes happen at random intervals and can't be prevented. To minimize damage from an earthquake, don't build cities on or close to hill terrain. If you do build a city on hill terrain, it could be destroyed by an earthquake, so don't build any wonders within those cities.

FIGHTING OTHER DISASTERS

Famine is a common problem that happens within cities, especially as your civilization grows. Building a Granary within each of your cities greatly minimizes the impact a Famine will have. If fire breaks out randomly within one of your cities, one City Improvement will be destroyed unless you've already built an Aqueduct Improvement within that city.

Any city built on or near a river terrain square runs the risk of experiencing a flood. To eliminate the possibility of disaster caused by floods, build a City Wall within cities located near rivers.

Plagues can be fought by obtaining the Knowledge Advance called Medicine or by building an Aqueduct Improvement within a city. Plagues, like famine, fires, and floods, happen at random during a simulation.

Volcanic eruptions can happen in cities built on or near mountain terrain squares. To protect your cities from this type of disaster, build a Temple within cities that are at risk.

AVOIDING NUCLEAR MELTDOWNS

In the later stages of a simulation, when nuclear weapons become commonplace, nuclear meltdowns grow to be a potential danger to any city containing a Nuclear Power Plant. If one of these cities enters a state of civil disorder, a meltdown can occur.

Simply by avoiding civil disorder is one way to cope with this problem. Still, be sure to work toward obtaining the Knowledge Advance known as Fusion Power. Meltdowns will instantly destroy half of a city's population and, at the same time, destroy multiple terrain squares surrounding that city. What will be left are terrain squares that are heavily polluted.

CIVNET SCORING

The Civilization Score screen appears at the end of a simulation. (An example is shown in Figure 10.32.) In addition to conquering the world or colonizing space, one of your goals in *CivNet* is to build up a point score of 1,000 points. It this possible? Yup! Is it easy? Nope. Here's how *CivNet* calculates your point score for a simulation: The only chance you have of earning 1,000 points is to reach one of the game's two ultimate goals between the years A.D. 2100 and 2020 (depending on the difficulty level you're playing at).

Civnet Scorecard

Destroy a rival civilization:	1,000 points each
Happy citizens:	2 points each
Content citizens:	1 point each
Wonders of the World (Built):	20 points each
Experience peaceful turns:	3 points each
Futuristic advances (available late in the simulation):	5 points each
Map squares containing pollution:	−10 points each
Destroy a rival civilization:	1,000 points each
Happy citizens:	2 points each
Content citizens:	1 point each
Wonders of the World (Built):	20 points each
Experience peaceful turns:	3 points each
Futuristic advances (available late in the simulation):	5 points each
Map squares containing pollution:	−10 points each

CIVNET PROGRAM UPDATES

When *CivNet* was first released, it was called Version 1.0. Since the program's release, MicroProse has fixed bugs and other problems and has released updates. At the time this strategy guide was written, Version 1.1 was being made available for download (free of charge) via the various on-line services that MicroProse Software supports. Version 1.1 may be downloaded as CivNet1.zip and should be placed in the main directory of the *CivNet* program. The default directory should be placed in C:\MPS\CivNet. Use the PKUnzip.exe utility to extract the compressed .zip file within the *CivNet* directory on your hard disk. This will automatically update your version of the game. MicroProse reports that the Version 1.1 update fixes the problems associated with network play, TrueType fonts, GPFs (General Protection Faults), and the hot seat game-play mode.

To find out more about *CivNet* software updates, call the MicroProse technical support phone number, access the company's on-line bulletin board system, or visit the MicroProse forums found on the World Wide Web (http://www.microprose.com), America Online (keyword: microprose), CompuServe (Go GAMBPUB), or Prodigy (Game Club). Update information is also posted on user-supported Internet sites. See Appendix C, *Civilization II and CivNet On-Line Resources* for specific *Civilization* Internet site information.

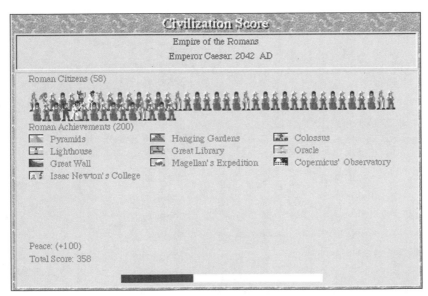

FIGURE 10.32: *CivNet's* Score screen appears at the end of a simulation, or when you retire.

Creating Worlds with the *Civilization II* MapEditor

As you already know, *Civilization II* allows you to create an empire and then become the sole ruler of all that you create. Before playing ruler, however, you can play master of the universe by first creating the world on which your simulations will take place. The *Civ II* Program CD comes with a map-editing program, which is separate from the *Civ II* and *CivNet* games. The MapEditor lets you create worlds from scratch, using your own imagination and creativity.

Gamers already familiar with the *Civ II* program will enjoy the added features and power that the MapEditor utility program offers. MapEditor you further customize your game-play experience. This section will show you how to create your own world from nothing, save it on your hard disk, and then load the world you create into *Civ II*, so that you can experience a simulation on that world.

STARTING MAPEDITOR

When you install *Civ II* onto your computer, the installation program creates a program group called Sid Meier's *Civilization II*, and within this group you will find two program icons. To run the MapEditor program, double-click on the MapEditor icon. If you're planning to create a custom world from scratch, this must be done *before* you begin a simulation.

Once you start this program, you'll be asked to select which language you want the text in the various menus displayed in. Select your option and then click on the OK button to continue.

Your next decision will be to select the size of the overall world that you want to create. There are three predefined choices (Small, Normal, and Large), plus there's a Customize option that allows you to enter a custom size for the world. The

> ### N O T E
> Don't confuse MapEditor with the Customize World option on the pregame menu in *Civilization II*. While the Customize World option allows you to change settings to the game-play environment, MapEditor allows you to create the entire simulated world *before* you begin playing.

size of the planet you're creating is measured in terrain squares (squares on the map). Creating a small world will result in a shorter simulation (which could still take many hours to complete). Choose the size of the world you wish to create, and then click on the OK button to continue.

The *Civ II* MapEditor's Main screen will now be displayed. This screen is somewhat similar to the Main Game screen of *Civ II* in that there's a Menu Bar at the top of the screen, a large Map area in the center of the screen, a small World Map in the upper-right corner of the screen, and a Status window in the lower-right corner of the screen. While the layout of this screen may look familiar, all the commands are different from what you'll find on the *Civ II* Main Game screen, or even in the *CivNet* Map Editor.

THE MAPEDITOR MENU BAR

> ### T I P
> If you're new to the *Civilization* game series, it's an excellent idea to spend some time mastering the game itself first, before you begin experimenting with what MapEditor offers.

The MapEditor has five pull-down menus: Editor, View, Map, Brush, and Tools. Using the commands available to you from these pull-down menus, along with the terrain tools located just below the Menu Bar, you will be able to create your own world. When you first load the MapEditor program, the large Map area in the center of the screen is a solid-blue color, with fish icons scattered randomly. This represents the ocean, which right now takes up the entire planet. It's your job to choose the size and shape of the continents, as well as to decide what type of terrain will make up the continents. Your secondary objective (which is optional) is to determine the starting location for every empire. Begin by exploring each of the commands available to you from the five pull-down menus.

The Editor Pull-Down Menu

From the Editor pull-down menu shown in Figure A.1, the following options are available to you:

- **New Map (Ctrl + N)**   Use this command to start your world creation process over again from scratch. This command will clear the Map area and return it to solid ocean.

- **Load Map (Ctrl + L)**   With this command, you can load a Map that you have already created and edit it. The *Civ II* Program CD comes with several predesigned maps that you can load using this command, and then edit (or modify) to create your custom world.

- **Save Map (Ctrl + S)**   Once you've created the world on which you want to experience your simulations, you must save the map to the computer's hard disk, and then reload the map once you begin running the actual *Civ II* program. If you fail to save the map, it will be erased when you exit MapEditor. When you save a map, you must choose a filename for the map. All maps created with MapEditor have the .mp extension.

- **Save Map As (Ctrl + A)**   This command gives you flexibility in how you save different versions of maps. You can save the same map using multiple

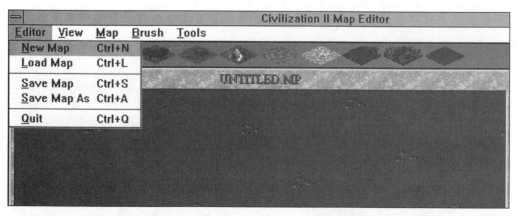

FIGURE A.1: The Editor pull-down menu contains commands for beginning, loading, and saving map files.

filenames, or you can use the same file to save multiple edited versions. If you've already saved a map under the filename Sample.mp, for example, you can then make changes to it and save them in a file with a *different* filename, which preserves (doesn't write over) the original map you saved in the Sample.mp file. In other words, use this command to give an updated map a new filename.

⊕ **Quit (Ctrl + Q)** After you have saved the map you create (or anytime for that matter), you can exit the MapEditor program by selecting this command.

The View Pull-Down Menu

From the View pull-down menu shown in Figure A.2, you can choose the viewing size of the Map area on the MapEditor's screen. By zooming in to a specific location, you can add details to areas of your map, such as rivers. To see a larger bird's-eye view of the map, you can zoom out. The following viewing options are available from this pull-down menu:

⊕ **Zoom In (Z)** Use this command to get a closer, more detailed view of a specific area of terrain in the Map area.

⊕ **Zoom Out (X)** With this command, you'll see less detail, but a slightly larger area of terrain, which makes everything in the Map area smaller.

Editor	View	Map	Brush	Tools

Zoom In   z
Zoom Out   x

Max Zoom In   Ctrl+Z
Standard Zoom   Shift+Z
Medium Zoom Out   Shift+X
Max Zoom Out   Ctrl+X

Arrange Windows
Center View   c

UNTITLED.MP

Civilization II Map Editor

FIGURE A.2: The View pull-down menu lets you change the Map area's viewing modes.

⊕ **Max Zoom In (Ctrl + Z)**   This command gives you the closest, most detailed view of a specific area of terrain that you can get. While this is an extreme close-up view, it is of a very small portion of the overall world.

⊕ **Standard Zoom (Shift + Z)**   This command returns you to the standard (default) viewing perspective of the map.

⊕ **Medium Zoom Out (Shift + X)**   This command allows you to see a slightly larger area of terrain than you would see using the Standard Zoom command.

⊕ **Max Zoom Out (Ctrl + X)**   For a bird's-eye view of the world, use this command. There is practically no detail, but you can see about 80 percent of the entire world.

⊕ **Arrange Windows**   The Main Map, Status window, and World Map are all independent windows that can be resized and moved using the mouse. To return all the windows to their original (default) sizes and locations, use this command.

⊕ **Center View (C)**   This command will instantly center your view (on the Main Map area) to where the white cursor box is placed on the map.

The Map Pull-Down Menu

As shown in Figure A.3, the Map pull-down menu provides several commands that give you some general assistance in rendering a new world.

⊕ **Generate Random Map (R)**   What, you're not feeling creative at the moment? Well, using this command, you can have the computer give you some assistance in generating a customized world. On selecting this option, you'll be asked to choose a size for your world (from the Select Size of World window). The available choices are: Small, Normal, Large, or Custom. Next, you must choose the size of each land mass (continent) in your world. The options are: Small, Normal, Large, or Random. You'll then be asked to choose a Land Form. Here, you can select: Archipelago, Varied, Continents, or Random.

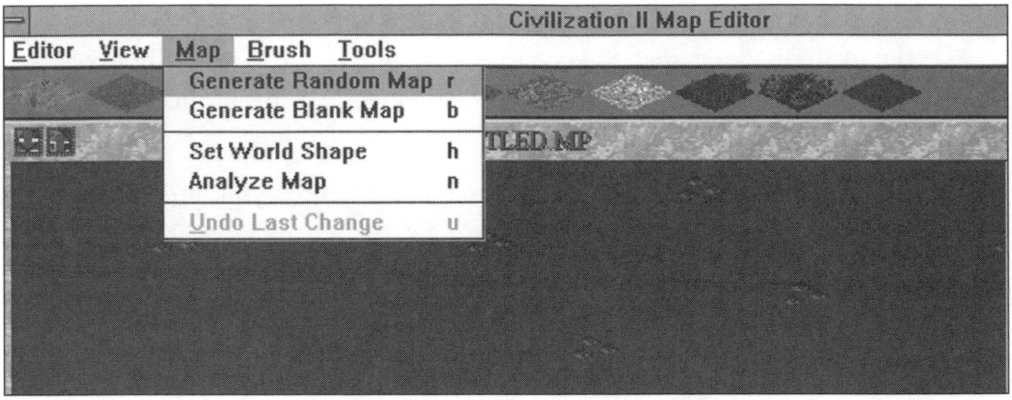

FIGURE A.3: The Map pull-down menu lets you set the general size and shape of your world map.

You must also select the overall climate (Arid, Normal, Wet, or Random) and the overall temperature (Cool, Temperate, Warm, or Random) for your world. Then you must select the age of the world (3, 4, or 5 billion years old). You can also select a random age. Also, is your world going to be flat or round? You will also need to make this decision when you select the Generate Random Map command. Based on these decisions, which are all made from command windows that appear on the screen, the computer will then generate a world. Once the world has been randomly created, you can still add a touch of creativity by editing it, before "saving" the world and starting a simulation.

⊕ **Generate Blank Map (B)**   This command erases everything currently in the Map area. So, if you want to start the creation process over again, use this command.

⊕ **Set World Shape (H)**   In the early days, many people thought the world was flat. (Some people probably still do.) In this game, you can choose to make your own world flat or round, using this command.

⊕ **Analyze Map**   Once you have created your map, this command analyzes your creation to ensure that once you begin a simulation, everything will run properly. While using this command is not mandatory, it's always a good idea to use it before "saving" your world and beginning a simulation. If everything is OK, a window will appear with the message "Map Analysis OK! The Map has been analyzed and no problems have been detected." If there are problems, a warning message will appear to inform you of the situation; for example, you might get a message telling you that the land mass or land masses that you created are too small.

⊕ **Undo Last Change (U)**   OOPS! If you make a mistake, use this command to undo the last thing you did. This command may become your best friend, but remember, when you're letting your creative juices flow and creating art, there is no such thing as a mistake.

The Brush Pull-Down Menu

This pull-down menu gives you the drawing tools you'll need to create your world. In this case, the *ink* you'll be using are the 11 main types of terrain squares (not including rivers) available in *Civ II*. From this menu, which is shown in Figure A.4, you can choose the thickness of the *paintbrush* you'll be using to paint terrain squares onto the Map. The white cursor box will change based on the size and shape of the *brush* you choose from this menu.

After choosing one of the following tools, you must select a type of terrain that you want to paint onto the Map area to create your custom world. You can mix and

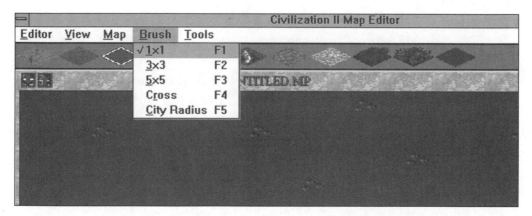

FIGURE A.4:   The Brush pull-down menu provides you with a variety of drawing tools.

match terrain types as often as you wish. It's also possible to overlap the land masses using these tools. The trick here is to be creative!

- **1 × 1 (F1)**   This command allows you to add one terrain square at a time to the map.

- **3 × 3 (F2)**   This command allows you to add blocks of terrain squares onto the map that measure three-by-three terrain squares each.

- **5 × 5 (F3)**   This command allows you to add blocks of terrain squares onto the map that measure five-by-five terrain squares each. This is an excellent tool for creating large blocks of land using one type of terrain.

- **Cross (F4)**   Instead of placing terrain squares, this command allows you to place blocks of five terrain squares onto the map, with the squares in the shape of a cross.

- **City Radius (F5)**   This tool allows you to place groups of 21 terrain squares at once onto the map, in a shape that resembles a city radius in *Civ II*.

The Tools Pull-Down Menu

As shown in Figure A.5, the Tools pull-down menu provides you with the following three map-editing environment tools:

- **Coastline Protect (P)**   When you activate this command's feature, once you create the outline for a continent, you can fill in the inside of the land mass without worrying about accidentally altering the coastline you created. This option *must* be turned off when you begin creating the world, or you will not be able to place any terrain squares on the map.

- **Autoscroll During Paint (A)**   When you are painting terrain squares onto the map with this command active, the screen will automatically scroll in whatever direction you are leading the cursor. Because you can only see a portion of the world from the Map area, this command makes creating large land masses faster and easier when it's activated.

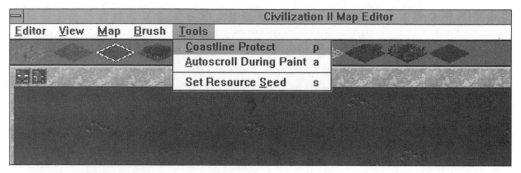

FIGURE A.5: The Tools pull-down menu provides commands for easier work within the MapEditor environment.

⊕ **Set Resource Speed (S)**   Special resources are randomly added to terrain squares as you paint them onto the map. Adjusting this feature, by changing the value to a number other than 1, alters the pattern in which these resources are placed on the map.

THE TERRAIN SQUARE PAINTING TOOLS

Located just below the MapEditor's Menu Bar are 11 terrain square icons. Each icon represents a different type of terrain that can be placed on the map using the *brush* you select from the Brush pull-down menu. Going from left to right, the types of terrain available to you are: desert, plains, grassland, forest, hills, mountains, tundra, glacier, swamp, jungle, and ocean. Using the mouse, you can place the white cursor on any of these terrain types to select it, and then begin *painting* that type of terrain square onto the Map, in any shape you choose.

Once the land masses (continents) for your world have been created, there are three additional icons located to the right of the terrain icons that allow you to further customize the world. Located to the right of the Ocean terrain icon is the River icon. Using this icon, you can *paint* over land masses to add rivers. Rivers are important because they allow for irrigation in the middle of a land mass. Of course, to create lakes, you can simply place one ocean terrain square in the middle of several other types of terrain. Next to the River icon is the Irrigation icon. Using this icon, you can add irrigated terrain squares to the world. This is normally a Terrain Improvement that Settler and Engineer Units must build during a simulation.

Now, let's take a look at the icon to the extreme right. This City icon allows you to place civilizations on the map. When you begin a new simulation, you're in control of one empire, while the computer controls between three and seven other empires that are randomly placed by the computer somewhere on the world map, before the simulation begins. Because MapEditor allows you to totally customize the world where your simulation will be taking place, using this City icon, you can predetermine where each civilization will begin in your world.

After you have created all your land masses and have added a few rivers, you can determine exactly where on your world map each empire will begin the simulation. Using the mouse, click on the City icon (located to the extreme right of the terrain icons), and then place the white cursor somewhere on one of the land masses you created. When you press the Enter key, a window will appear, asking you to select one of the 21 tribes built into the game, as shown in Figure A.6. This is where the tribe you select will begin the simulation. In other words, this is where that empire's very first Settler Unit will be placed when a simulation begins.

You can predetermine the starting location for any or all of the 21 tribes in the game. Any tribes you don't set a starting location for will be randomly placed by the computer.

MAPEDITOR'S STATUS WINDOW

The Status window constantly displays information about the world you're in the process of creating. At the top of this window, the world size and shape will be listed. Just below this information will be the exact location on the map of the white cursor. If, for example, you've created a world that is 50×80 terrain squares in size, and the cursor location is listed as 25×40, you know that the cursor is at the center of the world.

Below the cursor location is the type of terrain square you currently have selected. This is the type of terrain that you can now place on the map. Below this is the type of brush you have selected. Near the center of the Status window will be a graphic depiction of the terrain type you have selected and the brush type. So, if you have grassland as the active terrain type, and 3×3 as the active brush type, the graphic depiction you'll see in the center of the status window is of grassland terrain squares in a 3×3 block. At the bottom of the Status window are the keyboard commands you can use to paint the terrain onto the map.

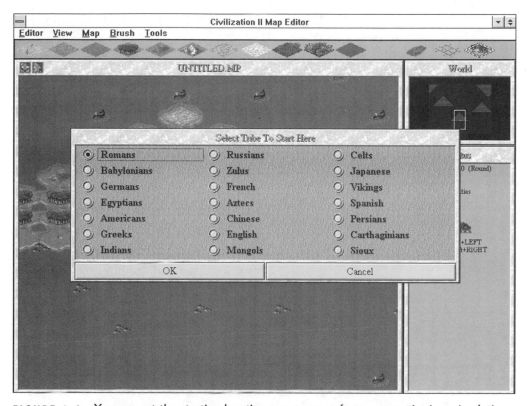

FIGURE A.6: You can set the starting location on your map for every empire in a simulation.

HERE'S HOW TO CREATE
A CUSTOMIZED WORLD

Now that you understand the tools and commands you'll be using to create a customized world, go ahead and create a sample world from scratch. Here are the steps you'll need to take:

1. From the Windows Program Manager, double-click on the MapEditor icon in the Sid Meier's *Civilization II* program group.

2. Choose the language in which you want all the text to appear. Click on the OK button to continue.

3. From the Select Size of World window, as shown in Figure A.7, choose Small (40 × 50 squares), Normal (50 × 80 squares), Large (75 × 120 squares), or Custom. Then click on the OK button to continue. For this example, choose a Normal size world.

4. The *Civ II* MapEditor screen will now appear. The white cursor box will be flashing in the center of the Map area, and this entire area will be blue (representing ocean), as shown in Figure A.8. Your job is to add the land masses.

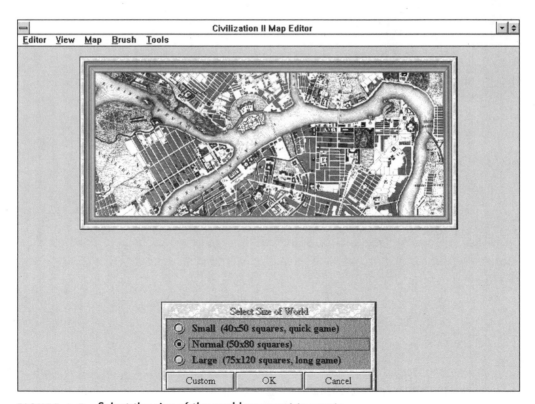

FIGURE A.7: Select the size of the world you want to create.

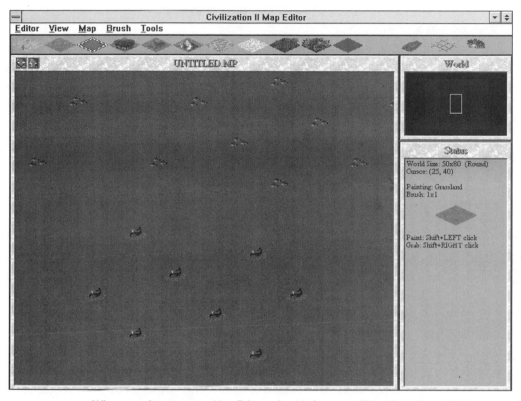

FIGURE A.8: When you begin using MapEditor, the Map area will be blank (a solid-blue color) because the entire planet is an ocean.

5. Click on one of the terrain icons, located just below the Menu Bar. For this example, choose the Grasslands icon (the third icon from the left).

6. Now, it's time to paint grassland terrain squares onto the Map area, in any shape you want. You can create land masses of any size. Right now, the default brush size is 1×1, which means you can paint one terrain square at a time.

7. For this example, several land masses were created using various terrain types and the 1×1 brush type, as shown in Figure A.9. All the land masses in this sample world are designed in the shape of pyramids. These pyramid continents were created by selecting various terrain types, one at a time, from the terrain icon menu, and then painting them onto the Main Map.

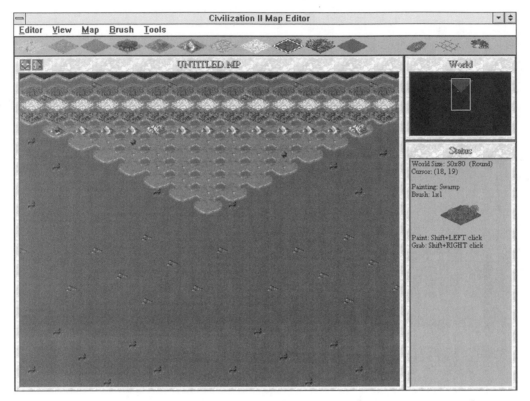

FIGURE A.9: Land masses in the shape of pyramids were created using various types of terrain.

8. To get a bird's-eye view of the world you've created, as you see in Figure A.10, select the Max Zoom Out command on the View pull-down menu. During the entire creation phase, you can also view a small representation of the entire world by checking out the small World Map that's located in the upper-right corner of the screen. After viewing the Main Map area from a bird's-eye perspective, use the Standard Zoom command to return the view to normal.

9. Once all the pyramid shaped continents are created, activate the City icon and place the starting location for each civilization somewhere on the map (spread out among the various continents), as shown in Figure A.11. If you know you're going to choose the American tribe when the simulation begins, you can set the starting location for this tribe to be on a large land mass, and then place all the other tribes very close together,

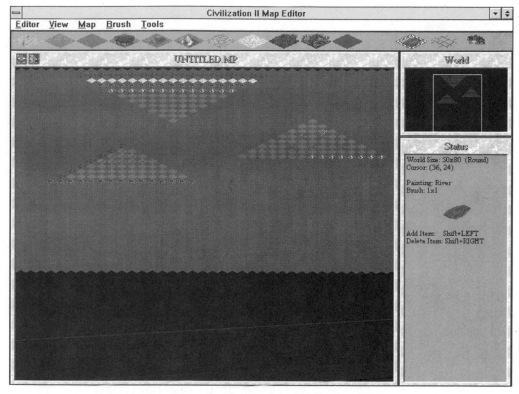

FIGURE A.10: Use the Max Zoom Out command to get a bird's-eye view of the world and see how the world is taking shape.

on other land masses. This will give you an advantage early in the game because the rival empire will battle and weaken each other, while your tribe (in this case, the Americans) are alone on a continent and can grow and prosper.

10. Now that the creation process is complete, use the Analyze Map command (on the Map pull-down menu) to ensure that this custom world will work properly in a simulation.

11. Select the Save Map command on the Editor pull-down menu to save the map to the computer's hard disk. For this example, you can use the file-name **sample.mp**. The location on the computer's hard disk where this map file is saved is the default location, c:\mps\civ2.

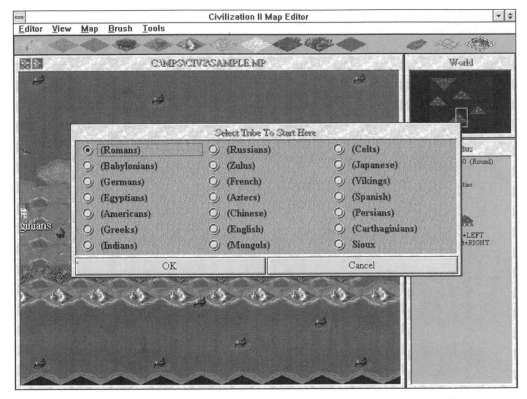

FIGURE A.11: The starting location of every civilization is determined after the land masses are designed.

12. Now that the map has been saved, use the Quit command to exit the MapEditor program. This will return you to the Windows Program Manager.

13. Begin the *Civilization II* program by double-clicking on the *Civilization II* program icon.

14. When *Civilization II*'s pregame menu appears, select the Start on Premade World option and then click on the OK button.

15. From the Select Map To Load window, choose the filename Sample.mp, which is the map you just created. You can type: **c:\mps\civ2\sample.mp** in the filename command box of this window, and then click on the OK button to load the map. As an alternative, you can load one of the other predesigned maps that comes with the *Civ II* game.

16. You will now be asked if you want to randomize the world's villages and resource squares. Villages are the hut icons that can provide bonuses during the game, and the resources are normally randomly placed throughout the map by the computer. If you choose Yes, both the villages and the resources will be randomly placed throughout the map. By selecting No, all the villages and resources will appear exactly where you saw them when you created the world using the MapEditor program.

17. The next window will ask if you want to randomly select the starting location of each civilization. By selecting Yes, the computer will determine where on the map the first Settler Unit for each empire will be placed at the start of the simulation. By selecting No, each empire will be placed where you positioned it when you created the world using the MapEditor program.

18. You will now be prompted with all the standard pregame options, which were discussed extensively in Chapter 2, *Getting a Simulation Started*. When the simulation actually begins, however, it will take place on the world that you created using the MapEditor program.

In addition to adding elements of fun, strategy, and creativity to the *Civ II* game, the MapEditor program allows you to experiment with different-sized land masses and veried types of terrain. You can create additional challenges for yourself by attempting to create an empire that thrives in a desert or a swamp environment. Using the MapEditor, your only limit is your own imagination!

If you create a world that's totally original or one that you're especially proud of, you can share it with other *Civ II* gamers by uploading the .mp file to one of the *Civ II* on-line forums. To find other gamers on-line, check out Appendix C, *Civilization II and CivNet Resources*, for World Wide Web site addresses on the Internet as well as for information about other on-line forums for the *Civilization* game series.

Installing *Civilization II*

Before playing *Civilization II*, you first must install the program onto your computer. This section tells you how to install the game so that it operates under Microsoft Window 3.1x or Windows 95.

HARDWARE
REQUIREMENTS FOR *CIV II*

To run this game, your computer must meet the following hardware specifications:

- A 486 (or better) PC-based computer that operates at a system speed of at least 33MHz (66MHz is ideal)

- Your computer must have a double-speed (or better) CD-ROM drive (running MSCDEX Version 2.2 or later)

- The Microsoft Windows 3.1x or Windows 95 Operating System

- At least 8MB RAM (16MB is highly recommended)

- SVGA graphics (256 color, 640×480 resolution graphics)

- A Microsoft-compatible mouse

- Between 11MB and 55MB hard disk drive space

When installing *Civ II*, you will have the option to perform a full installation, which will require between 39MB and 55MB, depending on the size of your overall hard drive. (If the total disk space on your hard drive is under 128MB, then the full installation of *Civ II* will require 39MB.) If you choose the Custom install option, the *Civ II* program is divided into three parts: Civilopedia, Required Game Files, and Recommended Game

Files. You can choose which parts of the *Civ II* program you want copied to your hard disk. The remaining program elements will be accessed directly from the program CD as they are needed.

Civ II now features multimedia animation that will not be copied to your computer's hard drive, even if you request a full installation. These files require vast amounts of disk space and can easily be run directly from the CD-ROM drive as they are needed during the game. The animation effects are simply eye candy. While they have no impact on the game itself, they're nice to look at once you acquire a Wonder of the World during the game.

If you happen to have one of those really, really big hard disks, and you want to copy the multimedia files from the program CD to your hard disk, you can do it manually. After installing the main program, create a directory called **c:\mps\civ2\video**. Now, copy all the files from the *Civ II* CD's directory called **d:\civ2\video** to the directory you just created on your hard disk. Next, create another directory on your hard disk called **c:\mps\civ2\kings**, and copy all the files from the *Civilization II* CD that are in the **d:\civ2\kings** directory.

If you're already familiar with how to install programs under the Window 3.1x or the Window 95 operating system, then installing *Civilization II* will be a quick and easy process. Should you have problems installing the software, consult your Windows 3.1x or Windows 95 manual, or call the MicroProse technical support telephone number that's listed in the game's manual.

INSTALLING *CIVILIZATION II* TO RUN WITHIN WINDOWS 3.1X

Assuming your computer meets the necessary hardware requirements, follow these steps to install *Civilization II* from Windows 3.1x:

1. Turn on your computer and load Windows 3.1x.

2. Open the Windows Program Manager.

3. Insert the *Civilization II* compact disc into your computer's CD-ROM drive.

4. Within Program Manager, select the Run command from the File pull-down menu.

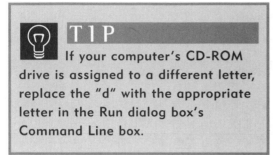

T I P

If your computer's CD-ROM drive is assigned to a different letter, replace the "d" with the appropriate letter in the Run dialog box's Command Line box.

5. When the Run dialog box appears, type: **d:\setup.exe** in the Command Line box, as shown in Figure B.1, and then click on the OK button.

6. When the *Civ II* language window appears, choose English, French, or Dutch, and then click on the OK button to continue.

7. The Sid Meier's *Civilization II* Installation Program dialog box shown in Figure B.2 will now appear on the screen. Select a directory on your computer's hard drive into which the installation program will copy the *Civ II* program files. The default option is **c:\mps\civ2**. Also, you must decide if you want to perform a full installation or a custom installation. Click on the appropriate button for the type of installation you desire. Full installation is recommended; however, if you have limited hard disk space, you can select which elements of the *Civ II* program you want copied to your hard disk, as shown in Figure B.3. To save hard disk space, you can skip copying the Civilopedia files.

The installation program copies all the files needed for *Civ II* to run on your computer. To save hard disk space, the installation program does not copy any of the new multimedia files, so when you're playing *Civ II*, if you want to experience all the awesome new graphics and animation, you must keep the *Civilization II* CD inserted in your computer's CD-ROM drive.

FIGURE B.1: Type the command to run the setup program on the *Civilization II* compact disc in the Windows 3.1x Run dialog box.

8. When the program files have been copied, the installation program will ask you to name the Windows program group in which the *Civ II* program icons will be placed. The default option is Sid Meier's *Civilization II*. To create the necessary program

FIGURE B.2: You can choose where you want the *Civ II* program files copied to your hard disk, as well as whether you want a full or custom installation.

icons, click on the Create button. At this time, instead of choosing to create a new program group, you can assign the *Civ II* program icons to be placed within an existing program group. For example, if you already have a program group called Games on your computer, you might want the *Civ II* program icons to be placed within this group.

When the installation process is complete, you'll be returned to the Windows Program Manager. You'll find that the installation program has created a program group called Sid Meier's *Civilization II*, as you can see in Figure B.4, and within this group are two program icons—*Civilization II* and MapEditor.

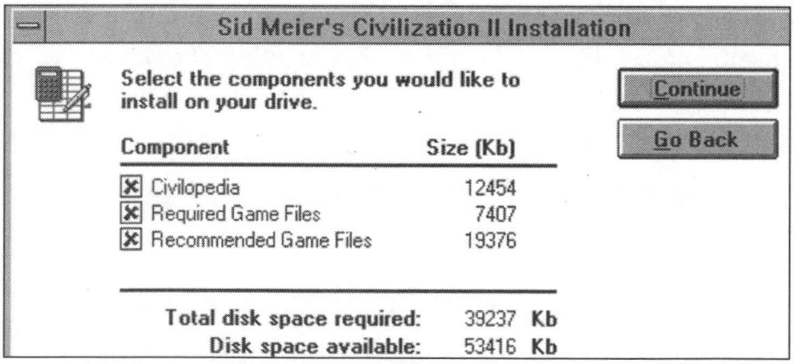

FIGURE B.3: Although you must copy the required game files, you can conserve hard disk space by removing the "X"s from the Civilopedia and Recommended Game Files check box options.

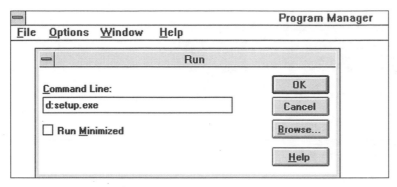

FIGURE B.4: When the installation process is complete, two program icons named *Civilization II* and MapEditor appear in the Sid Meier's *Civilization II* Program Group.

To begin playing *Civ II*, double-click on the *Civilization II* icon. Before the actual game begins, a window called *Civ II* Diplomatic Heralds will appear. Here, you must tell the computer if you have the 16MB of RAM necessary to view many of the new animated sequences built into the game. The game can be played, however, with only 8MB of RAM. After this window disappears, the game's opening animation will be displayed. At any time, click the left mouse button or press any key on the keyboard to skip this opening animation and go directly to the list of pregame options.

INSTALLING *CIVILIZATION II* TO RUN WITHIN THE WINDOWS 95 OPERATING SYSTEM

If your computer operates under the Microsoft Windows 95 operating system, there are two ways to get the *Civ II* installation program to run. You can use the Run command on the Start button's menu, or you can use the Add/Remove Programs utility in the Windows 95 Control Panel group. Follow these steps for installing *Civ II* onto your computer using the Run command:

1. Turn on your computer to load the Windows 95 operating system.

2. Click on the Start button, and select the Run command.

3. Insert the *Civilization II* CD into your computer's CD-ROM drive.

4. When the Run dialog box appears, enter the following command line: **d:\setup.exe** and then click on the OK button. The *Civ II* Installation Program will begin running.

5. You will have the option to choose full installation or custom installation, plus select the directory (folder) on your computer's hard disk where you want the *Civ II* program files to be copied. The default option is: **c:\mps\civ2**. The Full Install option is recommended, so click on the Full Install button to continue.

All the *Civ II* program files will now automatically be copied to your computer's hard drive. This will take several minutes.

6. When all the necessary program files have been copied to your computer's hard drive, the *Civ II* installation program will ask if you want to create a new Windows program group for the game. The default name is Sid Meier's *Civilization II*.

Click on the Create button to continue. At this time, instead of choosing to create a new program group, you can assign the *Civ II* program icons to be placed within an existing program group. For example, if you already have a program group called Games on your computer, you might want the *Civ II* Program icons to be placed within this group.

7. The *Civ II* Installation program will now create a program group called Sid Meier's *Civilization II*, and within it will be two program icons—*Civilization II* and MapEditor.

> **NOTE**
>
> During installation in either the Windows 3.1x or Windows 95 environment, the *Civ II* Installation Program might have to install WinG and Indeo Video for Windows, which are two programs that come on the *Civilization II* CD and are required to run this and many other game programs. If you play a lot of computer games on your PC, chances are these files already exist on your computer's hard disk and will not have to be copied there again. If these files do have to be copied to your hard disk, follow the prompts offered by the *Civ II* installation program. Before actually playing *Civ II*, you will have to reboot your computer after the installation process.

> **TIP**
>
> If your computer's hard disk is assigned to a letter other than "c," insert the appropriate letter when you're assigning the directory in which the *Civ II* program files will be stored.

8. At this time, you can create a shortcut for *Civ II* and place its shortcut icon on the Windows 95 desktop for easy access. You can also launch the program using the Taskbar's Start button. On the Programs menu, Sid Meier's *Civilization II* will now be listed.

Installing *Civ II* with the Windows 95 Add/Remove Programs Utility

Follow these steps to install *Civ II* with the Add/Remove Programs utility:

1. Turn your computer on to load Windows 95, and insert the *Civilization II* program CD into your computer's CD-ROM drive.

2. Double-click on the My Computer icon.

3. In the My Computer window, double-click on the Control Panel icon.

4. In the Control Panel window, double-click on the Add/Remove Programs icon.

5. In the Add/Remove Programs Properties dialog box, click the Install button.

6. Click on the Next > button that appears at the bottom of the Install Program From Floppy Disk or CD-ROM dialog box.

7. Check the Command line for installation program: box in the Run Installation Program dialog box to be sure you see the following command line: **d:\setup.exe**. Click on the Finish button.

8. Select the language you want *Civ II* to operate under (English, French, or Dutch), and click on the OK button. The *Civ II* Installation program will now begin running.

9. You will have the option to choose full installation or custom installation, plus select the directory (folder) where you want the *Civ II* program files to be copied. The default option is: **c:\mps\civ2**. Full installation is recommended, so click on the Full Install button to continue.

All the *Civ II* program files will now automatically be copied to your computer's hard drive. This will take several minutes.

10. When all the necessary program files have been copied to the directory **c:\mps\civ2** on your computer's hard drive, the *Civ II* Installation program will ask if you want to create a new program group for the game. The default name is Sid Meier's *Civilization II*. Click on the Create button to continue. At this time, instead of choosing to create a new program group, you can assign the *Civ II* program icons to be placed within an existing program group. For example, if you already have a program group called Games on your hard disk, you might want the *Civ II* program icons to be placed within this group.

The *Civ II* Installation program will now create a program group called Sid Meier's *Civilization II*, and within it will be two program icons—*Civilization II* and MapEditor.

11. At this time, you can create a shortcut for *Civ II* and place its shortcut icon on the Windows 95 desktop for easy access. You can also launch the program using the Taskbar's Start button. On the Programs menu, Sid Meier's *Civilization II* will now be listed.

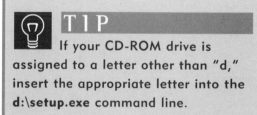

TIP
You can also open the Control Panel window by selecting the Settings command on the Start button's menu, and then selecting the Control Panel command on the Settings menu.

TIP
If your CD-ROM drive is assigned to a letter other than "d," insert the appropriate letter into the **d:\setup.exe** command line.

TIP
If your computer's hard disk is assigned to a letter other than "c," insert the appropriate letter when you're assigning the directory (folder) in which the program files will be stored.

To begin playing *Civ II*, double-click on the *Civilization II* icon. Before the actual game begins, a window called *Civ II* Diplomatic Heralds will appear. Here, you must tell the computer if you have the 16MB of RAM necessary to view many of the new animated sequences built into the game. The game can be played, however, with as little as 8MB of RAM. After this window disappears, the game's opening animation will be displayed. At any time, click the left mouse button or press any key on the keyboard to skip this opening animation and go directly to the list of pregame options.

Civilization II has now been copied to your computer's hard disk and is ready to be played! Get ready to begin your quest to dominate the world or colonize space. Good luck!

Civilization II and CivNet Resources

Have you developed strategies that you want to share with other *Civ II* gamers? Using the MapEditor program, have you created a world map that you think is wonderful? Do you have a question about *Civilization II* or *CivNet* that you hope another gamer will be able to answer? Well, if you have a modem and access to one of the major on-line services or the Internet, then you have the ability to communicate with other *Civ II* and *CivNet* gamers from around the world!

Also, if you want to share your *Civ II* or *CivNet* strategies with readers of future editions of this *Civilization II Strategies & Secrets* book, please e-mail them to the author at: **JR7777@aol.com**. You will be given credit within the book if your strategies are printed in a future edition.

WORLD WIDE WEB *CIVILIZATION II* AND *CIVNET*-RELATED SITES

- The MicroProse Web site: **http://www.microprose.com**

- Other Civilization-related Web site addresses: **http://www.gamesdo-main.co.uk** and **http://www.io.com/ ~ cgoodwin/civnet.htm**

To locate other World Wide Web sites that relate to *Civilization*, *Civilization II*, or *CivNet*, visit Yahoo! (**http://www.yahoo.com**), and do a keyword search, using words like: MicroProse, Civilization, Civilization II, or CivNet. Using Yahoo!, or a similar service, you can locate Web sites that have been created since this strategy guide was published.

The following are Internet newsgroups and mailing lists to subscribe to:

⊕ Internet newsgroup: **alt.games.civnet**

⊕ Mailing list: Send a message containing the words "Subscribe civnet-list" to **majordomo@jagunet.com**

CIVILIZATION II AND *CIVNET* INFORMATION ON THE MAJOR ON-LINE SERVICES

⊕ **America Online:** The keyword **MicroProse** accesses MicroProse's forum.

⊕ **CompuServe:** The command **GO GAMBPUB** accesses MicroProse's forum.

⊕ **Prodigy:** Visit the **Game Club** forum.

WHERE TO MEET OTHER *CIVNET* GAMERS

Thanks to the Information Superhighway, there are many places on-line where you can meet, chat with, exchange information, or compete against other *CivNet* fans. MicroProse has a strong on-line presence, and supports forums on all of the popular on-line services. (See the previous section for details.) There are also several user-supported places you can visit via the Internet:

⊕ **Two *CivNet*-related Internet newsgroups** can be accessed at the following addresses: **comp.sys.ibm.pc.games.strategic and alt.games.civnet**

⊕ **You can also join a *CivNet* mailing list** by sending an email message to: **majordomo@jagunet.com**. Within the body of your message, type: **"subscribe civnet-list"**

As for sites on the World Wide Web, here two places worth checking out:

⊕ **http://www.io.com/ ~ cgoodwin/civnet.htm**

⊕ **http://www.yahoo.com/recreation/games/computer_games/titles/civilization/civnet/**